MIND ONLY

The Society for Asian and Comparative Philosophy Monograph Series was started in 1974. Works are published in the series that deal with any area of Asian philosophy, or in any other field of philosophy examined from a comparative perspective. The aim of the series is to make available scholarly works that exceed article length, but may be too specialized for the general reading public, and to make these works available in inexpensive editions without sacrificing the orthography of non-Western languages.

MIND ONLY

A PHILOSOPHICAL AND DOCTRINAL ANALYSIS OF THE VIJÑĀNAVĀDA

Thomas E. Wood

MONOGRAPH NO. 9
SOCIETY FOR ASIAN AND COMPARATIVE PHILOSOPHY

University of Hawaii Press
Honolulu

Printed in the United States of America

Library of Congress Cataloging-in-Publication Data

Wood, Thomas E., 1946–
Mind only : a philosophical and doctrinal analysis of the Vijñānavāda/Thomas E. Wood.
p. cm.—(Monograph no. 9 of the Society for Asian and Comparative Philosophy)
Includes bibliographical references and index.
ISBN 0-8248-1356-1
1. Yogācāra (Buddhism) 2. Vijñaptimātratā. I. Title. II. Series: Monograph . . . of the Society for Asian and Comparative Philosophy : no. 9.
BQ7496.W66 1991
294.3'42—dc 20 90-41660
CIP

Camera-ready copy was prepared by the author.

University of Hawaii Press books are printed
on acid-free paper and meet the guidelines
for permanence and durability of the Council
on Library Resources

CONTENTS

ABBREVIATIONS

AA	Abhisamayālaṃkāra
AK	Abhidharma-kośa
AKB	Abhidharma-kośa-bhāṣya
AKSV	Sphuṭārthā Abhidharma-kośa-vyākhyā
AN	Aṅguttara-nikāya
CWSL	Cheng wei shilun
JNA	Jñānaśrīmitra-nibandhāvaliḥ
MBh	Vyākaraṇamahābhāṣya (Patañjali)
MMK	Mūla-madhyamaka-kārikā
MMKV	Mūla-madhyamaka-kārikā-vṛtti (Prasannapadā)
MN	Majjhima-nikāya
MV	Madhyānta-vibhāga
MVB	Madhyānta-vibhāga-bhāṣya
MVBṬ	Madhyānta-vibhāga-bhāṣya-ṭīkā
NB	Nyāya-bindu
NBṬ	Nyāya-bindu-ṭīkā
PS	Pramāṇa-samuccaya
PSV	Pramāṇa-samuccaya-(sva)-vṛtti
PV	Pramāṇa-vārttika
PVB	Pramāṇa-vārttika-bhāṣya (Prajñākaragupta)
PVin.	Pramāṇa-viniścaya
RNA	Ratnakīrti-nibandhāvaliḥ
SD	Saṃtānāntara-dūṣaṇa
SN	Saṃyutta-nikāya
SS	Saṃtānāntara-siddhi
TB	Tarka-bhāṣā (Mokṣākaragupta)
TS	Tattva-saṃgraha
TSN	Tri-svabhāva-nirdeśa
TSP	Tattva-saṃgraha-pañjikā

Trimś.	Trimśikā
TṬ	Trimśikā-ṭīkā
Vimś.	Vimśatikā
VV	Vimśatikā-(sva)-vṛtti

Introduction

The Vijñānavāda was one of the two major schools of Mahāyāna Buddhism. It flourished in India from the 4th to the 12th century C.E., when it disappeared — along with all the other Buddhist schools in India — during the period of the Muslim conquests.

The adherents of this school (called Vijñānavādins or Yogācārins) held that the world is nothing but mind or consciousness (*vijñāna-mātra, citta-mātra, vijñapti-mātra*). Since the Vijñānavādins held that the world is mind only, there are many similarities between the Vijñānavāda and other idealist philosophies, both Eastern and Western. Nevertheless, the Vijñānavāda was very much a Buddhist formulation of idealism, and it is as a specifically Buddhist idealism that the Vijñānavāda is unique.

(1) One thing that makes the Buddhist idealism of the Vijñānavāda different from most other forms of idealism is the doctrine of illusion (*māyā*). According to the Buddhist schools, all things are unstable, insubstantial, and impermanent (*anitya*). The Mahāyānists went even further than this, however, and maintained that the world is actually unreal (*asat, māyā*). The Vijñānavādin interpretation of this doctrine was that the mind, under the influence of a beginningless delusion or ignorance (*avidyā*), believes that it apprehends, in both the waking and dreaming states, objects which are external to it, when in fact it is only the mind itself which is projecting, or appearing, as something external. Hence, although mind is real, the world (i.e. what is thought to be *perceived* by the mind) is unreal.[1]

(2) The Vijñānavāda is also of interest because it does not fit neatly into any of the categories of either solipsism, theistic idealism or monism. First of all, the Vijñānavādins — as I shall later argue at some length — were not solipsists. Secondly, the Vijñānavādins did not believe that the world was in God's mind, nor did they believe it was in the mind of an Absolute. In this respect, the Vijñānavādins were simply orthodox Buddhists, for, though the Buddhists believed

in the existence of a rather large number of deities (*devas*), Buddhism is an atheistic religion (*an-īśvara-vāda*), in the sense that it does not believe in a God or Absolute which is infinite, omnipotent, omniscient etc. Consequently, the Vijñānavāda doctrine that the world is "nothing but mind" does *not* mean that the world is the manifestation or creation of some infinite or absolute mind.

If the world is mind only, and if the Vijñānavādins were neither solipsists, theists, nor absolutists, whose mind did they think the world was in? The answer, as I shall argue at some length in the text, is as follows:

> The world exists (at least at the level of relative truth) in a multiplicity of independent minds. The impression that these minds have of an external world which is public (i.e. perceived by other minds as well as their own) is entirely false. However, the experiences of these minds — or at least the experiences they have in the normal waking state — are coordinated with each other because these minds are in immediate, mind-to-mind contact. It is this coordination of normal waking experiences which gives rise to the erroneous impression of an external world. The world we seem to see in our waking state is in fact just as unreal as the things we dream about at night. The only difference is that objects seen in the normal, waking state are *collectively* hallucinated, whereas the things seen in dreams are not.

(3) Another important difference between the Vijñānavāda and other forms of idealism (both Eastern and Western) is that the Vijñānavādins, as Buddhists, were principally interested in the *cessation* of the mind (*pratisaṃkhyā-nirodha*). The Buddhist analysis of mind or consciousness, which makes this wholly negative evaluation of mind understandable, may be be described briefly as follows.

Buddhist philosophy, which holds that there is no self or soul (*ātman*), analyzes a person into the following five components or groups: form (*rūpa*), feeling (*vedanā*), impulses (*saṃskāras*), conception (*saṃjñā*) and consciousness (*vijñāna*). These five groups (*skandhas*), in turn, are broken down into a number of different constituent elements called *dharmas*.[2] The constituent elements of the mental group (*vijñāna-skandha*) were the various kinds of mental impressions or thoughts (*vijñapti*).[3] Since the Buddhists held that there is no underlying soul (*ātman*) or substance (*dravya*) to be found anywhere — and consciousness itself is no exception — no distinction can be drawn in Buddhist philosophy between mind, thoughts, ideas, impressions etc. It is therefore not strictly correct, according to the Vijñānavāda or any other Buddhist school, to say that a mind or a person *has* thoughts, because a mind (*vijñāna*) just *is* the stream of these thoughts (*vijñapti*).

Although there was disagreement within Buddhism over the classification and numbering of the constituent elements (*dharmas*) of the various groups, all Buddhists agreed that all the impermanent *dharmas* comprising a person involve suffering (*duḥkha*). As long as we are in this life, this suffering cannot be completely avoided. However, if one follows the way (*mārga*) laid down by the Buddha and practices the appropriate mental discipline, one can achieve the interruption (or at least the attenuation) of the stream of thoughts. The attainment of this state involves a temporary respite from suffering; it also tends to cut off the defilements that lead to future rebirths and future suffering. The Buddhist who has attained this "deliberate cessation" (*pratisaṃkhyā-nirodha*) of the stream of thoughts, and who has lived the Buddhist life and cut off all the "defilements" (*āsravas*), is called an Arhat. While he lives, the Arhat is said to have attained the "*nirvāṇa* with a basis still remaining" (*sopadhi-śeṣa-nirvāṇa*), i.e. the *nirvāṇa* in which the five groups of form, feeling, impulses, perception and consciousness still remain. However, the Arhat is also destined at his physical death to attain release from suffering forever. This total release from suffering is called the "*nirvāṇa* of total extinction" (*nirupadhi-śeṣa-nirvāṇa*).

While the foregoing can be taken as an accurate account of the Hīnayānist views about *nirvāṇa*, the Mahāyānist views about *nirvāṇa* are somewhat more complicated because the Mahāyānists introduced the doctrine that the Buddha (unlike the Arhats) had not entered the *nirvāṇa* of total extinction at the time of his physical death at Kuśinagarī.[4] They taught instead that the Buddha had entered what was called the "*apratiṣṭhita-nirvāṇa*," in which he continued to work for the salvation of all sentient beings suffering in *saṃsāra*.

Orthodox Buddhist doctrine had always drawn a very sharp distinction between *saṃsāra* (consisting of compounded (*saṃskṛta*) *dharmas*), on the one hand, and *nirvāṇa* (the cessation of *saṃsāra* or what is compounded), on the other. The doctrine of an active, post-Kuśinagarī Buddha consisting of the *skandhas* of form, feeling, impulses, conception and consciousness (or any combination of these) threatened to undermine this absolutely fundamental Buddhist teaching. According to the traditional teachings, in fact, the assertion that *nirvāṇa* could include any of these *skandhas* is virtually a contradiction in terms.

The difficulties that this Mahāyānist doctrine of an *apratiṣṭhita-nirvāṇa* raised for Buddhist doctrine appear quite clearly in some of the Vijñānavāda writings. The chapters of Part I ("Śūnyatā and the Doctrine of the Three Natures") and Part II ("Nirvāṇa and Buddhahood") are concerned with these doctrinal problems, and with the closely connected issues involving the Vijñānavāda doctrine of the three self natures (*tri-svabhāva-lakṣaṇa*) and the Vijñānavāda interpretation of the Buddhist doctrine of emptiness (*śūnyatā*).

Chapter 1 of Part I discusses the first chapter of the Madhyānta-vibhāga; chapter 2 discusses the Tri-svabhāva-nirdeśa; chapter 3 discusses the Triṃśikā; and chapter 4 of Part II discusses the views of the Triṃśikā and the Tri-svabhāva-nirdeśa on the related topics of *nirvāṇa* and Buddhahood. In these chapters I argue that the Mahāyānist doctrine of the *apratiṣṭhita-nirvāṇa* led to the development in the Vijñānavāda of a very peculiar notion of an Absolute. The Vijñānavāda "Absolute" was not mind (*vijñāna*) — not even absolute or nondual mind — but rather non-mind (*acitta*). (Mind, however, was its manifestation.) The Vijñānavādins identified this Absolute with emptiness, and its attainment was said to ensue upon the realization that mind is empty (*śūnya*), in the sense that it is devoid of the imagined and totally unreal external objects (i.e. matter).

Chapters 5-8 of Part III are concerned with the question of the existence of *other* minds and the closely related question of the

Buddha's omniscience. For the Vijñānavādins, the existence of other minds was somewhat problematic. The Buddhist scriptures (*sūtras*) clearly take the existence of other minds for granted, but they also attribute, both to "ordinary" *yogins* and to the Buddhas, the power of knowing other minds directly (i.e. telepathically). Furthermore, according to most of the Buddhist schools the Buddha is (or was) omniscient, and the Mahāyānists even held that the Buddha had transcended the subject-object distinction altogether. This raises some interesting questions. If the *yogins* and the Buddhas can know other minds directly, are the minds which appear to be separate from each other really separate? In particular, if the Buddha knows all other minds directly, and if his knowledge is nondual, how can it be said that for the *Buddha* there are other minds?

In the four chapters of Part III I argue that this doctrine of the nondual omniscience of the Buddha provided another impetus within the Vijñānavāda towards the development of a notion of an Absolute. I also contend that the Vijñānavādins did not succeed in reconciling their views on this point with orthodox, traditional Buddhist doctrines. (Given the nature of these orthodox, traditional doctrines, it is hard to see how this *could* have been done.) I also contend that these difficulties could not be resolved (as the Vijñānavādins attempted to do) by invoking the distinction between relative (*saṃvṛti*) and absolute (*paramārtha*) truth.

At the level of relative truth, at any rate, the Vijñānavādins believed in a multiplicity of different mind streams. According to the Vijñānavādins, the impressions of the various mind streams are coordinated with each other because the various minds are always in immediate mind-to-mind contact (*paras-parataḥ*) through a special causal efficiency.[5]

I refer to this doctrine of the coordination of a multiplicity of mind streams as the doctrine of Collective Hallucination. Chapter 9 of Part IV discusses this doctrine of Collective Hallucination as it is presented in Vasubandhu's Viṃśatikā and the Cheng wei shilun of Xuan Zang (Hsuan Tsang). Chapter 10 presents a critique of the doctrine. The main purpose of chapter 10 is to show that the Vijñānavādins did not find a philosophically convincing or viable alternative to materialism, on the one hand, and theistic idealism on the other. (Solipsism I do not consider in any detail as a philosophical doctrine, although I do contend that the Vijñānavādins could not possibly have been *consistent* solipsists for purely doctrinal reasons.) In this chapter I am not concerned to defend or advocate either materialism, idealism or dualism (in any version) as a philosophical doctrine. I do argue, however, that without adopting some version or other of theistic idealism (either monistic or dualistic) one cannot make any sense of the notion that the world is "nothing but mind."

The texts of the Vijñānavāda which I discuss in some detail are the first chapter of the Madhyānta-vibhāga [MV], the Triṃśikā [Triṃś.], the Tri-svabhāva-nirdeśa [TSN], the Viṃśatikā [Viṃś.], the Cheng wei shilun [CWSL], the Saṃtānāntara-siddhi [SS], the Saṃtānāntara-dūṣaṇa [SD] and the Tattva-saṃgraha-(pañjikā) [TS(P)]. My own translations of the MV, TSN, Triṃśikā and Viṃśatikā appear in chapters 1, 2, 3 and 5, respectively. Comprehensive synopses of the Saṃtānāntara-siddhi and of the Saṃtānāntara-dūṣaṇa are given in the Appendixes.

In Appendix I ("Authors and Texts"), I give a brief account of some of the authors and texts discussed in the book.

Appendix II contains a synopsis of the Saṃtānāntara-siddhi. This is based on a comparison of the two available English translations from the Tibetan by Th. Stcherbatsky and Hidenori Kitagawa.

In Appendix III ["A Note on the Tattva-saṃgraha-(pañjikā) as a Vijñānavāda Text"], I argue — against the Tibetan tradition and against some modern scholars who have apparently followed the Tibetan tradition — that the TS(P) is a *purely* Vijñānavāda work.

Appendix IV contains a comprehensive synopsis of the Saṃtānāntara-dūṣaṇa of Ratnakīrti.

The references to primary and secondary sources mentioned or used in the text are included in the Bibliography at the end of the work.

PART I:

ŚŪNYATĀ AND THE DOCTRINE OF THE THREE SELF NATURES

The doctrine of rebirth is largely identified in the popular mind of the West with the major Indian religions, Hinduism, Buddhism and Jainism. To some extent this is justified, since it is only in these major religious systems that the doctrine of rebirth is accepted as the orthodox view and, as such, plays a central role in religious belief. It is not always recognized, however, that in these religions rebirth is regarded as *undesirable*. All three of the religions are concerned with the attainment of liberation (*mukti*, *mokṣa*) from the cycle of rebirth (*saṃsāra*). In Hinduism, for example, the aim is to attain a state of merging or identity with God (*īśvara*) or the Absolute (*brahman*). The Buddha, on the other hand, taught a path that leads to *nirvāṇa*.

The term "*nirvāṇa*" refers to something that is blown out (as when one blows out the light of a lamp), extinct, vanished, calmed, quieted, or liberated from existence, or to the state in which this has occurred. There were disputes amongst the Buddhist schools about the subtleties of this "blowing out" or "extinction," but throughout the history of Buddhism in India the meanings of "cessation" or "destruction" were taken to be central to the meaning of the term "*nirvāṇa*." The Hīnayānist school that accepted the annihilationist meaning of the term the most unequivocally was perhaps the Sautrāntika school, for the Sautrāntikas maintained that *nirvāṇa* was not itself a state or thing, but only the extinction of all the conditioned factors of existence of what we refer to as a "person" or "individual." Their principal philosophical opponents, the Sarvāstivādins, maintained that *nirvāṇa* is a positive state which itself exists, but even this view appears to be annihilationist on closer examination, for even the Sarvāstivādins defined *nirvāṇa* as simply the state *in which* all the factors of existence are extinct.[1]

Any interpretation of *nirvāṇa* as a positive state of some sort would appear to be precluded by one of the most basic formulations of Buddhist doctrine, the four-fold noble truths (*ārya-satya*). These are: the truth of suffering (*duḥkha-satya*), the arising of suffering (*samudaya-satya*), the cessation of suffering (*nirodha-satya*) and the path leading to the cessation of suffering (*mārga-satya*). Here it is essential to realize that, according to Buddhist doctrine, *all* states of existence — even that of the highest gods — are impermanent and, as such, states of suffering (*duḥkha*). Since *nirvāṇa* is *defined* as the cessation of suffering, and since all states of existence are held to involve suffering, it would appear to follow that *nirvāṇa* is the cessation of all states of existence. If *nirvāṇa* were any kind of positive entity, the four-fold noble truths should have mentioned a positive state (*ens*) of non-suffering which is independent of the *saṃsāric* process of suffering, the arising of suffering, the cessation of suffering, and the path leading to the cessation of suffering. The oldest texts, however, never seem to refer to such a thing.[2] In the early Buddhist texts, at least, *nirvāṇa* is defined — as it is in the formulation of the four-fold noble truths — as simply the cessation of *saṃsāra*.[3]

Consider, for example, the Aggi-vacchagotta-sutta of the Pāli canon. In this *sutta*, a wanderer by the name of Vacchagotta asks the Buddha whether the world is eternal or not, whether the world is finite or not, whether the soul and the body are the same or different, and whether the Tathāgata exists after death, does not exist after death, both exists and does not exist after death, or neither exists nor does not exist after death. The Buddha tells Vacchagotta that he has no view on these questions. When asked why, the Buddha replies that these questions have nothing to do with leading the "*brahma*-faring": these views, he says, involve wrangling and fettering, and do not "conduce to turning away from, nor to dispassion, stopping, calming, super-knowledge, awakening, nor to *nibbāna*." Then Vacchagotta asks where the monk arises whose mind is thus freed. The Buddha says in reply that "arises" does not apply, that "not arises" does not apply, that "both arises and not arises" does not apply, and that "neither arises nor not arises" does not apply. When Vacchagotta expresses bewilderment at this teaching, the Buddha says that his teaching is hard to see and to understand, and that it is rare, excellent, beyond dialectic, subtle and comprehensible only by the intelligent. He then asks Vacchagotta whether a fire goes to the east, west, north or south when it is extinguished. Vacchagotta replies that this question does not apply, since the fire simply *goes out* (*nibbāna*) when it has exhausted its fuel. Then the Buddha says:

> Even so, Vaccha, that material shape, feeling, perception, impulses and consciousness by which one might define the Tathāgata — all have been got rid of by the Tathāgata, cut off at the root, made like a palm-tree stump that can come to no further existence in the future. Freed from reckoning by form, feeling, perception, impulses and consciousness is the Tathāgata: he is deep, immeasurable, unfathomable, as is the great ocean. "Arises" does not apply, "not arises" does not apply; "both arises and does not arise" does not apply and "neither arises nor does not arise" does not apply.

Note that in this *sutta* it is not the defilements (*kleśas*) of the Buddha which are said to "go out". What "goes out" is the Tathāgata himself.[4]

There are some passages in the oldest strata of Buddhist texts which are sometimes cited as evidence against the view that *nirvāṇa* is simply the complete cessation of existence. One passage which is frequently cited is Udāna VIII. i, which says:

> Monks, there exists that condition wherein is neither earth nor water nor fire nor air: wherein is neither the sphere of infinite space nor of infinite consciousness nor of nothingness nor of neither-consciousness-nor-unconsciousness; where there is neither this world nor a world beyond nor both together nor moon and sun. Thence, monks, I declare is no coming to birth; thither is no going (from life); therein is no duration; thence is no falling; there is no arising. It is not something fixed, it is immovable, it is not based on anything. That indeed is the end of ill.

Ud. VIII. ii adds the following:

> Hard is the infinite (*anattan*) to see; truth is no easy thing to see; / Craving is pierced by him who knows; for him who sees this nothing remains.

And Udāna VIII. iii adds to Ud. i and ii the following:

> Monks, there is a not-born, a not-become, a not-made, a not-compounded. Monks, if that unborn, not-become, not-made, not-compounded were not, there would be apparent no escape from this here that is born, become, made, compounded. But since, monks, there is an unborn etc., therefore the escape from this here that is born, become etc. is apparent.[5]

This passage begins by asserting "There is (*atthi*) a condition" etc. Ordinarily such a passage would assert that there is some *positive* entity with such and such qualities. In Udāna VIII, however, the descriptions that follow the phrase "There is..." are consistently negative. Furthermore, there are clear indications in the passage that it is to be understood in the context of the teaching of the four-fold noble truths, for Ud. VIII says explicitly that the condition described is the "end of ill" (i.e. *nirvāṇa*). Similarly, Ud. VIII. iii says that if there were not the not-born, not-become, not-compounded etc. there would be no escape from *saṃsāra*. This, too, is an unmistakable indication that Ud. VIII is to be understood simply in terms of the four-fold noble truths of suffering, the arising of suffering, the cessation of suffering, and the path leading to the cessation of suffering.

Interpretations of such passages which attribute a positive character to *nirvāṇa* appear to commit the philosophical error of "hypostasizing the negative." In ordinary language, if we want to say that there is no entity *x*, we can do so, if we like, by referring to the non-existence of *x*. But this does not mean that the non-existence of *x* is itself a real thing. Similarly, it appears that Ud. VIII simply restates at greater length the third of the four-fold noble truths, i.e. that there is an end of suffering, and that suffering is therefore neither necessary nor eternal. That this is the meaning that is intended is clear from the very wording of the third noble truth (*nirodha-satya*), for "*nirodha*" simply means "cessation" or "destruction."

The term "*śūnya*" (Pāli "*suñña*"), which is found in the older texts and becomes particularly important in the texts of the Mahāyāna, is closely related in meaning to the terms "*nirodha*" and "*nirvāṇa*." The adjective "*śūnya*" means 1) empty, void; 2) vacant; 3) non-existent; 4) lonely, desolate, deserted; 5) utterly devoid or deprived of; 6) bare or naked. The corresponding nominatives "*śūnyam*" and "*śūnyatā*" mean 1) vacuum, void, blank; 2) sky, space, atmosphere; 3) non-entity or absolute non-existence. It is also relevant here that the Indian mathematicians who discovered the number zero called it "*śūnyam*."

The foregoing definitions (all of which are closely connected in meaning) also apply to the terms "*śūnya*," "*śūnyam*" and "*śūnyatā*" as they were used in the Buddhist texts. These terms, which are connected with the notions of "absence," "lack," "devoidness," "non-existence" etc., were invested in Buddhism with religious significance because, according to Buddhist doctrine, all states of existence involve suffering. The ultimate aim of the Buddhist life, at least in the earliest texts, was the cessation of all suffering, the attainment of which was called *nirvāṇa*. "*Nirvāṇa*" means "blowing out," and is a synonym of the term "*nirodha*," which means extinction. *Nirvāṇa*, therefore, is the attainment of the state of *śūnyam* or *śūnyatā*, i.e. a state of emptiness or voidness in which all of the suffering connected with all states of existence is entirely absent.

The religious significance of the term "*śūnya*" and its connection with the notion of *nirvāṇa* is the theme of the Cūḷa-suññata-sutta of the Majjhima-nikāya.[6] In this *sutta* the Buddha teaches that the cessation of suffering depends on the cessation of being and becoming. In this connection he describes for his interlocutors a series of stages or planes which moves progressively from consciousness to unconsciousness, and from being to non-being:

(a) Consciousness of humanity
(b) Consciousness of the forest
(c) Consciousness of the earth
(d) Consciousness of the infinity of space
(e) Consciousness of the infinity of thought
(f) Consciousness of nothingness (*ākiñcaññāyatana-saññā*)
(g) Consciousness of neither consciousness nor unconsciousness
(h) Objectless cessation of consciousness
(i) The supreme, ultimate void (*paramānuttarā suññatā*).

There is a passage in this *sutta* which describes emptiness (P. *suññatā*) in terms of the analogy of the forest. Life in the forest — the traditional refuge of Indian religious men who had renounced worldly life — is extolled because it is held to be free of the cares and suffering attendant on worldly life. However, it is not any of the *positive* qualities of the forest or life in the forest which are extolled in the *sutta*, but the mere fact that the forest is devoid (*śūnya*) of the those things which trouble people in the cities and towns.[7] Since it is the mere voidness or emptiness (*suññatā*) which gives forest dwellers some release from suffering, the *sutta* concludes that earth itself, which is devoid of even the vegetation of the forest, should provide an even greater release from suffering [cf. consciousness of the earth, stage (c) above]. The *sutta* then proceeds through the succeeding states (d) through (i) above, arriving ultimately at the view that the final release from suffering (*duḥkha*) is attained when the Buddhist attains the supreme, ultimate void (*paramānuttarā suññatā*). This is the stage that ensues after the attainment of the "objectless cessation of consciousness."

There are passages in the early texts which state that the *world* is itself empty (*suñña*). However, these texts specify that the world is empty in the sense that it is "empty of self or what belongs to a self." The schools of the Hīnayāna took this to mean, not that the world itself was unreal or literally void, but that there is no self or soul in a person or sentient being.[8] In lieu of a soul-theory, the early Buddhist texts described a person or sentient being in terms of the five groups (*skandhas*) of form (*rūpa*), feeling (*vedanā*), perception (*saṃjñā*), impulses (*saṃskāras*) and consciousness or mind (*vijñāna*).[9] A useful analogy — one that is found in the Hīnayāna work called the Milinda-pañha — is that of a chariot. Just as, it is said, it would be an error to think of a chariot as an entity apart from its constituent parts like the axle, the hub, the wheel and so on, so it is an error to think that there is an entity or substance — a self — apart from the constituent elements of form, feeling, perception, impulses and consciousness. On this view, the self (*ātman*) is unreal. What really exists is only an ever-changing stream of constituent elements or *dharmas*.

The Mahāyānists rejected this interpretion of emptiness (*śūnyatā*), or to be more precise, thought that it did not go far enough. According to the *sūtras* and *śāstras* of the Mahāyāna, even these purported constituent elements are unreal and void (*śūnya, abhāva*). This theme can be traced back to the very earliest Mahāyāna texts. In the Aṣṭa-sāhasrikā-prajñā-pāramitā, for example, the statement that all *dharmas* are signless, wishless, unaffected, unproduced, unoriginated and *non-existent* (*abhāva*) appears as a *leitmotif* at least six different times.[10] This doctrine of the voidness of all *dharmas* (*sarva-dharma-śūnyatā*) raises the following question: If the world is unreal, what is that we *seem* to experience? The two major schools of the Mahāyāna diverged over the answer to this question. According to the Vijñānavādins, the world is nothing but mind (*vijñāna-mātra*). On this view, mind as such is real, and it is only external objects which are unreal. The Vijñānavāda, therefore, had an answer to the question "What is it that we actually experience?" The answer is: "What we see is a mere illusion (*māyā*) or appearance (*ābhāsa*) of the mind." The other school — the Śūnyavāda or Madhyamaka — was more radical. According to the Śūnyavādins or Mādhyamikas, even the teaching that the world is mind only is a provisional truth. In the final analysis, even the mind itself is non-existent, empty and void (*śūnya*). Even experience is unreal.[11]

Support for both interpretations of the doctrine of the voidness of all *dharmas* can be found in the Mahāyāna texts. On the one hand, there are many passages in the Mahāyāna *sūtras* which state that the world is nothing but the false ideation of the mind, like a dream.[12] On the other hand, there are numerous passages which state that all *dharmas* are void (*sarva-dharma-śūnyatā*), and since mind (*vijñāna*) itself is just a group of *dharmas,* according to Buddhist doctrine, it should follow that mind itself is strictly void. The two schools, therefore, differed about which interpretation was the highest or direct teaching (*nītārtha*) and which was the provisional or indirect teaching (*neyārtha*). According to the Śūnyavādins, the mind only teachings of the Mahāyāna scriptures were addressed by the Buddha to those disciples who could not grasp or accept the teaching that everything (including the mind) is totally unreal and void. People of the ordinary sort will always insist on asking: "How can the world be totally unreal when it is perfectly obvious that I am seeing *something*?" According to the Mādhyamikas, the Buddha replied to this sort of person: "What you see is merely a mental creation (*viparyāsa*, *māyā*)." According to the Śūnyavādins, however, the correct and final teaching of the Buddha is: "You are not seeing anything at all. Everything is non-existent and void." It was only when an individual was unable to grasp this teaching that the Buddha met the person halfway by saying that what the person saw was real, but only as an appearance (*ābhāsa*) of the mind.[13]

The Mādhyamikas were clearly the more radical school of the Mahāyāna, for while it might make sense to say that there is no external world, it is not at all obvious how it could make any sense to say that both the world *and* the mind that seems to perceive it are non-existent.[14] Furthermore, the Vijñānavādins also maintained that the Mādhyamika doctrine was doctrinally or soteriologically objectionable. The Buddhist scriptures state that the aim of the Buddhist religion (*buddha-dharma*) is to lead sentient beings from *saṃsāric* suffering to the liberation from suffering which is found in *nirvāṇa*. The Vijñānavādins argued that none of these teachings make any sense on the view that the mind — and therefore suffering itself — is unreal and totally non-existent (*abhāva*). The Vijñānavādins, therefore, interpreted the statement in the *sūtras* that all *dharmas* are void to mean that everything is mind only. This view, which interprets the doctrine of emptiness to mean that what does exist (i.e. mind) is *devoid of* any material object or thing, may be called the doctrine of "other emptiness," as opposed to a doctrine of emptiness as such.

This would appear to be a less plausible interpretation of the Mahāyāna doctrine of the emptiness of all *dharmas* than the Mādhyamika one, though it is one that is far more defensible — and even far more intelligible — on philosophical grounds. Furthermore, the Vijñānavādin interpretation can be more easily reconciled with the earlier texts which were recognized as canonical by all of the Buddhist schools. According to all the Buddhist schools, mind or consciousness (*vijñāna*), as one of the five groups of *dharmas*, is destroyed in the final *nirvāṇa* of total extinction (*nirupadhi-śeṣa-nirvāṇa*).[15] The Vijñānavādins believed that the mind continues to exist and that *saṃsāra* continues to be real, at least as a mental phenomenon, as long as the *nirupadhi-śeṣa-nirvāṇa* has not been attained. The only difference between the Hīnayānists and the Vijñānavādins on *this* point was that the Vijñānavādins, unlike the Hīnayānists, maintained that *saṃsāra* is purely ideal or mental.

The terms "emptiness" (*śūnyatā, śūnyam*) and "mind only" (*vijñapti-mātra*) are treated as closely related terms in the Vijñānavāda. This can be seen in the first chapter of the Madhyānta-vibhāga ("The Discrimination between the Middle and the Extremes").

This work is ascribed either to a Maitreyanātha or to Ārya Asaṅga (fl. 350 C.E.), who in the Buddhist tradition is said to have been the half-brother of Vasubandhu (the real founder of the school) and the individual responsible for converting Vasubandhu to the Mahāyāna. There is also a commentary (*bhāṣya*) on the text which is ascribed to Vasubandhu (MVB), and another commentary (*ṭīkā*) on Vasubandhu's commentary by Shiramati (MVBT). If the *bhāṣya* on the MV is authentic, it means that the MV itself is probably an older text than even the Viṃśatikā or Triṃśikā of Vasubandhu.

Chapter 1 (*lakṣaṇa-pariccheda*) of the Madhyānta-vibhāga consists of two parts. Verses 1-11 are principally concerned with the subject of what is called "false ideation" (*abhūta-parikalpa*); verses 12-22 are principally concerned with the topic of emptiness (*śūnyatā*). This is a rather rough division, however, for both of these are regarded as interconnected concepts. (The concept of *śūnyatā*, for example, actually occurs in the definition of the false imagination which is given in the first verse.) The connection between these two concepts is contained in the doctrine of the three self natures (*tri-svabhāva-lakṣaṇa*). These three self natures are:

(1) The purely imagined nature (*kalpita, parikalpita*). This is the nature of the supposed external objects. According to the Vijñānavādins, these are entirely non-existent (*abhāva*).

(2) The other-dependent nature (*paratantra-svabhāva*). This is another name for the mind (*vijñāna*) and the false imagination (*abhūta-parikalpa*). It is essentially what appears as the external objects, or what causes the appearance of the external objects. Although it appears to be something that it is not (i.e. an external object) it is not itself unreal.

(3) The perfected nature (*pariniṣpanna*). This is identified by MV 1.14 — at least by implication — with emptiness (*śūnyatā*), suchness (*tathatā*), the reality limit (*bhūta-koṭi*), the signless and the causeless (*animitta*), the absolute reality (*paramārtha*) and the fundamental reality (*dharma-dhātu*).

The text and a translation of the first chapter (*lakṣaṇa-pariccheda*) of the Madhyānta-vibhāga are given below:

THE DISCRIMINATION BETWEEN THE MIDDLE AND THE EXTREMES

FALSE IDEATION (ABHŪTA-PARIKALPA)

1. False ideation (*abhūta-parikalpa*) exists. Duality does not exist in it. However emptiness (*śūnyatā*) does exist in the false ideation, and false ideation also exists in emptiness.

   abhūta-parikalpo 'sti dvayaṃ tatra na vidyate /
   śūnyatā vidyate tv-atra tasyām-api sa vidyate //

2. Because of existence, non-existence and again existence [i.e. because of the existence of the false ideation, the non-existence of duality in the false ideation, and the existence of that non-existence] everything is said in the Mahāyāna to be neither void (*śūnya*) nor non-void. This is the middle path (*madhyamā pratipad*).

   na śūnyaṃ nāpi cāśūnyaṃ tasmāt sarvaṃ vidhīyate /
   sattvād-asattvāt sattvāc-ca madhyamā-pratipac-ca sā //

3. Consciousness (*vijñāna*) arises in the appearance of things, sentient beings, self (*ātman*) and ideas (*vijñapti*); its external object (*artha*) does not exist, and because of the non-existence of the external object, mind itself is false (*asat*).

artha-sattvātma-vijñapti-pratibhāsaṃ prajāyate /
vijñānaṃ nāsti cāsyārthas-tad-abhāvāt-tad-apy-asat //

4. Hence the nature of the false ideation is established. Because the mind is not, in this way, totally non-existent, liberation (*mukti*) is said to be from the destruction of the mind.

abhūta-parikalpatvaṃ siddham-asya bhavaty-ataḥ /
na tathā sarvathābhāvāt tat-kṣayān-muktir-iṣyate //

5. The imagined (*kalpita*), the dependent (*paratantra*) and the perfected (*pariniṣpanna*) are taught on account of external things, false ideation and the non-existence of duality (*dvayābhāva*).

kalpitaḥ paratantraś-ca pariniṣpanna eva ca /
arthād-abhūtakalpāc-ca dvayābhāvāc-ca deśitaḥ //

6. On the basis of perception of mind only, non-perception of external objects arises. Based on the non-perception of external objects, non-perception of mind only arises.

upalabdhiṃ samāśritya nopalabdhiḥ prajāyate /
nopalabdhiṃ samāśritya nopalabdhiḥ prajāyate //

7. Hence it is established that perception has the nature of non-perception. Hence the identity (*samatā*) of perception and non-perception is known.

upalabhdes-tataḥ siddhā nopalabdhi-svabhāvatā /
tasmāc-ca samatā jñeyā nopalambhopalambhayoḥ //

8. The three realms (*dhātus*) are false ideation and the mental associates (*citta-caittas*). Mind is perception (*dṛṣṭi*) with respect to the external object; the mental associates are the perception of what is different from the external object.

abhūta-parikalpaś-ca citta-caittās-tridhātukāḥ /
tatrārtha-dṛṣṭir-vijñānaṃ tad-viśeṣe tu caitasāḥ //

9. The mind is consciousness as condition (*pratyaya-vijñāna*) and the second (the mental associates) is the experiencing or enjoying consciousness. In it the mental phenomena are experience, discrimination and volition.

ekaṃ pratyaya-vijñānaṃ dvitīyaṃ caupabhogikam /
upabhoga-pariccheda-prerakās-tatra caitasāḥ //

10,11. Because of completing, because of the definite perception caused by the three, because of enjoyment, projection, fitting, confronting with and suffering, the world is defiled. Because of the false ideation, there is the three-fold, the two-fold and the seven-fold defilement.

chādanād-ropaṇāc-caiva nayanāt-saṃparigrahāt /
pūraṇāt tri-paricchedād-upabhogāc-ca karṣaṇāt //

nibandhanād-ābhimukhyād duḥkhanāt kliśyate jagat /
tredhā dvedhā ca saṃkleśaḥ saptadhābhūta-kalpanāt //

EMPTINESS

12. Now the characteristics (*lakṣaṇa*), the synonyms (*paryāya*), the meaning (*artha*) of the synonyms, the discrimination (*bheda*) and the realization (*sādhana*) of emptiness (*śūnyatā*) are to be fully understood.

lakṣaṇaṃ cātha paryāyas-tad-artho bheda eva ca /
sādhanaṃ ceti vijñeyaṃ śūnyatāyāḥ samāsataḥ //

(the characteristics of emptiness) *(lakṣaṇa):*

13. The essence of emptiness (*śūnyam*) is the non-existence of duality (*dvayābhāva*) and the existence of this non-existence (*abhāvasya bhāva*). Neither existence nor non-existence (*na bhāvo nāpi vābhāvaḥ*), emptiness has neither the nature of being different *(pṛthaktva)* nor the nature of being the same (*eka-lakṣaṇa*).

dvayābhāvo hy-abhāvasya bhāvaḥ śūnyasya lakṣaṇam /
na bhāvo nāpi vābhāvaḥ na pṛthaktvaika-lakṣaṇam //

(the synonyms of emptiness: *śūnyatā-paryāya*):

14. Summarily, the synonyms of emptiness are: suchness (*tathatā*), the reality limit (*bhūta-koṭi*), the signless *(animitta)*, the absolute reality (*paramārtha*) and the fundamental reality (*dharma-dhātu*).

tathatā bhūta-koṭiś-cānimittaṃ paramārthatā /
dharma-dhātuś-ca paryāyāḥ śūnyatāyāḥ samāsataḥ //

(the meaning of the synonyms: *paryāyārtha*):

15. Immutability, non-erroneousness, the destruction (*nirodha*) of the sign or cause, the field of activity of the noble (*ārya-gocara*) and the cause of the noble *dharmas* (*ārya-dharmas*): these are the meanings of the synonyms of emptiness which follow in due order.

ananyathāviparyāsa-tan-nirodhārya-gocaraiḥ /
hetutvāc-cārya-dharmāṇāṃ paryāyārtho yathā-kramam //

(the discrimination of emptiness: *prabheda*):

16. Emptiness is defiled and purified, and it is pure and impure. Its purity is said to be like the purity of water, gold and space.

saṃkliṣṭā ca viśuddhā ca samalā nirmalā ca sā /
ab-dhātu-kanakākāśa-śuddhivac-chuddhir-iṣyate //

17. The emptiness of the enjoyer, the emptiness of the enjoyed, the emptiness of the body thereof, the emptiness of any thing (*vastu*), and that by which emptiness is perceived, the way in which it is perceived and the object which is perceived: all these are just emptiness.

bhoktṛ-bhojana tad-deha-pratiṣṭhā-vastu-śūnyatā /
tac-ca yena yathā dṛṣṭaṃ yad-arthaṃ tasya śūnyatā //

18. Emptiness is the object (*artha*) of attaining the two purifications, in order to help all sentient beings, in order to not renounce *saṃsāra*, and in order to attain the inexhaustible goodness (*akṣaya-kuśala*).

śubha-dvayasya prāpty-arthaṃ sadā sattva-hitāya ca /
saṃsārātyajanārthaṃ ca kuśalasyākṣayāya ca //

19. In order to purify the lineage of the Buddha, in order to attain the principal and the secondary marks, and in order to purify the *buddha-dharmas*, the Bodhisattva practices.

gotrasya ca viśuddhy-arthaṃ lakṣaṇa-vyañjanāptaye /
śuddhaye buddha-dharmāṇām bodhisattvaḥ prapadyate //

20. The non-existence of the self (*pudgala*) and the non-existence of all *dharmas* is one emptiness. The real existence (*sad-bhāva*) of that non-existence is the other emptiness (*sā śūnyatāparā*).

pudgalasyātha dharmāṇām-abhāvaḥ śūnyatātra hi /
tad-abhāvasya sad-bhāvas-tasmin sā śūnyatāparā //

(the realization of emptiness: *sādhana*):

21. If defilement did not exist, all creatures would be liberated. If purity did not exist, all effort would be in vain.

saṃkliṣṭā ced-bhaven-nāsau muktāḥ syuḥ sarva-dehinaḥ /
viśuddhā ced-bhaven-nāsau hy-āyāso niṣphalo bhavet //

22. Emptiness is neither defiled nor non-defiled, neither pure nor impure, because the mind (*citta*) is innately pure and the defilements are adventitious.

na kliṣṭā nāpi cākliṣṭā śuddhāśuddhā na caiva sā /
prabhāsvaratvāc-cittasya kleśasyāgantukatvataḥ //

Even without the reference to the non-renunciation of *saṃsāra* in MV 1.18 it would be clear that the above verses are from a Mahāyāna text. In the early, canonical Buddhist texts, the highest state of attainment (*nirvāṇa*) was not identified with reality or the nature of things (*paramārtha*) or the way things really are (*yathā-bhūtam*). It was simply the state of extinction and peace which ensues — at least at death — for the individual who has *realized* the way things really are. *Nirvāṇa* in the early Buddhist texts is pure void (*śūnyatā, śūnyam*), as in the Cūḷa-suññata-sutta, where it is described as the supreme, ultimate void (*paramānuttarā suññatā*), and in the Vacchagotta-sutta, where it is conceived as the mere going out of a fire. Since the world is certainly real in the original teachings, there is no question in early Buddhism of identifying the *saṃsāric* world of dependent co-origination (*pratītya-samutpāda*) with the void (*śūnyam, śūnyatā*), which would entail that it was somehow unreal.

In the Madhyānta-vibhāga, however, some identification of this kind is made. Here, the concept of emptiness is linked with the concept of reality. As a corollary, the text wishes to show that emptiness (*śūnyam, śūnyatā*) is not mere non-existence or negation, but is itself a reality (*abhāvasya bhāva, sad-bhāva*), as in MV 1.13 and 1.20. Even more strikingly, it wants to argue that emptiness is in some sense both existence *and* non-existence.

Note that there is one thing in these verses that clearly corresponds to emptiness in the sense in which "*śūnya*," "*śūnyatā*" etc. were used in Sanskrit and in the early Buddhist texts, and that is the imagined nature (*parikalpita*). MV 1.5 identifies the imagined nature with the external object (*artha*), and MV 1.3 says that this external object does not exist (*nāsti cāsyārtha*). Since "*x* is non-existent" is one of the possible meanings of "*x* is *śūnya*," and since the imagined nature (i.e. the external object) is said to be non-existent, it would be perfectly natural on purely semantic grounds to identify the non-existent external object or *parikalpita* with emptiness (*śūnyatā*). This, however, the MV does not do.

The question whether the *dependent* nature is void (*śūnya*) is more complicated. According to one meaning, "*śūnya*" is a two-place predicate (i.e. a relation), and according to another meaning it is a one-place predicate. Thus, one could say that a purported entity is entirely non-existent and void; it is in this sense that a married bachelor or the son of a barren woman or the horn of a hare is *śūnya*. In this use, "*x* is *śūnya*" is a one-place predicate. On the other hand, one could say that a jar is *śūnya*, in the sense that the jar is empty of water. This would use "*x* is *śūnya*" as a two-place predicate, i.e. as a relation.

The MV says that the mind is empty in the second sense because it is *devoid of* the non-existent external object. It holds that everything is mind only, and that the appearance of external objects is just an illusory appearance of the mind. In other words, what does exist (i.e. mind) is devoid of external objects, just as one might say that a jar is empty of water. As in the case of the jar example, the mind only teachings of the MV do not mean that mind is empty in the sense that mind is unreal, as the Mādhyamikas contended. MV 1.1, for example, says that the false imagination exists, and since the text takes "false imagination" to be one of the synonyms of mind (*vijñāna*), the MV is committed to the view that mind itself is not unreal.

MV 1.4 appears to qualify MV 1.1 somewhat, for it says that the false imagination (i.e. the mind) is not totally non-existent (*na tathā sarvathābhāva*). However, the point of this qualification appears to be that the mind is unreal in the sense that *it appears to be something that it is not.* According to the Vijñānavāda, it is an essential characeristic of the mind that it *appears* as external objects, hence the mind is *deceptive* in the sense that it appears to be something that it is not. The MV concludes that one must say that the mind itself is "not totally unreal," presumably because what is real about the mind is not the same thing as what is *thought* to be real about it.

Thus, two senses of *"śūnya"* are involved in the MV's use of the word "*asat.*" In Sanskrit the word "*asat*" can mean "false" in the sense of "deceptive," or it can mean "non-existent." If something does not exist as what it appears to be, it may be said to be *asat* in the first sense but not the second, i.e. it may be said to be deceptive but it is not itself non-existent.

Consider, for example, the rope-snake illusion — one of the most common examples in Indian epistemology. If a person is walking along in the dusk and takes a rope in the path to be a snake, then the snake as such is *asat* in the sense that it is unreal or non-existent. It would make no sense to ask of this "snake" questions like: How and when was it born, where did it come from, where did it go, how much did it weigh? etc. In this example, however, something really does exist, i.e. the rope which is misperceived. Therefore the rope may be said to be *asat* (in the sense of "false" or "deceptive") in the conditions in which it is perceived. Something real is "false" or "unreal" in this sense when it is the basis for an illusory appearance. According to the Vijñānavādins, mind is *asat* in the sense of this twilight-rope: i.e. it appears as an external object, but this object, according to the Vijñānavāda, is totally unreal. Nevertheless, mind is still *śūnya* — at least in one sense — for it is empty of the thing it appears to be, just as a desert is empty of the water that appears to exist when we see a mirage.

Note, however, that the notion of "other emptiness" which is applied to the mind does not give us what the MV regards as emptiness (*śūnyatā*) itself, any more than the imagined nature (*parikalpita*) does. Even if the Vijñānavāda is right in maintaining that the mind is nondual in the sense that it appears as external objects which are non-existent, this nondual mind would still not give us the *śūnyatā* which is identified by MV 1.14 with suchness (*tathatā*), the reality limit (*bhūta-koṭi*), the signless (*animitta*), the absolute reality (*paramārtha*) and the fundamental reality (*dharma-dhātu*). Emptiness is invested by the MV, and the Mahāyāna generally, with religious significance, and is equated with *nirvāṇa*, enlightenment, the true nature of things, or all of these simultaneously. All these are connected, not with the other dependent nature (*paratantra*) or the imagined nature (*parikalpita*), but with the perfected nature (*pariniṣpanna*).

MV 1.13 defines *śūnyatā* in the following way:

> The essence or characteristic of *śūnya* is the non-existence of duality and the existence of this non-existence. Neither existence (*bhāva*) nor non-existence (*abhāva*), it has neither the nature of being different nor the nature of being the same.[16]

A closely related definition of *śūnyatā* is given in MV 1.20, which says:

> The non-existence of self and *dharmas* is one emptiness; the real existence (*sad-bhāva*) of that non-existence there [i.e. in the self and *dharmas*] is the other emptiness (*sā śūnyatāparā*).

Note that there are two parts to these definitions. First, *śūnyatā* is said to be the non-existence of duality or the external objects, i.e., as the non-existence of the self and the *dharmas*.[17] Secondly, emptiness is said to be the existence of this non-existence. I shall refer to the two parts of these definitions of *śūnyatā* in MV 1.13 and 1.20 as D1 and D2:

D1 Emptiness is the non-existence of duality (i.e. the non-existence of the external object, either self or *dharmas*).

D2 Emptiness is the existence of this non-existence (i.e. the existence of the non-existence of the external objects).

Since the perfected nature (*pariniṣpanna*) is defined in MV 1.5 as the non-existence of duality, D1 of MV 1.13 and MV 1.20 (and presumably D2 as well) must be intended as definitions of the perfected nature, as well as definitions of emptiness. Nevertheless, MV 1.13 and MV 1.20, and D1 and D2, will not do as definitions of *śūnyatā* and the perfected nature.

Consider the following three notions:

(a) The external objects, also called duality (*dvaya*).
(b) The non-existence of the external objects.
(c) The existence of the non-existence of the external objects.

The MV's definitions presuppose that it is meaningful to assume that each of (a) - (c) refers to something different, but this is surely incorrect. First of all, no distinction can be drawn (at least in the actual world) between a non-existent object and its non-existence; consequently, no distinction can be drawn between (a) and (b). For similar reasons, it doesn't make any sense to speak of the existence of the nonexistence of something, either.

To get a clearer view of the philosophical point that is involved here, consider the following two sentences:

(1) The present king of France exists.
(2) The present king of France is bald.

If (1) and (2) are uttered when there is a king of France, (1) will be true, and (2) will be true if he is bald. Both these sentences have the grammatical structure of subject-predicate sentences, i.e. from a purely grammatical point of view (1) attributes the predicate "*x* exists" to the king of France, and (2) attributes the property "*x* is bald" to the king of France. However, the view that the grammatical structure of these sentences actually gives the meaning or logical structure of the sentences leads to difficulties which emerge as soon as we try to analyze the meaning of these sentences or the meaning of the sentence

(3) The king of France does not exist.

when (as in 1990) there is no king of France.

Like (1) and (2), (3) has the grammatical form of a subject-predicate sentence, i.e. grammatically speaking it predicates the expression "does not exist" of the king of France, or at least denies that the predicate "*x* exists" is true of the king of France. But what is the *logical* meaning of the sentence? For example, what makes the sentence true when it is true? It would be odd to suppose that when the sentence is true it is true because there is a property Non-existence which is true of the king of France, and also odd to suppose that when the sentence is true it is true because the property Existence does *not* apply to the king of France — for the simple reason that if the sentence is true there *is* no king of France.

Bertrand Russell (1905) pointed out that this kind of problem dissolves under analysis as soon as one recognizes that "*x* exists" — unlike, for example, "*x* is bald" — is not a genuine predicate.[18] Russell argued persuasively that (3), despite its grammatical appearance, is not a subject-predicate statement about the king of France at all; instead, it simply denies that there is an entity *x* such that *x* is the king of France. In Russell's analysis of the sentence, the referring expression "the king of France" and the predicate "*x* does not exist" no longer appear. The predicate "*x* does not exist" is replaced by the expression "It is not the case that there is an *x*" and the referential expression "the king of France" is replaced by the predicate expression "is a king of France."

When (3) is interpreted in the way Russell suggested — i.e. as meaning that there is no *x* such that *x* is the king of France — it is quite easy to see how it could be true. Similarly, it is easy to see why (2) is false when it is uttered when there is no king of France, for according to Russell (2) simply means (roughly):

(4) There is an *x* (and only one *x*) such that *x* is the king of France and *x* is bald.

and this assertion is simply false.

According to Russell's analysis, it clearly makes no sense to speak (as MV 1.13 does) of the "existence of the non-existence" of something. What would the phrase "the existence of the non-existence of the present king of France" mean? Note that this phrase cannot even be translated à la Russell. Perhaps the closest thing we can get (and it is definitely *not* a Russellian analysis) is something like: "It is the case that it is not the case that there is an entity *x* such that *x* is the present king of France." If this is what the words "the existence of the non-existence of *x*" mean, then they simply entail the non-existence of *x*. In other words, the phrase "the existence of the non-existence of *x*" can only mean the non-existence of *x*. But if *this* is what the phrase means, it makes no sense to say, as MV 1.20 does, that the existence of the non-existence of *x* is a reality in its own right (*sad-bhāva*).

Suppose, on the other hand, that one treats the expression "the present king of France" as a referring expression and the expression "*x* exists" as a predicate (as some philosophers in the Western analytic tradition after Russell have continued to do). This actually makes matters worse, for MV 1.13's definition of the perfected nature then turns out to be contradictory.

Consider first the following three sentences:

(5) The jar is blue.
(6) The blueness of the jar is beautiful.
(7) The beauty of the jar's blueness was noted by Devadatta.

It is natural to analyze these sentences grammatically in the following way. In (5) "the jar" is the grammatical subject of the sentence, and refers to an entity which possesses the property Blue. In (6) this property Blueness is itself referred to by the grammatical subject of the sentence, and this property is said to be beautiful. In (7) the property Beauty is made the grammatical subject of the sentence. It therefore corresponds grammatically to the first-order property Blue in (6), and in (7), therefore, it could be said that it is referred to as a second-order property.

Now consider the following three phrases:

8. the present king of France (uttered when, as in 1990, there is no king of France)
9. the non-existence of the present king of France
10. the existence of the non-existence of the present king of France.

Analyzing (10) along the lines of (5)-(7), the property Existence of (10) becomes a second-order property, and the corresponding first-order property is Non-existence. Now we must ask: Does it make any sense to apply the second-order property Existence to the first-order property Non-existence? One would think not. Clearly, (10) is unacceptable in a way that (7) is not, for while it is perfectly natural to speak of the beauty of the color Blue, it is patently senseless to speak of the "existence of the non-existence" of something. There is no reason to think that this phrase makes any more sense than it does to speak of the non-blueness (or the redness) of the color Blue or the non-circularity (or triangularity) of a circle.

What the MV seems to imply is that there is a real thing (*sadbhāva*) called *śūnyatā* which is in some way an Absolute and the true nature (*paramārtha*) of things. The problem is that the assertion that emptiness is itself a thing contradicts the plain meaning of "*śūnya*," "*śūnyatā*" etc. in ordinary Sanskrit and in the Buddhist texts themselves. If *śūnyatā* were a positive entity (i.e. an existent thing) then *śūnyatā* would be a counter-example to the plain meaning of the early Buddhist texts, all of which assert that everything that exists is suffering. The MV attempts to evade these difficulties by speaking of emptiness as the non-existence of duality and as the existence of the non-existence of this duality, but as we have just seen, this apparently makes no sense.

What about the other dependent nature (*paratantra*)? Is there a way of construing *it* as the true nature of things (*paramārtha*), the reality limit, the immutable suchness (*tathatā*) etc.? In one respect it would be natural to expect such an identification, for the Vijñānavādins asserted that everything is mind only. Nevertheless, it is clear, on examination, that mind cannot be the same thing as *śūnyatā* either.

The Madhyānta-vibhāga's doctrines on the nature of the mind are not very clear, and perhaps not even consistent. Consider MV 1.21 and 1.22. The first part of MV 1.21 says that the defiled, false imagination exists because otherwise all sentient beings would be liberated by nature and there would be no *saṃsāra*. (This assertion is directed against the Mādhyamikas, who held that everything — even the mind — is totally void.) The MV's assertion that the defiled, false imagination exists is consistent with the traditional Buddhist teachings, according to which what we call mind or consciousness is in fact just an aggregate (*skandha*) of *dharmas,* and as such one of the essential links in the cycle of suffering and rebirth. However, MV 1.22 and the second part of MV 1.21, which asserts that *purity* exists, are more problematic.

MV 1.22 says that the essential nature of the mind is purity. A very natural way of interpreting the doctrine of the innately pure mind is to say that mind, or at least the dualistic mind which distinguishes between subject and object, is defiled (and is therefore different from emptiness), but that the pure mind, or the nondual mind, is not defiled and is not different from emptiness. However, this would imply that mind in its true nature is not *saṃsāric*, and as I have just pointed out, this contradicts fundamental Buddhist doctrines. Furthermore, there are at least two passages in the Vijñānavāda literature which show that passages like MV 1.22 were not taken by the Vijñānavādins to mean what they might seem to mean. One of these is Xuan Zang's commentary (CWSL) on Triṃśikā 2, and another is Sthiramati's commentary on MV 1.22 (MVBT 1.22).

(a) Xuan Zang was a member of the Dharmapāla school of the Vijñānavāda. According to Dharmapāla, impure *dharmas* cannot give rise to pure *dharmas*; consequently, if pure "seeds" or "potentialities" (*bījas*) were not innate in the mind from the beginning the very thought of enlightenment (*bodhi-citta*) could not occur. After Xuan Zang has endorsed this view in CWSL 2, he has an opponent suggest another possibility: that the mind is by its very nature pure. Xuan Zang characterizes his opponent's view in the following way: "They believe," he says, "that the nature of the mind is 'essentially immaculate' (*prakṛti-viśuddha*); but, being defiled by impurities, the adventitious (*āgantuka*) dusts, the mind is said to be defiled; when it is separated from the defilements, it becomes pure (*anāsrava*)." He then launches into a criticism of this doctrine:

> [Xuan Zang]: "We ask: what is the meaning of the expression 'the nature of the mind'? Is it a question of voidness (*śūnyatā*), i.e. of the true nature of things or *bhūta-tathatā*? This is not the *cause* of mind; being unconditioned (*asaṃskṛta*) and immutable, it cannot be the seed of the pure *dharmas*, because it is always the same in the future as it was in the past."[19, 20]

Xuan Zang then raises the following additional objections to the idea that the mind itself is innately pure:

1. The view that the mind is immutable and unique in its nature, but that it nevertheless evolves with respect to its characteristics, is the view of the non-Buddhist school of the Sāṃkhya, and is therefore heretical and false.
2. If the mind were essentially pure, then the bad mind and the mind which is non-defined (i.e. neither good nor bad) would also be good, which is absurd.
3. If the impure mind were pure, then the pure mind would also be impure, and this is not the result that is desired.

The question is then raised by the opponent: "What, then, is the meaning of the *sūtras* (e.g. the Vimalakīrti, the Śrīmālā etc.) that speak of the immaculate nature of the mind?" Xuan Zang's reply is as follows:

> The *sūtra* refers to the true nature of things (*bhūta-tathatā*) which the voidness (*śūnyatā*) of the mind manifests, because the true nature of things (*bhūta-tathatā*) is the true nature of the mind. Or else, what the *sūtra* says is that 'the nature essentially immaculate' (*prakṛti-viśuddha*) is the principle of the substance of the mind, because the principle or the substance of the mind is free from the impurities (*kleśas*). The nature of the impure mind is not called 'essentially immaculate' because it would then be pure (*anāsrava*).

In other words, Xuan Zang rejects the idea that the mind as such could be essentially immaculate, and allows only that the *śūnyatā* or *bhūta-tathatā*, or something he calls the "principle" or the "substance" of the mind (Ch. *di*) could be innately pure.

When one looks carefully at this passage, it is clear that Xuan Zang is saying that mind and purity, or mind and emptiness, are *necessarily* two different things. According to Xuan Zang, therefore, mind cannot really be pure; only the essence of what is *not* mind can be pure.[21] To be sure, Xuan Zang's interpretation of the doctrine of the innately pure mind leaves that doctrine rather mysterious. This, however, is probably inevitable, since this doctrine contradicts other Buddhist teachings about the nature of *saṃsāra* and *nirvāṇa* which are absolutely fundamental. For example, the traditional Buddhist teachings clearly assert that the mind itself (and not just its defilements) is *saṃsāric*, defiled and involved in suffering. Otherwise passages like Udāna III (cited above) would presumably have asserted that only the mind's *defilements* are extinguished in *nirvāṇa*; instead, the texts plainly assert that it is mind *itself* that is extinguished. Furthermore, the very distinction between the essence of mind and its (defiled) properties is a distinction which cannot be made within Mahāyānist philosophy, for the Mahāyānists rejected the distinction between substance and properties.

(b) Like Xuan Zang, Sthiramati (MVBT 1.22) denies that mind is innately pure; instead, he interprets MV 1.22 to mean that the *essence* of mind (*citta-dharmatā*) is innately pure. Here it is important to note that MV 1.22 occurs in the second set of verses of the chapter, i.e., it occurs in the set of verses that is concerned *principally* with the subject of emptiness (*śūnyatā*). Hence when Sthiramati says that it is the essence of mind (*citta-dharmatā*) that is innately pure, what he undoubtedly means is that the essence of mind is just emptiness, and therefore that *emptiness* is innately pure. This is in fact what we might have expected from the meaning of "*śūnya*" in ordinary Sanskrit, for non-existence (*abhāvatva*) can in a sense be said to be "pure." This interpretation, furthermore, is supported by all the early texts that were regarded by canonical by all of the Buddhist schools. According to the earliest teachings, the only state that is free from defilement is *nirvāṇa*. This is defined, as we have seen, as the cessation or extinction (*nirodha*) of *all* states of existence, since all states of existence are necessarily implicated in suffering. In one sense, therefore, it is natural for Sthiramati to argue that the essence of mind, interpreted as *śūnyatā*, is pure. However, Sthiramati's interpretation of MV 1.22, like Xuan Zang's interpretation of Triṃś. 2, is problematic, because it appears to equate the emptiness/non-emptiness distinction with the substance/property distinction. If emptiness is construed as the essence or substance of mind, then both mind and the essence of mind should be non-existent, and this not the result that the Vijñānavādins wanted.[22]

The fundamental problem that Sthiramati and Xuan Zang faced in interpreting verses like MV 1.22 is that in traditional Buddhist teachings mind is *intrinsically* bound up in *saṃsāra*. The Vijñānavāda teaching that matter and external objects are entirely unreal, and that everything is mind only, should not in itself be taken as a denial of these fundamental teachings. To the traditional teachings the Vijñānavāda simply added the assertion that all *dharmas* are mental *dharmas* (i.e. that the *rūpa-skandha* as such does not exist). It also taught that the *saṃsāric* aspect of the mind — the one that keeps the whole *saṃsāric* process going — is the tendency for the mind to project itself in the form of non-existent objects (i.e. the self and *dharmas*). This teaching of the nonduality of mind does not make the mind itself intrinsically pure.[23] According to fundamental Buddhist principles one could say that mind is pure (*anāsrava, prabhāsvara*) only to the extent that it is true that the mind is literally void. The "other emptiness" interpretation of the mind does not show that the mind is void in this sense. (For example, the proposition that a jar is empty of water asserts that there is no *water* in the jar, and not that the jar is itself void.) To show that the mind is itself characterized by emptiness, the Vijñānavādins would have had to show that the mind is *śūnya* in the sense in which "*śūnya*" is a one-place predicate. This is the sense in which the Mādhyamikas used the word, and when the word in this sense was applied to all the *dharmas* it entailed that *saṃsāra* was unreal. The author of the MV, however, evidently regarded this conclusion as absurd.

Has the MV found a viable interpretation of the Mahāyāna doctrine that all *dharmas* are void (*sarva-dharma-śūnyatā*)? According to MV 1.2, the doctrine of "other emptiness" shows that *dharmas* are void in a way that does not contradict the Buddhist teaching of a middle path between the extremes of existence and non-existence. However, all that is shown by the MV's doctrine of other emptiness is that mind is *asat* in the sense that it is false or deceptive. Since something has to exist in order to be false and deceptive in this sense, and since MV 1.1 says categorically that the mind does exist, it seems to me that the MV fails to show (as it apparently claims to do) that the mind is neither existent nor non-existent.[24]

Finally, neither the Mādhyamika nor the Vijñānavādin view seems to correctly represent the doctrine of the middle path as it is found in the teachings of early Buddhism. In fact, I think that it can be seen that the attempt by the Mahāyānists to show that things are empty in themselves is a heresy according to the earliest accounts of the Buddhist teaching of the "middle path."

Consider, for example, the Kaccāyana-sutta of the Pāli canon.[25] This *sutta* is concerned specifically with teaching a middle path between the extremes of existence and non-existence, and it undoubtedly represents a very early teaching of the Buddhist tradition. According to the Mahāyānists, at least *one* of the things asserted by this *sūtra* is that things cannot be said to really exist. If we look at the version of the *sūtra* which is found in the Pāli canon, however, it is clear that it does not assert this at all; in fact it quite explicitly *denies* it.

This *sutta* begins when a man by the name of Kaccāyana asks the Buddha to define what is the "right view." The Buddha replies that the world usually bases its views on two things: existence and non-existence. But, the Buddha says, he who with right insight sees the uprising of the world as it really is does not adhere to the view that the world is non-existent. Similarly, he who with right insight sees the passing away of the world as it really is, does not adhere to the existence of the world. He then critizes those philosophers who imprison themselves in dogmas and go in for system-building, all of which is based on the delusion of a self. The wise man, however, does not grasp at things or at a self; he simply thinks: "What arises is suffering (*duḥkha*); what passes away is suffering." Then the Buddha says:

> Everything exists: this is one extreme. Nothing exists: this is the other extreme. Not approaching either extreme the Tathāgata teaches you a doctrine of the middle way: Conditioned by ignorance activities come to pass, conditioned by activities consciousness; thus conditioned arises name-and-shape; and then sensation, contact, feeling, craving, grasping, becoming, birth, decay-and-death, grief and suffering...this is the uprising of this great mass of suffering. But from the utter fading away and ceasing of ignorance there is the cessation of activities, and thus there comes about the cessation of this entire mass of suffering.

Here it is quite clear that the view that nothing exists is held to be a false view. Furthermore, the view that things *exist* is held to be a false view *only* in the sense that things are not eternal. This is perfectly clear from the way the *sutta* ends, for the alternative to the view that "everything exists" is that things arise and perish according to the law of eternal co-origination. In other words, things come to be and exist, but they are impermanent — perhaps even momentary, although the *sutta* does not actually say this.

This teaching of a middle path between 1) "existence" and 2) "non-existence" is therefore a teaching that 1) things are impermanent (rather than eternal) and 2) that the world is not non-existent. In other words, what this middle path amounts to is simply a middle way between *eternalism* and *nihilism*.

This *sutta* indicates that both nihilism and eternalism must have been taught as philosophical doctrines in the Buddha's time. That there were philosophers at this time who were eternalists (*śāśvatavādins*) is not surprising, since eternalist doctrines are undoubtedly of great antiquity in India. The fact that there were philosophers in India who were nihilists, and who held that *nothing* exists, is perhaps more surprising, but even apart from the Kaccāyana-sutta there is evidence that nihilism was present as a philosophical alternative in India from a very early period. K. N. Jayatilleke (1963: 256) has pointed out, for example, that the Lokāyata philosopher Jayarāśi denied both the validity of all means of knowledge and the reality of the world. The date of Jayarāśi, the author of the Tattvopaplava-siṃha, is uncertain, but he probably flourished around 650 C.E. This of course is much later than the time of the Buddha (by about a thousand years); nevertheless there is nothing intrinsically implausible in the suggestion that Jayarāśi is simply a medieval representative of a much older tradition of nihilism in India. In any case, one cannot make any sense of the Kaccāyana-sutta unless one supposes that there was such a school of nihilists in India even in the Buddha's time.

It is easy to see why the Buddha thought it important to teach a middle path between eternalism and nihilism. The very essence of his enlightenment is said to have been the insight that everything is suffering and that suffering arises depending upon causes and conditions (*pratītya-samutpāda*). Neither eternalism nor nihilism is compatible with this doctrine. Note, however, that the teaching of the Buddha implies that things *do* arise and perish, and this in turn implies that things *do* exist, even if they are impermanent or even momentary. This is the very proposition that the Mahāyānists, in one fashion or another, wished to deny. In so far as they denied it, however, they were embracing a doctrine which the Kaccāyana-sutta plainly condemns.[26]

The Tri-svabhāva-nirdeśa (TSN) is usually ascribed to Vasubandhu, but this attribution is questionable for a number of reasons.

(1) There are four manuscript sources — two in Sanskrit and two in Tibetan [Tola and Dragonetti (1983)]. One of the Tibetan texts attributes the work to Vasubandhu and the other attributes it to Nāgārjuna. Nāgārjuna, of course, has nothing to do with the matter, but the very fact that a text of the TSN in the Bstan-'gyur is ascribed to him throws some doubt on Vasubandhu's authorship of the text.

(2) There are differences (*vide infra*) between the TSN and the Triṃśikā, which *was* written by Vasubandhu the Vijñānavādin.

(3) Unlike most of the major writings of the Vijñānavādins, the TSN has no commentary on it. This would be somewhat unusual if it were in fact a work of Vasubandhu's.

Since the TSN was certainly not written by Nāgārjuna and may not have been written by Vasubandhu, it cannot be said for certain who wrote it. Nevertheless, the TSN is an important work of the Vijñānavāda. It consists basically of a lengthier account of the doctrine of the three self natures (or three non-self natures) than is found in either the Madhyānta-vibhāga or the Triṃśikā.

The Sanskrit text and a translation of it are given below.

THE ANALYSIS OF THE THREE SELF NATURES

1. The imagined (*kalpita*), the other dependent (*paratantra*) and the perfected (*pariniṣpanna*): these are the three natures which are to be thoroughly understood by the wise.

   kalpitaḥ paratantraś ca pariniṣpanna eva ca /
   trayaḥ svabhāvā dhīrāṇāṃ gaṃbhīraṃ jñeyam iṣyate //

2. The dependent nature (*paratantra*) is that which appears; that which is imagined (*kalpita*) is the manner in which the

dependent nature appears. The dependent nature is so-called because its modifications arise on the basis of causes and conditions; the imagined nature is so-called because it is only imagination (*kalpanāmātra*).

yat khyāti paratantro 'sau yathā khyāti sa kalpitaḥ /
pratyayādhīna-vṛttitvāt kalpanāmātra-bhāvataḥ //

3. The eternal non-existence of that appearance in the manner in which it appears (*yathākhyānam*) is known as the self nature of the perfected nature (*pariniṣpanna-svabhāva*), because it is unchanging (*ananyathātva*).

tasya khyātur yathākhyānaṃ yā sadāvidyamānatā /
jñeyaḥ sa pariniṣpannaḥ svabhāvo 'nanyathātvataḥ //

4. What then appears? A false idea (*asatkalpa*). How does it appear? As a duality. What is the non-existence (*nāstitā*) of this duality? It is that in virtue of which there is the nature (*dharmatā*) of being devoid of duality (*advaya-dharmatā*).

tatra kiṃ khyāty asatkalpaḥ kathaṃ khyāti dvayātmanā /
tasya kā nāstitā tena yā tatrādvaya-dharmatā //

5. What is the imagination of the non-existent (*asatkalpa*)? It is the mind (*citta*), because whatever is imagined as an object and whatever causes such imagination is entirely false.

asatkalpo 'tra kaś cittaṃ yatas tat kalpyate yathā /
yathā ca kalpayaty arthaṃ tathātyantaṃ na vidyate //

6. The mind (*citta*) is two-fold, as cause (*hetu*) and effect (*phala*). As cause it is called the store consciousness (*ālaya-vijñāna*), and as effect it is called the evolved consciousness (*pravṛtti-vijñāna*). The latter is seven-fold.

tad dhetu-phala-bhāvena cittaṃ dvividham iṣyate /
yad ālayākhya-vijñānaṃ pravṛttyākhyaṃ ca saptadhā //

7. The *ālaya-vijñāna* is called "*citta*" because it collects the seeds (*bījas*) of the impurities and impulses (*vāsanās*). The second (i.e. the *pravṛtti-vijñāna*) is called "mind" (*citta*) because it evolves as the diverse appearances of things.

saṃkleśa-vāsanā-bījaiś citatvāc cittam ucyate /
cittam ādyaṃ dvitīyaṃ tu citrākāra-pravṛttitaḥ //

8. Collectively all eight consciousnessness are called the false imagination (*abhūta-kalpa*), and it is said to be three-fold: the fruition (*vaipākika*), the causal (*naimittika*) and the mere appearance (*prātibhāsika*).

samāsato 'bhūta-kalpaḥ sa caiṣa trividho mataḥ /
vaipākikas tathā naimittiko 'nyaḥ prātibhāsikaḥ //

9. The *ālaya-vijñāna* is called the root consciousness (*mūla-vijñāna*) because it is the fruit. The other two (i.e. the causal and the mere appearance) are called the evolved consciousnesses because they are modifications that depend on the distinction of the seer, the seen and knowledge.

prathamo mūla-vijñānaṃ tad vipākātmakaṃ yataḥ /
anyaḥ pravṛtti-vijñānaṃ dṛśya-dṛg-vitti-vṛttitaḥ //

10. The profundity of the three natures consists in being and non-being, duality and nonduality, impurity and purity, and non-difference of the characteristics.

sad-asattvād dvayaikatvāt saṃkleśa-vyavadānayoḥ /
lakṣaṇābhedataś ceṣṭā svabhāvānāṃ gabhīratā //

11. The imagined nature (*kalpita-svabhāva*) is said have the characteristic of existence (*sat*) and non-existence (*asat*),

because it is thought to exist, but is totally non-existent (*atyantābhāva*).

sattvena gṛhyate yasmād atyantābhāva eva ca /
svabhāvaḥ kalpitas tena sad-asal-lakṣaṇo mataḥ //

12. The other dependent nature (*paratantra-svabhāva*) is said to have the characteristic of existence and non-existence because it exists as an illusion (*bhrānti*) but does not exist in the manner in which it appears.

vidyate bhrānti-bhāvena yathākhyānaṃ na vidyate /
paratantro yatas tena sad-asal-lakṣaṇo mataḥ //

13. The perfected nature (*niṣpanna-svabhāva*) is said to have the characteristic of existence and non-existence because it is the nature of nonduality and is the non-existence of duality.

advayatvena yac cāsti dvayasyābhāva eva ca /
svabhāvas tena niṣpannaḥ sad-asal-lakṣaṇo mataḥ //

14. The nature which is imagined (*kalpita-svabhāva*) by the ignorant is said to be both dual and unitary, because the object that is imagined has a two-fold nature and because the existence of that non-existence (*tad-asattvaika-bhāva*) is unitary .

dvaividhyāt kalpitārthasya tad-asattvaika-bhāvataḥ /
svabhāvaḥ kalpito bālair dvayaikatvātmako mataḥ //

15. The other dependent nature (*paratantra-svabhāva*) is both dual and unitary because its appearance as a duality exists, and because its existence as a mere appearance (*bhrānti-mātra*) is singular.

prakhyānād dvaya-bhāvena bhrānti-mātraika-bhāvataḥ /
svabhāvaḥ paratantrākhyo dvayaikatvātmako mataḥ //

16. The perfected nature is said to be both dual and unitary because it is essentially the existence of duality and also because it is essentially a single nonduality.

dvaya-bhāva-svabhāvatvād advayaika-svabhāvataḥ /
svabhāvaḥ pariniṣpanno dvayaikatvātmako mataḥ //

17. The imagined nature and the other dependent nature are characterized by impurity; but the perfected nature is characterized by purity.

kalpitaḥ paratantraś ca jñeyam saṃkleśa-lakṣaṇam /
pariniṣpanna iṣṭas tu vyavadānasya lakṣaṇam //

18. The perfected nature is to be understood as non-different from the imagined nature, for the imagined nature is essentially the unreal duality, and the perfected nature is essentially the non-existence of that duality.

asad-dvaya-svabhāvatvāt tad-abhāva-svabhāvataḥ /
svabhāvāt kalpitāj jñeyo niṣpanno 'bhinna-lakṣaṇaḥ //

19. The imagined nature is to be understood as non-different from the perfected nature, for the perfected nature is essentially nondual, and the imagined nature is essentially the non-existence of that duality.

advayatva-svabhāvatvād dvayābhāva-svabhāvataḥ /
niṣpannāt kalpitaś caiva vijñeyo 'bhinna-lakṣaṇaḥ //

20. The perfected nature is non-different from the other dependent nature, because the other dependent nature exists differently from the way in which it appears, and

because the perfected nature is essentially the non-existence of that appearance.

yathākhyānam asad-bhāvāt tathāsattva-svabhāvataḥ /
svabhāvāt paratantrākhyān niṣpanno 'bhinna-lakṣaṇaḥ //

21. The other dependent nature is to be understood as non-different from the perfected nature, because the perfected nature is essentially the unreality of duality, and because the other dependent nature lacks the nature of existing as it appears.

asad-dvaya-svabhāvatvād yathākhyānāsvabhāvataḥ /
niṣpannāt paratantro 'pi vijñeyo 'bhinna-lakṣaṇaḥ //

22. A particular order of the natures is set out according to the conventions about them and according to the order in which they are entered. They are as follows.

krama-bhedaḥ svabhāvānāṃ vyavahārādhikārataḥ /
tat-praveśādhikārāc ca vyutpatty-arthaṃ vidhīyate //

23. The imagined nature is that which exists only conventionally (*vyavahāra*); the dependent nature is the cause (*vyavahartrātmaka*) of that which exists only conventionally; the perfected nature is that which destroys that which exists only conventionally.

kalpito vyavahārātmā vyavahartrātmako 'paraḥ /
vyavahāra-samucchedaḥ svabhāvaś cānya iṣyate //

24. One enters first into the other dependent nature which is the non-existence of duality; then one enters into the imagined nature, the unreal duality which exists in it.

dvayābhāvātmakaḥ pūrvaṃ paratantraḥ praviśyate /
tataḥ praviśyate tatra kalpamātram asad-dvayam //

25. Then one enters the perfected nature which is in (*atra*) the dependent nature. The perfected nature is the existence of the non-existence of duality (*dvayābhāva bhāva*); consequently it, too, is said to exist and to not exist.

tato dvayābhāva-bhāvo niṣpanno 'tra praviśyate /
tathā hy asāv eva tadā asti nāstīti cocyate //

26. These three self natures have the characteristic of being nondual and ungraspable, because the imagined nature does not exist, the other dependent nature does not exist as such (i.e. in the way that it appears), and the perfected nature is essentially the non-existence of this manner of appearance.

trayo 'py ete svabhāvā hi advayālabhya-lakṣaṇāḥ /
abhāvād atathābhāvāt tad-abhāva-svabhāvataḥ //

27. It is like a magically produced elephant which appears through the power of a *mantra*. The elephant is a mere appearance (*ākāra-mātra*). It does not exist at all.

māyā-kṛtaṃ mantra-vaśāt khyāti hasty-ātmanā yathā /
ākāra-mātraṃ tatrāsti hastī nāsti tu sarvathā //

28. The imagined nature is the elephant; the other dependent nature is the apparitional form of the elephant; the perfected nature is the non-existence of the elephant in the other dependent nature (*tatra*).

svabhāvaḥ kalpito hastī paratantras tad-ākṛtiḥ /
yas tatra hasty-abhāvo 'sau pariniṣpanna iṣyate //

29. Due to the root consciousness (*mūla-citta*), the false imagination (*asatkalpa*) appears as a duality. That duality is entirely unreal. All that exists there is a mere apparitional form (*ākṛtimātra*).

asatkalpas tathā khyāti mūla-cittād dvayātmanā /
dvayam atyantato nāsti tatrāsty ākṛti-mātrakam //

30. The root consciousness (*mūla-vijñāna*) can be compared to the *mantra*; suchness (*tathatā*) to the piece of wood; imagination (*vikalpa*) to an appearance of the elephant; and duality to the elephant.

mantravan mūla-vijñānaṃ kāṣṭhavat tathatā matā /
hasty-ākāravad eṣṭavyo vikalpo hastivad dvayam //

31. As soon as one understands the three characteristics and the true nature of things (*artha-tattva*), there occurs — simultaneously — knowledge, abandonment and attainment.

artha-tattva-prativedhe yugapal lakṣaṇa-traye /
parijñā ca prahāṇaṃ ca prāptiś ceṣṭā yathākramam //

32. There, knowledge is non-perception, abandonment is non-appearance, attainment is perception without any object as cause. The last is direct realization.

parijñānupalambho 'tra hānir akhyānam iṣyate /
upalambho 'nimittas tu prāptiḥ sākṣāt-kriyāpi sā //

33. Duality disappears through the non-perception of duality; through the disappearance of duality, the perfected nature, which is the non-existence of duality, is understood.

dvayasyānupalambhena dvayākāro vigacchati /
vigamāt tasya niṣpanno dvayābhāvo 'dhigamyate //

34. Similarly, in the case of magic, the non-perception of the elephant, the disappearance of its form, and the perception of the piece of wood, take place simultaneously.

hastino 'nupalambhaś ca vigamaś ca tad-ākṛteḥ /
upalambhaś ca kāṣṭhasya māyāyāṃ yugapad yathā //

35. Through the restraint of thought, through the perception that discriminative intelligence (*buddhi*) is useless, through the adherence to the three-fold knowledge, through the effortless attainment of liberation (*mokṣa*):

viruddha-dhī-kāraṇatvād buddher vaiyarthya-darśanāt /
jñāna-trayānuvṛtteś ca mokṣāpatter ayatnataḥ //

36. By means of the perception of "mind only" (*citta-mātra*), there is the non-perception of the external object which is known; through the non-perception of the external object, there is the non-perception of mind (*citta*).

cittamātropalambhena jñeyārthānupalambhatā /
jñeyārthānupalambhena syāc cittānupalambhatā //

37. From this two-fold non-perception, there is the perception of the fundamental nature of things (*dharma-dhātu*); through the perception of the fundamental nature of things there is the perception of that which is all-pervading (*vibhutva*).

dvayor anupalambhena dharmadhātūpalaṁbhatā /
dharmadhātūpalambhena syād vibhutvopalambhatā //

38. Having perceived the all-pervading and having attained the good of oneself and others, the sage attains the supreme enlightenment (*anuttarā-bodhi*) which consists of the three bodies of the Buddha.

upalabhda-vibhutvaś ca sva-parārtha-prasiddhitaḥ /
prāpnoty anuttarāṃ bodhiṃ dhīmān kāya-trayātmikām //

One of the main themes of the TSN is that the three self natures are non-different (TSN 10c: *lakṣaṇābheda*; TSN 18-21: *abhinna-lakṣaṇa*). Tola and Dragonetti (1983: 243) have noted that the TSN teaches that the three natures are identical, but to my knowledge no commentator to date has pointed out that this doctrine is actually logically inconsistent.[1]

The following are some of the contradictions in the text to which the TSN's definitions give rise:[2]

1. According to TSN 16a, the perfected nature is the existence of duality (*dvaya-bhāva-svabhāvatva*). This contradicts all the assertions in the TSN cited in a) on p. 44 below (i.e. TSN 4c; 13b; 18b; 28cd; and 33cd), which assert that the perfected nature is the *non*-existence of duality.

2. TSN 24ab *defines* the dependent nature as the non-existence of duality (*dvayābhāvātmaka*). Note, however, that it is typically the *imagined* nature that is defined as the non-existence of duality, e.g., TSN 18a (*asad-dvaya*); TSN 19b (*dvayābhāva-svabhāva*). Furthermore, the imagined nature is said to be non-existent [e.g. TSN 11b (*atyantābhāva*); TSN 26c (*abhāvāt*); TSN 27d (*hastī nāsti tu sarvathā*); TSN 29c (*dvayam atyantato nāsti*)]. Hence it follows that the *dependent* nature must be non-existent.

Spelled out step by step, this contradiction is derived as follows:

(1) The dependent nature = the non-existence of duality (TSN 24ab).

(2) The non-existence of duality = the imagined nature (TSN 18a; TSN 19b).

(3) The imagined nature is non-existent (TSN 11b; 26c; 27d; 29c).

(1)-(3) together lead to the conclusion that the dependent nature does not exist. This, however, contradicts other assertions in the Vijñānavāda writings, e.g. MV 1.1, which asserts that the mind (*vijñāna* = *abhūta-parikalpa* = *paratantra*) *does* exist.

3. TSN 20-21 maintain that the perfected nature is non-different (*abhinna-lakṣaṇa*) from the dependent nature. This raises the following problem. According to Buddhist doctrine, mind is essentially changing and *saṃsāric*. (As TSN 17 says, of the three

natures, only the perfected nature is pure.) If the perfected nature were non-different from the dependent nature, therefore, one would get the contradiction that the perfected nature is both pure and impure.

4. TSN 19 equates (*abhinna-lakṣaṇa*) the imagined nature and the perfected nature. Note, however, that the imagined nature is defined as the non-existence of duality; as such, the imagined nature is said not to exist at all. (Cf. TSN 11b, 26c, 27d and 29c, cited in (2) above.) It follows, therefore, that the perfected nature is non-existent. This, however, contradicts other passages which assert that the perfected nature exists and that it is a real entity. [Cf. TSN 25a, cited in b) on p. 44 below.]

In other words, the TSN asserts both that:

(1) The perfected nature is identical with (*lakṣaṇābheda*; *abhinna-lakṣaṇa*) the imagined nature (TSN 19)

and

(2) The imagined nature is non-existent (TSN 11b, 26c, 27d and 29c).

By (1)-(2), one is led to the conclusion that the perfected nature is non-existent. But this is not the conclusion that is wanted, and furthermore it contradicts other statements in the TSN.

5. Note, finally, the *self*-contradiction of TSN 16, which asserts that the perfected nature is essentially the existence of duality and that it is also essentially a single nonduality.

What accounts for all these contradictions? The explanation probably lies in the fact that the Vijñānavādins were confronted with irreconcilable doctrinal demands when they formulated the doctrine of the three self natures.

According to the Vijñānavādins, the mind exists. (For example, MV 1.1 asserts that it exists, and MV 1.4 says that liberation comes from the destruction of the mind.) The Vijñānavādins also interpreted the Mahāyāna doctrine of the voidness of all *dharmas* (*sarva-dharma-śūnyatā*) to mean that everything is mind only, i.e. that there are no external objects. (Hence the imagined nature — the *parikalpita* — is said to be non-existent.) Neither the dependent nature nor the imagined nature, however, was held to be the absolute (*tathatā*, *śūnyatā* etc.), which was identified instead with the perfected nature (*pariniṣpanna*). The *pariniṣpanna*, therefore, was the central object of the Vijñānavādins' religious and soteriological concern. But what is it actually?

On the one hand, the Vijñānavādins clearly wanted to think of the perfected nature, *tathatā*, *śūnyatā* etc. as a real entity in some sense (cf. TSN 25a, cited in b) on p. 44 below). However, they were actually precluded from doing so by Buddhist doctrine, which held that any view which asserted or entailed the existence of an eternal and unchanging entity or substance was an eternalist (*śāśvata*) doctrine and hence pernicious and false. (Much less could the Vijñānavādins as orthodox Buddhists have identified the perfected nature with an absolute and unchanging *mind*, for this would have made their views virtually indistinguishable from the Vedānta.) This, I think, is the real cause of the ambivalence shown in the TSN towards the concept of the perfected nature, and also the ultimate cause of the inconsistencies that are found in the text. It is also what accounts for the fact that it proves to be impossible, upon examination, to say what the perfected nature is.[3]

It is easy to miss these points because the analogy that the TSN uses in TSN 27-28 to explain its doctrine of the three self natures actually suggests a substantialist notion of an absolute. On closer examination, however, this analogy proves to be misleading, at least when one considers it in terms of the actual *definitions* which the TSN gives of the three self natures.

The analogy used in TSN 27-28 is that of an imaginary elephant. These verses compare the imaginary elephant to the imagined nature (*parikalpita*), the dependent nature (*paratantra*) to the apparitional form (*ākṛti*) of the elephant, and the perfected nature (*pariniṣpanna*) to the elephant in the dependent nature (*yas tatra hasty-abhāva*).

The part of this passage that concerns the imagined nature and the dependent nature is clear enough. An hallucinatory elephant is not an elephant. What does exist is only a mental event or phenomenon. According to the TSN, the imagined nature is the totally unreal external object, and the dependent nature is the appearance of that object.

But what about the perfected nature? According to TSN 28, there is a third thing in the picture which is the "non-existence of the elephant in the mind." What could this mean? Consider the example, already discussed in chapter 1, of the referring expression "the present king of France" when there is no king of France. Should we, for example, say that in the year 1990 there is a certain something — the non-existence of the king of France — in the palaces of the Louvre and Versailles etc? If we committed ourselves to an affirmative answer to this question, then presumably we would have to say that there is also the non-existence of the queen of France, the non-existence of the king and queen of Germany, the non-existence of Hamlet the prince of Denmark etc. in these palaces as well. In this way real places would get populated with every non-existent entity that could possibly exist. The same idea does not seem to be any more appealing when it is applied to the mind than when it is applied to physical locations.

TSN 30 expands on the analogy of the illusory elephant. This verse appeals to the notion of the magical efficacity of spells (*mantras*) etc. in explaining perceptual illusions. It says that in the case of an illusory elephant the store consciousness (*ālaya-vijñāna*) is the *mantra* or magic spell, suchness (*tathatā*) is the piece of wood, imagination (*vikalpa*) is the appearance or illusion of an elephant, and duality (*dvaya*) — the supposed external object — is the imagined nature.

The appeal to the magical efficacity of spells introduces some unnecessary complexities into the philosophical issues at this point. All the essential points would appear to remain the same if we considered instead a more standard analysis of perceptual illusion, like the rope mistaken in the dusk for a snake. In terms of this more standard example, TSN 30 tells us that suchness or emptiness is the rope, that the mind is the *appearance* of the snake (i.e. a sense datum), and that the non-existent snake is the imagined nature.

In this example, the piece of rope, which is a real entity, is the analogue of the perfected nature. The analogy, therefore, suggests that emptiness, the perfected nature etc. is a real, existent entity (*sad-bhāva*). However, insofar as passages like MV 1.13, MV 1.20, TSN 3 etc. define these terms purely negatively, suchness, emptiness, the perfected nature etc. are indistinguishable from sheer non-existence. What the analogy of perceptual illusions strongly suggests is therefore not confirmed by what the *definitions* offered in the TSN and other texts actually say. In the case of perceptual illusions (as opposed to hallucinations) we can point to a real thing (e.g. a rope or a piece of wood) which is in some sense the basis (*ādhāra, āspada*) of the illusory appearance. Although the Vijñānavāda texts clearly want to treat suchness and *śūnyatā* as a real entity of this sort, the actual definitions of the perfected nature which are given do not support such an interpretation.

The TSN actually offers four different definitions of the perfected nature. Sometimes the perfected nature is defined as the non-existence of duality; sometimes it is defined as the existence of the non-existence of duality; sometimes it is defined as the nature of nonduality; and sometimes it is defined as the non-existence of the mind in the manner in which it appears. Cited below are some examples of each of these different definitions.

a) The perfected nature is defined as the non-existence of duality in TSN 4c-d (*tasya kā nāstitā tena yā tatrādvaya-dharmatā*); TSN 13b (*dvayasyābhāva*); TSN 18b (*tad-abhāva-svabhāva*); TSN 28cd (*yas tatra hasty-abhāvo 'sau pariniṣpanna*); and TSN 33cd (*niṣpanno dvayābhāva*).

b) The perfected nature is defined as the existence of the non-existence of duality in TSN 25a (*dvayābhāva-bhāva*).

c) The perfected nature is defined as the nature of nonduality in TSN 4d (*advaya-dharmatā*); TSN 13a (*advayatva*) and TSN 16b (*advayaika-svabhāva*).

d) The perfected nature is defined as the non-existence of the mind in the manner in which it appears in TSN 3 and TSN 26d.

There are a number of reasons why these definitions will not do as definitions of the perfected nature.

So far as a) is concerned, the phrase "the non-existence of duality" simply defines the non-existent, imagined object. Since this is said to be entirely unreal (*atyantābhāva*), the imagined nature cannot be the same thing as the perfected nature. Similarly, as was shown in the previous chapter, b), which defines the perfected nature as the existence of the non-existence of duality, also reduces to sheer non-existence (insofar as it can be given any meaning at all); therefore the phrase "the existence of the non-existence of duality" cannot refer to the perfected nature either. Finally, so far as d) is concerned, the definitions given in TSN 3 and 26d suffer from ambiguity. What could it mean to define the perfected nature as the non-existence of the mind *in the manner in which it appears*? If this expression refers to the non-existence of duality (i.e. of the *parikalpita*), then the expression simply refers to something that is non-existent. On the other hand, if the expression is taken to refer to the mind (*paratantra*), then the definition is problematic for other reasons. For example, TSN 2 asserts that the modifications of the mind (*paratantra*) arise depending on causes and conditions. This effectively precludes identifying the perfected nature with mind, for the perfected nature is by definition immutable.

Given all these contradictions, and the general view that the three self natures are non-different from each other (*lakṣaṇābheda*, *abhinna-lakṣaṇa*), it is perhaps not very surprising that the author of the TSN also wanted to show in TSN 11-13 that each of the three natures is "*sad-asal-lakṣaṇa*." If one interpreted these verses literally, they would violate the law of non-contradiction, because something cannot both exist and non-exist. On examination, it turns out that TSN 11-13 do *not* violate or provide counterexamples to this fundamental logical law. What they do instead is to equivocate between two very different senses of the terms "*sat*" and "*asat*."

As was previously mentioned, one can use the Sanskrit phrase "*x* is *asat*" to mean either that *x* is non-existent or that *x* is deceptive. (These two meanings, of course, are mutually exclusive, for only an existent entity can be *asat* in the second sense.) When one is careful to distinguish these two meanings of the term "*asat*" in verses 11-13, it is clear that none of these verses provides a counterexample to any logical laws, for it turns out that the imagined nature is simply non-existent and that the dependent nature exists (although it is also deceptive).

TSN 11 says that the imagined nature has the characteristic of existence because it is thought to exist, and that it has the characteristic of non-existence because it is in fact totally non-existent.[4] Note that the first part of TSN 11 implies that one can infer from the fact that someone *thinks* that something exists that it does exist (or that there is a sense in which it exists). This, however, is untenable. Consider the rope-snake illusion. In the dusk I may mistake a rope for a snake, and even "see" a snake (in some sense of the word "see"). However, it does not follow from this that there *is* a snake; indeed, it does not even follow from this that there is in *some sense* a snake. It makes no sense, for example, to ask questions like: where did the snake come from? where did it go? how much did it weigh? when and where was it born? etc. In this example, what may be inferred from the fact that someone *thinks* there is a snake or that someone "sees" a snake is that there is an *illusion* of a snake. However, an illusory snake is not a snake — it is a mental event or phenomenon, rather than an external object. In short, in cases of perceptual illusions the apparent external objects are non-existent, though illusions as *mental* events or phenomena do exist. This is quite different from what TSN 11 appears to assert, which is that one and the same thing both exists and does not exist.[5]

The same considerations which have just shown that the imagined nature cannot be an existent thing (*sat*) also go to show that there is no respect in which the *dependent* nature can be said to be *non*-existent, as TSN 12 claims. According to TSN 12, the other dependent nature is existent/non-existent (*sad-asal-lakṣaṇa*) because it exists as an illusion but does not exist in the manner in which it appears. To see why this claim does not show what the TSN wants it to show, consider once again the example of the rope-snake. In this analogy one's impression of the rope-snake is presumably what "exists as an illusion but does not exist in the manner in which it appears." The problem is that unless one wants to deny the reality of mind (which the Vijñānavādins did not want to do), one still has to say that this mental impression exists. So far as existence per se is concerned, there would appear to be no distinction between the existence of a veridical and a non-veridical impression. The only difference between a veridical impression and a non-veridical one, presumably, is that there is a public object corresponding to one's veridical impression but no such object for one's non-veridical impression. Clearly, this distinction does not mean that there is a sense in which the mental impression *per se* is non-existent.

TSN 12, in other words, has simply conflated two very different meanings of the term "*asat*" (i.e. "false" or "deceptive" versus "non-existent)." TSN 12, therefore, has failed to show that there is a sense in which the mind or other dependent nature is non-existent (*asat* = *abhāva*) in the sense that is needed. The most that it could be taken to show is that the mind is *asat* in the sense of "false" or "deceptive."[6]

The Thirty Verses (Triṃśikā) of Vasubandhu is one of the most important texts of the Vijñānavāda. Xuan Zang's magnum opus is his commentary on the Triṃśikā, called the Cheng wei shilun (Sk. Vijñaptimātratā-siddhi), which is the root text or foundational text of the *wei shi* (Consciousness Only) school of Chinese Buddhism. There is also a commentary (*ṭīkā*) on the Triṃśikā by Sthiramati. Fortunately, a Sanskrit manuscript of the Triṃśikā and Sthiramati's Ṭīkā was discovered by Prof. Sylvain Lévi in Nepal in the 1920s.

The Triṃśikā will be discussed in this chapter and the next. This chapter continues the discussion of the Vijñānavādins' doctrines about emptiness (*śūnyatā*) and the three self natures (*tri-svabhāvas*). The next chapter will focus on what the Triṃśikā says about *nirvāṇa* and Buddhahood.

The first verse of the Triṃśikā states the general philosophy: what are called selves (*ātman*) and entities (*dharmas*) are simply the transformations of consciousness (*vijñāna-pariṇāma*). Verses 2-18 give some of the details of these transformations, which are said to be three-fold: i.e. the store consciousness (*ālaya-vijñāna*), the thinking consciousness (*mano-vijñāna*), and the six sense-based consciousnesses. Verses 20-24 present the doctrine of the three self natures (also called the three non-self natures). Verses 25-30 return to the general topic of mind only (*vijñaptimātratā*). The two concluding verses describe the ultimate reality which is attained by the Buddhas.

THE THIRTY VERSES (TRIṂŚIKĀ)

1. The usages of the terms "*ātman*" and "*dharma*" are manifold, but both terms just refer to the transformations of consciousness (*vijñāna-pariṇāma*). That transformation is three-fold.

ātma-dharmopacāro hi vividho yaḥ pravartate /
vijñāna-pariṇāme 'sau pariṇāmaḥ sa ca tridhā //

2. The three-fold transformations are fruition, thinking and representations of objects. The first, which is also known as the store consciousness (*ālaya-vijñāna*), is the fruition (*vipāka*) of all the seeds.

vipāko mananākhyaś-ca vijñaptir-viṣayasya ca /
tatrālayākhyaṃ vijñānaṃ vipākaḥ sarva-bījakam //

3. The store consciousness is the perception, abiding in, and grasping of what is unperceived (*asaṃviditaka*). It is always associated with touch, attentiveness, knowledge, conception and willing.

asaṃviditakopādi-sthāna-vijñaptikaṃ ca tat /
sadā sparśa-manaskāra-vit-saṃjñā-cetanānvitam //

4. The feeling that pertains to it is that of indifference. The store consciousness is undefiled and undefined. Touch etc. are also indifferent in feeling. The store consciousness is constantly evolving like a torrent of water.

upekṣā vedanā tatrānivṛtāvyākṛtaṃ ca tat /
tathā sparśādayas-tac-ca vartate srota-saughavat //

5. In the state of Arhatship there is a turning away (*vyāvṛtti*) from the store consciousness. The second transformation of consciousness, called the *mano-vijñāna*, evolves when it takes the store consciousness as an object and support. The essential nature of the *mano-vijñāna* is to think.

tasya vyāvṛttir-arhatve tad-āśritya pravartate /
tad-ālambaṃ manonāma vijñānaṃ mananātmakam //

6. It is always associated with the four defilements which are obscured and undeveloped: self-regard, self-delusion, self-pride and self-love.

kleśaiś-caturbhiḥ sahitaṃ nivṛtāvyākṛtaiḥ sadā /
ātma-dṛṣṭy-ātma-mohātma-mānātma-sneha-saṃjñitaiḥ //

7. Wherever the *mano-vijñāna* arises there are the associated mental states of touch etc. which are of the same nature. The *mano-vijñāna* does not exist in the Arhat, nor in the state of cessation (*nirodha-samāpatti*), nor in the world transcending path (*lokottara mārga*).

yatra-jas-tanmayair-anyaiḥ sparśādyaiś-cārhato na tat /
na nirodha-samāpattau mārge lokottare na ca //

8. This is the second transformation of consciousness. The third transformation of consciousness is the perception of the six-fold objects. The *mano-vijñāna* is good, bad and neither (*advaya*).

dvitīyaḥ pariṇāmo 'yaṃ tṛtīyaḥ ṣaḍ-vidhasya yā /
viṣayasyopalabdhiḥ sā kuśalākuśalādvayā //

9. These six-fold objects are the mental associates (*caittas*) that are universal, specific and good, as well as the primary defilements, secondary defilements and the three kinds of feelings.

sarvatragair-viniyataiḥ kuśalaiś-caitasair-asau /
saṃprayuktā tathā kleśair-upakleśais-trivedanā //

10. The universal mental associates are touch etc. The specific mental associates are desire, resolve and memory, together with concentration and thought. The good mental associates are faith, sense of shame, fear of censure,

ādyāḥ sparśādayaś-chandādhimokṣa-smṛtayaḥ saha /
samādhi-dhībhyāṃ niyatāḥ śraddhātha hrīr-apatrapā //

11. the triad of non-covetousness etc., courage, equanimity, vigilance and harmlessness. The primary defilements are attachment, anger, delusion,

alobhādi-trayaṃ vīryaṃ praśrabdhiḥ sāpramādikā /
ahiṃsā kuśalāḥ kleśā rāga-pratigha-mūḍhayaḥ //

12. pride, false views and doubt. The secondary defilements are anger, enmity, jealousy, spite, envy, parsimony, deceit,

māna-dṛg-vicikitsāś-ca krodhopanahane punaḥ /
mrakṣaḥ pradāśa īrṣyātha mātsaryaṃ saha māyayā //

13. deception, intoxication, harmfulness, pride, shamelessness, lack of integrity, sluggishness, restlessness, lack of faith, laziness, idleness, forgetfulness,

śāṭhyaṃ mado 'vihiṃsā hrīr-atrapā styānam-uddhavaḥ /
āśraddhyam-atha kausīdyaṃ pramādo muṣitā smṛtiḥ //

14. distraction and thoughtlessness. Remorse, sleepiness, reasoning and analysis, which are of two kinds, are also secondary defilements.

vikṣepo 'saṃprajanyaṃ ca kaukṛtyaṃ middham-eva ca /
vitarkaś-ca vicāraś-cety-upakleśā dvaye dvidhā //

15. The five sense-consciousnesses arise in the store consciousness — either together or separately — depending on causes and conditions, just as waves originate on water.

pañcānāṃ mūla-vijñāne yathā-pratyayam-udbhavaḥ /
vijñānānāṃ saha na vā taraṅgāṇāṃ yathā jale //

16. The *mano-vijñāna* arises at all times, except in the case of those who are born in the realms of beings without thought (*asaṃjñika*), those who are in the two mindless trances

(*samāpatti*), or those who are in states of stupor or unconsciousness (*acittaka*).

manovijñāna-saṃbhūtiḥ sarvadāsaṃjñikād-ṛte /
samāpatti-dvayān middhān mūrchanād-apy-acittakāt //

17. This three-fold transformation of consciousness is imagination (*vikalpa*). What is imagined (*yad vikalpyate*), therefore, does not exist. Consequently, everything (*idaṃ sarvam*) is nothing but representations of consciousness (*vijñapti-mātraka*).

vijñāna-pariṇāmo 'yaṃ vikalpo yad-vikalpyate /
tena tan-nāsti tenedaṃ sarvaṃ vijñaptimātrakam //

18. Since there is the store consciousness which contains all seeds, there are the transformations of consciousness; these transformations proceed depending upon mutual influences. From this imagination arises.

sarva-bījaṃ hi vijñānaṃ pariṇāmas-tathā tathā /
yāty-anyonya-vaśād yena vikalpaḥ sa sa jāyate //

19. Due to the habit-energy (*vāsanā*) of actions and the two-fold grasping, as soon as a previous maturation has been exhausted another maturation arises.

karmaṇo vāsanā grāha-dvaya-vāsanayā saha /
kṣīṇe pūrva-vipāke 'nyad-vipākaṃ janayanti tat //

20. Whatever thing (*vastu*) is imagined by whatever imagination is purely imaginary (*parikalpita*). That which is purely imaginary has no self nature (*svabhāva*).

yena yena vikalpena yad-yad vastu vikalpyate /
parikalpita evāsau svabhāvo na sa vidyate //

21. Imagination itself, which arises depending on causes and conditions, has a self nature, which is that of being dependent (*paratantra-svabhava*). The perfected nature (*parinişpanna*), on the other hand, is that which is the eternal absence (*rahitatā*) of the purely imagined nature in the dependent nature.

paratantra-svabhāvas-tu vikalpaḥ pratyayodbhavaḥ /
niṣpannas-tasya pūrveṇa sadā rahitatā tu yā //

22. For that very reason, the perfected nature is neither the same nor different from the dependent nature. It is like impermanence etc. As long as the perfected nature is not seen, the dependent nature is not seen, either.

ata eva sa naivānyo nānanyaḥ paratantrataḥ /
anityatādivad vācyo nādṛṣṭe 'smin sa dṛśyate //

23. Corresponding to the three-fold nature (*svabhāva*) there is the three-fold absence of self nature (*niḥsvabhāvatā*). The absence of self nature of all *dharmas* was taught by the Buddha with a secret intention (*saṃdhāya*).

trividhasya svabhāvasya trividhāṃ niḥsvabhāvatām /
saṃdhāya sarva-dharmāṇāṃ deśitā niḥsvabhāvatā //

24. The imagined nature is without self nature by definition. The dependent nature, again, does not come into existence by itself, and accordingly lacks a self nature. The perfected nature is absence of self nature itself (*niḥsvabhāvatā*).

prathamo lakṣaṇenaiva niḥsvabhāvo 'paraḥ punaḥ /
na svayaṃ-bhāva etasyety-aparā niḥsvabhāvatā //

25. The true nature of mind only (*vijñaptimātratā*) is the true nature (*paramārtha*) of all *dharmas*, because, remaining as

it is at all times (*sarvakālaṃ tathā-bhāvāt*) it is suchness (*tathatā*).

dharmāṇāṃ paramārthaś-ca sa yatas-tathatāpi saḥ /
sarva-kālaṃ tathābhāvāt saiva vijñaptimātratā //

26. As long as consciousness does not abide in mind only (*vijñaptimātratva*), the attachment of the subject-object distinction will not cease.

yāvad-vijñaptimātratve vijñānaṃ nāvatiṣṭhati /
grāha-dvayasyānuśayas-tāvan-na vinivartate //

27. If a person places something before himself, thinking "This is consciousness only," he does not abide in consciousness only.

vijñaptimātram-evedam-ity-api hy-upalambhataḥ /
sthāpayann-agrataḥ kiṃcit tanmātre nāvatiṣṭhate //

28. When the mind no longer seizes on any object (*ālambana*) whatever, then the mind is established in the nature of mind only (*vijñānamātratva*). When there is nothing that is grasped, that is mind only, because there is no grasping.

yadā tv-ālambanaṃ vijñānaṃ naivopalabhate tadā /
sthitaṃ vijñānamātratve grāhyābhāve tad-agrahāt //

29. That is the supreme, world-transcending knowledge (*jñāna*), without mind (*acitta*) and without support or object (*anupalambha*). From the abandonment of the two-fold faults, there occurs the revulsion (*parāvṛtti*) of the store-consciousness.

acitto 'nupalambho 'sau jñānaṃ lokottaraṃ ca tat /
āśrayasya parāvṛttir dvidhā dauṣṭhulya-hānitaḥ //

30. That alone is the pure realm (*dhātu*), unthinkable, good, unchanging, blissful, the liberation body (*vimukti-kāya*), the *dharma*-body (*dharma-kāya*), so-called, of the great sage.

sa evānāsravo dhātur-acintyaḥ kuśalo dhruvaḥ /
sukho vimuktikāyo 'sau dharmākhyo 'yaṃ mahāmuneḥ //

Triṃś. 29 asserts that the supreme, world transcending knowledge of the Buddha is devoid of mind (*acitta*). This verse raises a couple of fairly obvious questions. First of all, how could any knowledge (*jñāna*) be said to be devoid of mind? And secondly, how could the state of Buddhahood — or anything else for that matter — be said to be devoid of mind (*acitta*), given that the Vijñānavādins held that everything is mind only?

It is fairly easy to see the *doctrinal* motivations for this assertion. According to fundamental Buddhist teachings, mind consists of an ever-changing aggregate of conditioned *dharmas*. That is why in the early Buddhist teachings it was held that one had to extinguish the mind (along with all other conditioned and compounded *dharmas*) in order to escape from what is conditioned, impermanent and *saṃsāric*. Therefore, insofar as the Vijñānavādins wished to maintain the orthodoxy of their own teachings, or at least to show their continuity with the earlier teachings, they were necessarily committed to the view that the highest world transcending knowledge (*nirvikalpa jñāna*) is *acitta*.

Although the doctrinal motivation for Triṃś. 29 is clear enough, the assertion that everything is mind only, on the one hand, and the assertion that Buddhahood is *acitta*, on the other, are pretty clearly inconsistent. Other (though related) inconsistencies show up in a number of different places in the Triṃśikā. Consider Triṃś. 25, for example. This verse says: "The nature of mind only (*vijñaptimātratā*) is the true nature (*paramārtha*) of all *dharmas* because, remaining as it is at all times, it is suchness (*tathatā*)." This verse, in other words, identifies the essence of mind only (*vijñaptimātratā*) with what is immutable and unchanging (i.e. suchness, *śūnyatā* etc.) However, Triṃś. 21 asserts that it is of the essence of mind that it is mutable (lit. that it "arises depending on causes and conditions" (*pratyayodbhava)* and that it has the "self nature of being dependent on causes and conditions" (*paratantra-svabhāva*).

The problem, then, is that the Triṃśikā asserts three propositions that as a set are inconsistent:

(1) Triṃś. 21 and 24: The essence of mind (*paratantra-svabhāva*) is that it arises and perishes depending on causes and conditions.

(2) Triṃś. 25(a)-(b): The true nature of things (*dharmāṇāṃ paramārthaḥ*) is immutable and unchanging (and therefore does not depend on causes and conditions).

(3) Triṃś. 25(d): The nature of mind only (*vijñaptimātratā*) is identical with the true nature of things.

Note that in Sanskrit the essence (*svabhāva*) of an entity *x* is the same thing as the abstract property that is designated by adding the suffix *-tā* to "*x*." For example, the essence of Blue (*nīla-svabhāva*) is the same thing as Blueness (*nīlatā, nīlatva*). For exactly the same reason, the essence of mind (*vijñapti-svabhāva*, *vijñāna-svabhāva*, *paratantra-svabhāva*) is the same thing as *vijñāna(mātra)tā* or *vijñapti(mātra)tā*. The inconsistency in (1)-(3) above is that Triṃś. 21 asserts that the former is mutable, whereas Triṃś. 25(d) — in conjunction with 25(a) — asserts that the latter is immutable.

The identity of the essence (*svabhāva*) of mind with *vijñapti(mātra)tā* is just a matter of what is meant by these words, i.e. it is just a truth of semantics. Nevertheless, it is of interest to note that the equation between the essence (*svabhāva*) of a thing *x* and the abstract property *x-tā* or *x-tva* was explicitly recognized in the Indian tradition. For example, in Aṣṭādhyāyī 5.1.119, Pāṇini states as a meaning rule (*tasya bhāvas-tva-talau*) that the suffixes "*-tā*" and "*-tva*" have the sense of "the nature of (*bhāva*)." Explicit recognition of this equation was also given by the Buddhist tradition. For example, in his autocommentary on the *svārthānumāna-pariccheda* of the Pramāṇa-vārttika (67), Dharmakīrti lays it down as a condition of adequacy of any theory of language that it should be able to account for the fact that the "essential nature of the sky is skyness" (*khasya svabhāvaḥ khatvam*). In short, the contradiction described in (1)-(3) involves a violation of a rule of language (or logic) which was explicitly recognized, not only by the greatest of the Indian grammatical authorities, but by later Buddhist writers as well.[1]

Since (1)-(3) above is an inconsistent set of propositions, one can derive from it the further contradiction that *vijñaptimātratā* (the essence of mind only) is *acitta*, i.e. that mind (only) is essentially non-mind. Oddly enough, Vasubandhu seems to have accepted this consequence. Evidence for this can be found in the passages that connect Triṃś. 29 with Triṃś. 25. Thus, Triṃś. 28 says that when the mind (*vijñāna*) no longer seizes on an object, it is established in mind only; when this happens, the verse says, there is no grasping, since there is nothing to grasp. Then Triṃś. 29 says: "This is the world-transcending knowledge (*lokottara-jñāna*) which is devoid of mind (*acitta*)." Clearly, the Triṃśikā means to identify this ultimate, world-transcending knowledge which perceives the true nature of things with the *vijñaptimātratā* of Triṃś. 25, which is identified with the true nature of all *dharmas*. But since the world-transcending knowledge is said to be devoid of mind, Triṃś. 29 leads to the conclusion that the true nature of mind only (*vijñaptimātratā*) is that everything is devoid of mind!

It might be objected that this contradiction is only an apparent one, since, strictly speaking, what Vasubandhu actually says is that it is the essence of mind *only* (*vijñapti*mātratā) which is said to be immutable and unchanging, rather than the essence of mind (*vijñaptitā*, *vijñaptitva*) simpliciter. Vasubandhu, therefore, may have thought that there was no contradiction between asserting that 1) *vijñaptimātratā* is immutable and 2) that the essence of mind is mutable, on the grounds that mind only (*vijñaptimātra*, *vijñāna-mātra*) is something different from mind simpliciter (*vijñapti*, *vijñāna*). [Presumably the reason would be that mind only (*vijñaptimātra*), unlike mind simpliciter, is devoid of the illusion of an external object.] However, this way of avoiding the difficulty will not work, for if it is the case that 1) the essence of mind is that it is mutable and arises and perishes depending on causes and conditions, and 2) that there is mind but no external objects (i.e. everything is just mind only), then what we must conclude, as a matter of logic, is that the essence of the *non*dual mind is that it is mutable and dependent on causes and conditions. In other words, one must conclude that even *vijñaptimātratā* itself is dependent on causes and conditions and is mutable, and this contradicts what is stated in Triṃś. 21, which says that *vijñaptimātratā* is identical with the immutable suchness.

There are, incidentally, signs in Sthiramati's and Xuan Zang's commentaries on the Triṃśikā that both of these commentators felt the impossibility of interpreting Triṃś. 25 and 29 together in a consistent way. Sthiramati's commentary on Triṃś. 25, for example, clearly shows signs of strain in the following passage:

> The being (*bhāva*) of the dependent nature is *māyāvic*, because it arises depending upon causes and conditions; therefore it is said that it does not really arise at all; therefore the dependent nature is said to be the non-self nature of origination. Since that is the true nature of all *dharmas* it is said to be suchness. The supreme, world-transcending knowledge, because it is the highest, is the realization of the *paramārtha*. Or else it may be said to be like space, being all-pervading, stainless and formless.
>
> The self nature of the perfected nature is the true nature of things. Since the perfected nature is the true nature of the *dharmas* which are essentially dependent on causes and conditions — that is, because such is the very nature of things (*dharmatā*) — the perfected nature alone is the self nature of things. In truth, everything lacks a self nature (*paramārtha-niḥsvabhāvatā*) in virtue of the non-existent self nature (*abhāva-svabhāvatvāt*) of the perfected nature.[2]

This is an unusually murky passage, but its murkiness must be due, at least in part, to the fact that Sthiramati is trying to explain how the true nature of mind only (*vijñaptimātratā*) can be identified with the true nature of things (*paramārtha*) and with the perfected nature. The problem is that (according to the Mahāyāna texts) the *paramārtha* must be unoriginated, unchanging, void like space, formless etc., just as Triṃś. 25 asserts, whereas the orthodox Buddhist teachings (and Triṃś. 21 as well) held that it is of the essence of the mind to be changing. Sthiramati, therefore, is trying in this passage to do the impossible, i.e., to make sense of a verse which asserts that the essence of mind (*vijñaptimātratā*) is defined by qualities which mind as such (according to traditional Buddhist teachings) could not have.

Xuan Zang's commentary on Triṃśikā 29 is even more interesting in this respect. According to Poussin (1928-48: 606), Xuan Zang translated Triṃś. 29 as follows:

> The supramundane knowledge is without any perceived object (*anupalambha*) and is incomprehensible (*acintya*); thus by the abandonment of the two-fold faults (incapacity), one obtains the revulsion of the basis (*āśraya-parāvṛtti*).

Poussin seems to have been puzzled that Xuan Zang used the Chinese term for "incomprehensible" in this verse, for, as he noted, the Sanskrit MS. discovered by Sylvain Lévi in Nepal in the 1920s has "*acitta*" (devoid of mind), and Sthiramati's Ṭīkā on the Triṃśikā (also discovered by Lévi) confirms this reading (*acitto 'nupalambho 'sau*). There can, therefore, be no doubt that Xuan Zang's translation and interpretation of Triṃś. 29 fails to give the exact meaning of the original.

It is interesting to speculate about CWSL ad Triṃś. 29. This passage could simply be a case of inaccuracy in translation, of course, but another possibility is that Xuan Zang deliberately changed the "*acitta*" of the Sanskrit to "*acintya*" because he himself felt the philosophical difficulties involved in the literal reading of the original Sanskrit passage. One problem is that it would appear to make no sense to speak of a knowledge that is *acitta*. Another problem is that, due to Triṃś. 29's linkage with Triṃś. 25 through Triṃś. 26-28, the Sanskrit of Triṃś. 29 leads to the unacceptable conclusion that *vijñaptimātratā* is *acitta*, i.e., that mind is essentially non-mind.

PART II:

NIRVĀṆA AND BUDDHAHOOD

It is easy to see that the Triṃśikā, like the Madhyānta-vibhāga, is a Mahāyāna text. Although the *nirvāṇa* of the Arhat is acknowledged in Triṃś. 5, it is never referred to again. The main concern of the treatise is the doctrine that the world is nothing but mind (*vijñaptimātratā*), the realization of which is said to lead, not to the *nirvāṇa* of the Arhat, but to the state of Buddhahood.

According to the Mahāyānists, the Arhat (i.e. the one who attains the end of the Hīnayāna or "Lesser Vehicle") realizes the selflessness (*nairātmya*) of the person (*pudgala, ātman*), but — unlike the Buddha — does not realize the selflessness of all the *dharmas* (*sarva-dharma-śūnyatā*). In order to realize the selflessness of all the *dharmas*, it is necessary to follow the path that leads to Buddhahood, and this, according to the Vijñānavādins, essentially involves realizing the truth that everything is mind only. The Hīnayānist who follows the Lesser Vehicle attains *nirvāṇa*, but the Mahāyānist who follows the Mahāyānist path of the Greater Vehicle attains Buddhahood. As we shall see, the state of Buddhahood, which involves the realization that everything is mind only (*vijñaptimātratā*), is more than merely the cessation or extinction of the *saṃsāric* process, and is therefore very different from anything that is described in the early Buddhist teachings. This becomes quite clear when one examines Xuan Zang's Cheng wei shilun, which (among other things) is concerned to reconcile Vasubandhu's teachings with the traditional Buddhist teachings.

According to the Mahāyāna *sūtras*, the teaching that the Buddha entered the final *nirvāṇa* of total extinction (*nirupadhi-śeṣa-nirvāṇa*) at the time of his physical death at Kuśinagarī is only a provisional teaching for those who are incapable of grasping a much greater truth. In the sixteenth chapter of the Sad-dharma-puṇḍarīka-sūtra (Lotus of the Good Law), for example, Buddha tells his most advanced disciples that he has been a Buddha for countless ages and that he lives forever, working for the salvation of all sentient beings. He explains to the advanced disciples that he tells the deluded people that he must enter the *nirupadhi-śeṣa nirvāṇa* because this will make them cherish the precious teachings of the *dharma*, which they would otherwise be inclined to take for granted. On hearing the teaching of the *nirupadhi-śeṣa-nirvāṇa*, deluded people come to believe that it is very difficult to see a Tathāgata, and therefore cherish a desire to see him and follow his teachings. Therefore, though the Tathāgata does not in reality become extinct, he announces his extinction to others.

The conception of an active *nirvāṇic* Buddhahood is usually called in the Mahāyāna the "*a-pratiṣṭhita-nirvāṇa*," to distinguish the Buddha's *nirvāṇa* from the *nirupadhi-śeṣa-nirvāṇa* of the Hīnayāna. The Sanskrit term "*apratiṣṭhita*" can mean 1) not placed or situated; 2) not firm, fixed, rooted, or supported; 3) not having reached; and 4) uncompleted or unfinished. An *apratiṣṭhita-nirvāṇa*, therefore, is a *nirvāṇa* that is either 1) not firmly fixed, situated or supported, 2) not reached or attained, or 3) partial or unfinished.

This doctrine of an *apratiṣṭhita-nirvāṇa* led to numerous doctrinal problems and interpretational difficulties, for it threatened to undermine the distinction (which was fundamental to the older, pre-Mahāyāna texts) between the conditioned and the unconditioned, between *saṃsāra* and *nirvāṇa*, and between suffering and release. The traditional teachings analyzed all the factors of *saṃsāric* existence into five groups (*skandhas*) of *dharmas*: form, feeling, perception, impulses and consciousness. How is the teaching of an active *nirvāṇic* Buddha, working for the salvation of all beings, to be explained in terms of this doctrine? On the one hand, the view that the Buddha had not completely destroyed the five groups of *dharmas* and become extinct (*nirodha*) contradicts the plain meaning of the earliest and oldest texts, which state unequivocally 1) that the possession of any of the *dharmas* in these five groups necessarily involves suffering and 2) that the Buddha attained the complete liberation from suffering when he attained his final *nirvāṇa* (*parinirvāṇa*) at the time of his physical death at Kuśinagarī. On the other hand, the view that he does *not* have any of the *dharmas* belonging to these five groups appears to contradict the plain meaning of the Mahāyāna texts, which hold that he renounced the total release from suffering associated with the *nirvāṇa* of total extinction in order to work for the welfare and salvation of all sentient beings.

In the Mahāyāna at least five different views were developed in response to this dilemma. Two of the views maintained that there is in fact only one goal and one path (*ekayāna*); the other three views maintained that there are two paths and two goals.

(1) According to the *ekayāna* doctrines, the teachings of the *sūtras* which refer to the *nirvāṇa* of the Arhat are purely provisional teachings. There is no *nirvāṇa* of total extinction as it is conceived in the Hīnayāna, i.e. no *nirupadhi-śeṣa-nirvāṇa*. According to this view, the *nirvāṇa* of the Arhat and the teachings that are connected with it are so ignoble and inferior to Buddhahood that the former is not a state of real liberation, much less real enlightenment, at all. In short, the canonical texts describe something called the *nirvāṇa* of final extinction, but there really is no such thing. The Śrī-mālā-devī-sūtra, for example, says that the noble truth of the cessation of suffering (*nirodha-satya*) is beyond the object of perception of all sentient beings, is inconceivable and is not within the domain of knowledge of any Śrāvaka or Pratyeka-buddha.[1]

(2) The most natural way of reading the Śrī-mālā-devī-sūtra is that there is no *nirupadhi-śeṣa-nirvāṇa*, and that the only real liberation and real enlightenment lies in Buddhahood. Another possible view, however, is that the *nirupadhi-śeṣa-nirvāṇa is* the true *nirvāṇa*, but that it is attained only by the Buddha. This, too, would be a "one vehicle" (*ekayāna*) doctrine.

This seems to have been the view of the Mādhyamikas. As was previously noted,[2] Candrakīrti says that the teaching that all the factors of existence are extinct (*nirodha*) in the *nirupadhi-śeṣa-nirvāṇa* is taught in all of the Buddhist schools. Candrakīrti, however, believed that all *dharmas* are always non-existent and unreal, like the the proverbial snake in the rope-snake illusion. It would appear to follow that on this view only the Buddhas attain *nirvāṇa*, since only they realize that all *dharmas* are entirely void (*sarva-dharma-śūnyatā*) in this sense.

(3) The *nirvāṇa* of the Buddha is incomplete or partial. This was undoubtedly the interpretation of Buddhahood in the earliest Mahāyāna texts. On this view, the Buddha rejected the peace of the

nirvāṇa of total extinction in favor of a limited and partial *nirvāṇa* in which he could still work for the salvation and release from suffering of other sentient beings. Buddhahood, therefore, is at least to some extent a *saṃsāric* state, because it involves renouncing the absolute release from suffering which is attained with the *nirvāṇa* of total extinction. The Buddha's *nirvāṇa* is sublime and pure in relation to our own experience, of course, but it nevertheless belongs to the conditioned realm of experience and is therefore impure and *saṃsāric* in relation to the *nirvāṇa* of total extinction of the Arhat.

Adherents of this view disagreed about the duration of the incomplete or partial *nirvāṇa* of the Buddha. Some held that all sentient beings were destined for enlightenment and *nirvāṇa*, and that when all sentient beings had been saved the Buddha would himself enter the *nirupadhi-śeṣa-nirvāṇa*. Other Mahāyānists — like Xuan Zang and the Dharmapāla school generally — held that there were some sentient beings who had "cut off the roots of goodness" or who had never had the potential for enlightenment or *nirvāṇa* in the first place. Since such beings could never attain *nirvāṇa*, the Buddha's *apratiṣṭhita-nirvāṇa*, which was dedicated to the alleviation of the suffering of all sentient beings, was also eternal.

(4) Buddhahood is *apratiṣṭhita* in the sense that it is "not situated" or "not fixed"; specifically, it is fixed in neither *saṃsāra* nor *nirvāṇa*. This is the view of the Laṅkāvatāra-sūtra and many other Mahāyāna texts.

The problem with this interpretation is that the notion of a state which is neither *saṃsāric* nor *nirvāṇic* is a contradiction in terms according to traditional Buddhist teachings. According to these teachings, anything which is *saṃsāric* is eo ipso compounded (*saṃskṛta*), impure (*āsrava*), impermanent (*anitya*) and involved in suffering (*duḥkha*). *Nirvāṇa*, on the other hand, is *defined* in the oldest texts as what is *not saṃsāric*, compounded, impure, impermanent and involved in suffering. It is attained by the destruction of *all* the elements of existence, i.e. by the cessation of *saṃsāra*.

(5) Closely connected with the fourth interpretation is the view that Buddhahood has two different *aspects*. According to this view, Buddha attained the *nirvāṇa* of the Arhat, but unlike the Arhat he also has all the great qualities (*mahā-guṇa-dharmas*) which are

attained only by the Buddhas. These *mahā-guṇa-dharmas* are sometimes said to comprise the *dharma* body (*dharma-kāya*) and the enjoyment or ornamented body (*saṃbhoga-kāya*) of the Buddha. The extinction and voidness of the *nirupadhi-śeṣa-nirvāṇa*, however, is the basis (*āśraya*), in some sense, of the active aspect of the Buddha as he continues to work for the welfare of others.

Xuan Zang's commentary on the Triṃśikā (CWSL) deals at some length with the foregoing interpretations of the *apratiṣṭhita-nirvāṇa* in connection with Triṃś. 29-30's description of Buddhahood. Xuan Zang's discussion of the terms "pure realm" (*anāsrava-dhātu*); "*kuśala*" (good), "*dhruva*" (unchangeable), "*sukha*" (blissful), "*vimukti-kāya*" (liberation body) and "*dharma-kāya*" (*dharma* body) in this part of the CWSL shows just how difficult it is to reconcile the last two verses of Vasubandhu's work with the traditional Buddhist teachings about *saṃsāra* and *nirvāṇa*.

(a) *anāsrava-dhātu*. In Buddhist philosophy, purity (*anāsravatva*, *asaṃkleśatva*) and impurity (*āsravatva*, *saṃkleśatva*) are usually associated with *nirvāṇa* and *saṃsāra*, respectively. In the strictest sense, that which is pure (*anāsrava*) is essentially that which is is uncompounded and unconditioned (*asaṃskṛta*). Sometimes, it is true, the term is used to describe the "purified" components of conditioned existence. The purity of these conditioned elements, however, is very largely a mere *façon de parler*, for while they are "pure" in comparison with the totally impure elements of unenlightened existence, they are impure in relation to the absolutely uncompounded and unconditioned (*asaṃskṛta*).[3]

Xuan Zang's interpretation of the term "*anāsrava dhātu*" in Triṃś. 30 attempts to combine two concepts of purity in a single doctrine. According to Xuan Zang, the revolution of the basis of Triṃś. 29 can be interpreted in two ways: on the one hand, it is the revolution or transformation of the store consciousness, and on the other it is the revolution or transformation of the true nature of reality (*bhūta-tathatā*), since the latter is in some sense the basis (*āśraya*) for both *saṃsāra* and *nirvāṇa*. The revolution of the store consciousness, which is attained by the Arhat, produces *nirvāṇa*; the revolution of the *tathatā* produces supreme enlightenment (*mahā-bodhi*), which he defines as the "diverse classes of mind associated with the four supernatural wisdoms (*jñāna*) of the Buddha."[4] He says that these four wisdoms "comprise all the conditioned qualities of the realm (*bhūmi*) of the Buddhas." He also gives the following description of the *nirvāṇa* of total extinction which is attained by the Arhat of the Lower Vehicle:

> There remains only pure Suchness, exempt from the ten signs (*nimittas*), the same, tranquil, destroyed, blissful (*sukha*). One says, therefore, from the viewpoint of Suchness, that the saints of the two vehicles are not different from the Buddhas: but they do not have great wisdom (*bodhi*), nor the activities directed to the salvation of others, and they are therefore different from the Buddhas.[5]

On Xuan Zang's interpretation, therefore, the two-fold revolution of the basis of the Mahāyāna produces two related things: the *nirvāṇa* of the Lesser Vehicle, which is unconditioned, and the great wisdom of the Greater Vehicle, which is conditioned. Accordingly, he interprets Triṃś. 30 as meaning that the enlightenment of the Mahāyāna involves two different kinds of purity (*anāsrava*): one that is compounded, and one that is uncompounded. These are really two different (though related) things, which are simply given the same name.

Xuan Zang attempts to defend his view against the following objection. The opponent concedes that there are Mahāyāna texts which refer to an element (called the *dharma-dhātu*) which is pure (*śuddha*, *anāsrava*). However, the opponent argues that it makes no sense to say that the minds associated with the four wisdoms of the Buddha are also exclusively pure, presumably because wisdom (*jñāna*) is a function or aspect (*caitta*) of mind, which is regarded in Buddhist philosophy as an aggregate of compounded *dharmas*.

This objection and Xuan Zang's answer to it, which I have translated into English from Poussin's French, goes as follows:

> [Objection]: "It is all right to say that the pure *dharma-dhātu* is pure (*anāsrava*). But how can the minds associated with the four *jñānas* be exclusively pure (*anāsrava*)?

> [Xuan Zang]: Because all that is comprised in the Way (*mārga-satya*), i.e. the qualities (*saṃskṛta-guṇas*) and the bodies and lands (*kṣetras*) of the Buddha, are engendered by the pure "seeds" (*bījas*), and because the Buddha has completely rejected all the seeds of the impure *dharmas*. No doubt the Buddha manifests the actions, defilements etc. which produce a *saṃsāric* body: one says that there is "suffering" and "production of suffering." But all these manifestations are really pure (*anāsrava*), and form part of the noble path.[6]

The opponent then objects that an authoritative text, the Abhidharma-samuccaya, says that the five sense-organs, the five objects of sensory consciousness and the five sense-consciousnesses themselves (making fifteen elements or *dhātus* in all) are exclusively impure. Must we believe, he asks, that the Tathāgata, who is entirely pure, does not have sense-organs, sensory conciousness or objects of sensory perception? To this pointed question, Xuan Zang outlines three possible answers:

(1) There are aggregates (*skandhas*) etc. which belong to the Buddha in *nirvāṇa*. However, these are not like the aggregates and conditioned *dharmas* which are enumerated in the traditional Abhidharma of the Buddhist teachings and which belong only to the minds and bodies of non-Buddhas. The Abhidharma lists only the impure *dharmas* and aggregates; the pure *dharmas* and aggregates of *dharmas* of the Buddha are entirely different from these. The pure *dharmas* are "born from the *dharma-dhātu*" (*dharma-dhātu-ja*) and proceed from the Buddha's uninterrupted meditation.

(2) According to another view, Buddhahood and the *nirvāṇa* of total extinction of the Hīnayāna are the same: i.e. the Buddha is in the *nirvāṇa* of total extinction described in the traditional texts, but he is also active. Since in this state the Buddha has no mind or any other aggregate of *dharmas*, no sense-fields etc., he is not impure. Xuan Zang describes this view as follows:

> The qualities, bodies and lands of the Tathāgatas are very profound, beautiful, are neither existent nor non-existent, are apart from all imagination (*vikalpa*), transcend all names or words (*prapañcātīta*), and are not comprised among the aggregates, sense-fields and elements. Therefore one can say,

without contradicting the Abdhidharma, that the Buddha is not impure.[7]

(3) The third view is that the aggregates of the Buddha are the same as the aggregates which are enumerated in the Abhidharma, but the aggregates of the Buddha, unlike those of the non-Buddhas, are exclusively pure. (This is the view that Xuan Zang favored.) On the face of it, this doctrine repudiates the well-established Buddhist teaching that only the uncompounded can be really pure. Xuan Zang himself is not willing to repudiate such a well-established teaching, and attempts to reconcile his own view with the traditional teaching by drawing a distinction between "gross objects" and "superficial knowledge," on the one hand, and the supernatural wisdoms of the Buddha, on the other. The relevant passage on this point from the CWSL is as follows:

> The qualities (*guṇas*) and the bodies and lands of the Tathāgatas are comprised in the aggregates, sense-fields and elements, which is as it should be (*yathā-yogam*). But the aggregates etc. can be pure or impure. In fact, the Abhidharma-samuccaya teaches that fifteen elements are exclusively impure, but this declaration has in view the gross objects (*viṣaya*, *artha*) and the "superficial *vijñānas*" of the two vehicles, and not the fifteen elements of the Buddha. Among the eighteen aggregates, sense organs and elements of the non-Buddhas, only the last three can be pure, but, in regard to the Buddha, the eighteen are pure and unknowable by the saints of the two vehicles. In truth, some texts (Mahāprajñā etc.) say that the qualities, bodies etc. of the Buddhas are not comprised in the elements because these qualities etc. do not resemble the elements which are known by the mediocre knowledge of the adherents of the two vehicles. But it is certain that the qualities, bodies etc. of the Buddha are comprised among the elements.—Why? Because, according to all the texts, all the *saṃskṛtas* are comprised in the five *skandhas*, all the *dharmas* are comprised in the eighteen elements and the twelve sense-fields. And if, as the opponent says, the fruit of the Buddha (Buddha-*phala*), because it is beyond words (*prapañcātīta*) is not elements etc., then one cannot say that it is the 'pure *dhātu*, good, immutable, blissful, the liberation body' (Triṃś. 30), because isn't *that* pure verbal designation (*prapañca*)?[8]

In these three views we may see the underlying problems confronting the Mahāyānist conception of Buddhahood very clearly, for there are weighty objections to all *three* views.

(1) The first view flatly contradicts the traditional teachings of the Abhidharma, because it says that there are more than eighteen *dhātus*. This view makes the traditional teaching that all conditioned *dharmas* are impure, impermanent and essentially connected with suffering literally untrue. According to this interpretation, the correct view is: only those *dhātus* which belong to the *non*-Buddhas are impure, impermanent and essentially connected with suffering. This view is therefore highly unorthodox.

(2) The second view is identified by Kui Ji in his commentary on the CWSL with that of the Three Treatises school, i.e. with the Mādhyamikas. This interpretation is the most radical of all. In the first and third theories, the *dharma* theory is held to be incomplete in some way. According to this view, however, the whole theory is fundamentally false, because this view asserts that someone can be active in the state of Buddhahood and not consist of *dharmas* at all. From the standpoint of the traditional Buddhist teachings this makes no more sense than speaking of a married bachelor or a round square.

(3) The third view (which is Xuan Zang's) attempts to reconcile two different notions of purity. However, the view that the Buddha is comprised of the eighteen *dhātus* of the traditional teachings *and* is also pure in the strict sense contradicts the traditional teaching that all conditioned *dharmas* are impure (at least in comparison with the *asaṃskṛta dharmas*).[9] As a result, Xuan Zang has to resort to two different notions of purity — a conditioned one and an unconditioned one. Furthermore, his notion of "conditioned purity" is hard to reconcile with the early Buddhist texts.

(b) *kuśala, dhruva, sukha*. The term "*kuśala*" means "right," "proper," "good," "auspicious," "happy," "prosperous" etc. The term "*dhruva*" means "fixed," "firm," "immovable," "stable," "permanent," and "unchangeable." The term "*sukha*" means "happy," "pleasant," "easy," and "joyful."

Clearly, Vasubandhu intends to describe by these terms a state which is the very opposite of the world of suffering described in the first of the four-fold noble truths (*duḥkha-satya*). The state described is not *saṃsāric*, so the interpretation of Buddhahood, according to which it is "incomplete," is ruled out. At the same time, the state Vasubandhu is describing is not the *nirvāṇa* of total extinction of the Hīnayāna. So again one is confronted with the same problem: qualities of the conditioned and unconditioned realms are being mixed together in a quite untraditional and unorthodox way. Terms are applied to the active, post-Kuśinagarī conception of the Buddha in a way which seems to contradict the fundamental Buddhist teaching that all the factors (*dharmas*) of conditioned existence involve suffering.

Perhaps the clearest instance of this is Vasubandhu's use of the term "*sukha*." In traditional Buddhism no state of conditioned existence is free from suffering, and consequently no state of conditioned existence can strictly be said to be "*sukha*." Of course, even the Hīnayāna texts frequently describe the "*nirvāṇa* with a residue remaining" (*sopadhi-śeṣa nirvāṇa*), in which the Arhat resides after his enlightenment and before his death, as "*sukha*" in a purely derivative or secondary sense. It is not entirely inappropriate, when comparing the Arhat or the Buddha when he is alive with the state of unenlightened beings, to say that, in comparison with them, the Arhat or Buddha is "*sukha*," for in their case the delusion of self etc. is extinguished, they have attained mental and spiritual clarity, and they know that they will be released on the death of the body. They are therefore at peace (*upaśama*). But there is no place in the traditional conception of the *nirvāṇa* of total extinction for saying that it is "*sukha*" even in this sense, for in this state, by definition, all the aggregates, sense-fields and elements are completely extinguished. As we have seen, the *nirvāṇa* of total extinction is described purely negatively. Therefore, as applied to the *nirvāṇa* of total extinction, the term "*sukha*" can *only* mean that it does *not* involve suffering, but since Vasubandhu is describing the active Buddhahood of the Mahāyāna, he must intend the term "*sukha*" to mean more than this.

The problems that this entails can be seen clearly in a passage from the Buddha-bhūmi-śāstra which is cited by Poussin. According to fundamental Buddhist principles, any state of existence in which the Buddha could work for the salvation of others would be compounded and relative, and therefore would inevitably involve suffering. This raises the question of how such an act of supererogation could be justified, as well as the question why the Buddha exhorted others to strive for the same renunciation. The Buddha-bhūmi-śāstra attempted to deal with this problem in the following passage:

> [Opponent]: The root of the sacred teaching (*ārya-deśanā*) of the Tathāgatas is that beings should leave the sufferings of *saṃsāra*. Now the Śrāvakas, when they attain the state of the Arhat (*aśaikṣa*), leave *saṃsāra* entirely: the sacred teaching of the Tathāgatas is therefore well accomplished (*su-pratipannā*). If this is so, why teach them the *dharma* anew?
>
> [Reply]: In order that they may turn (*pariṇam*) towards supreme enlightenment.
>
> [Opponent]: But the Śrāvakas, in that state of Arhatship, when they have exhausted this last unique existence (*vipāka*), will certainly enter the complete destruction (*nirodha*) of the *nirvāṇa* of total extinction. Now the treatises teach that the 'bliss of tranquility' (*vyupaśama-sukha*) of this *nirvāṇa* does not differ from that of the Buddha. Why does the Buddha turn the Śrāvakas towards supreme enlightenment, towards the long suffering of supreme enlightenment?
>
> [Reply]: There is no sensation of suffering (*duḥkha-vedanā*) in the supreme enlightenment. Therefore the objection has no force.
>
> [Opponent]: It does have force, because this existence involves the suffering of the habitual tendencies (*saṃskāra-duḥkhatā*), i.e. the pain which consists in the character which all existence has of being dependent on causes and conditions and therefore of being impermanent.
>
> [Reply]: The Arhats who become Bodhisattvas endure this suffering (*duḥkhatā*). But, by means of that, they obtain the three

bodies of the Buddha, the qualities (*guṇas*), the great joy, the great bliss (*mahā-sukha*) of the Tathāgatas.

[Opponent]: None of the great blisses (*mahā-sukhas*) surpasses that of *nirvāṇa*. What is there which is lacking in it that the Arhats should seek supreme enlightenment?

[Reply]: Nirvāṇa involves the 'bliss of tranquility,' but it does not involve the feeling-awareness of bliss (*sukha-saṃvedanā*), or the bliss of supreme enlightenment (*saṃbodhi-sukha*); it cuts off innumerable qualities (*guṇas*), awareness of bliss etc.

[Opponent]: What good is the compounded bliss of supreme enlightenment, which is penetrated by the suffering of the habitual impulses (*saṃskāra-duḥkhatā*)?

[Reply]: The pure compounded (*anāsrava saṃskṛta*) is like *nirvāṇa*; being pure, it is not comprised in the *saṃskāra-duḥkhatā*. Besides, the Śrāvakas who turn towards supreme enlightenment do so in order to be able to lead innumerable beings from *saṃsāra*.[10]

The vacillation in this passage between the teaching that the *apratiṣṭhita nirvāṇa* of the Buddha is a state of suffering and the teaching that it is a state of bliss is revealing. After some hesitation, the passage ends up adopting the view — as Xuan Zang did later — that the Buddha-*dharmas* are pure (*anāsrava*). This position is unorthodox, however, for it implies that there is an impermanent and conditioned realm which does not involve suffering.

(c) *vimukti-kāya*. As is shown by the following passages, the term "liberation body" (*vimukti-kāya*) was usually used in the Buddhist writings as a synonym for the *nirvāṇa* of total extinction of the Arhats:[11]

[Abhidharma-kośa]: "The unconditioned liberation (*asaṃskṛta vimukti*) is the deliberate and final destruction (*prati-saṃkhyā-nirodha*) of the impurities (*kleśas*).

[Saṃdhi-nirmocana-sūtra]: "Bhagavat, is the revolution (*parāvṛtti*) obtained by the Śrāvakas and the Pratyeka-buddhas called the *dharma-kāya* or not? — No. — What is it called? — It is called the *vimukti-kāya*. From the point of view of the *vimukti-kāya*, the Śrāvakas and Pratyeka-buddhas, on the one hand, and the Buddhas, on the other, are the same.

[Yoga-śāstra]: "*Vimukti* is, as one says, the deliberate extinction (*prati-saṃkhyā-nirodha*) obtained by the knowledge of the non-existence of the self or person (*pudgala-śūnyatā*); it is a body (*kāya*) in the sense of being its support and its nature; the *vimukti-kāya* is the Suchness which is realized by the knowledge of the non-existence of the self (*pudgala-śūnyatā*).

[Buddha-bhūmi]: "When the Śrāvakas and Pratyekas of the determined lineage (i.e. who are predestined to the Hīnayānist *nirvāṇa*) are in the state of Arhatship, since they aspire to peace (*upaśama*), since they have completely destroyed the covering (*āvaraṇa*) of the defilements (*kleśas*) which motivate actions and promote rebirth, when they arrive at the spontaneous disappearance of the body-mind (*rūpa-citta*) created by anterior acts: then all the conditioned *dharmas*, pure or impure, manifested or potential, perish also. There remains only the 'revolution of the basis' (*āśraya-parāvṛtti*), suchness immaculate and beyond designation (*niḥprapañca-lakṣaṇa*), the pure *dharma-dhātu*, the *vimukti-kāya*. It is what is called the *nirupadhi-śeṣa-nirvāṇa*, firm, blissful, final, tranquil, which cannot be reasoned about (*na saṃkhyāṃ gacchati*), incomprehensible, exactly like the Tathāgatas (Buddhas). But it lacks the ornaments of the pure conditioned qualities *(anāsrava saṃskṛta)*, it lacks the service of others. Therefore, it is not like the Tathāgatas.

In the texts of the Mahāyāna, this *vimukti-kāya* is often contrasted with the *dharma-kāya*:

(d) *dharma-kāya*. One of the meanings of the word "*dharma*" is "teaching." Originally the term "*dharma-kāya*" probably referred simply to the body or corpus of teachings of the Buddha. In Saṃyutta-nikāya (SN) iii, p. 120, for example, a distinction is drawn between the physical body of the Buddha, which perished at his *mahā-nirvāṇa* at Kuśinagarī, and the teaching (P. *dhamma*) of the Buddha, which was given through his physical form. In this passage the Buddha says to a certain monk by the name of Vakkali: "What point is there in viewing the physical body of decay and putrefaction? He who sees the *dhamma* (i.e. the truth of the Buddhist teachings), he is the one who really sees me...". Similarly, in another early work, the Divyāvadāna, it is said: "I have seen the Bhagavat, not in his physical form (*rūpa-kāya*), but in his *dharma* body (*dharma-kāya*)" (i.e. in his teachings). At this early stage there is no question of the survival of the Buddha as a person in an *apratiṣṭhita-nirvāṇa*, but only the view that the Buddha can still be contacted — in a purely figurative sense — in the body or corpus of teachings that he left behind.

Later, however, the term "*dharma-kāya*" was given a more metaphysical meaning. According to the Mahāyānists, for example, the *dharma* body is obtained when one is born among the saints. It was thought to be the product or consequence of following the discipline that leads to Buddhahood rather than a body that was "born of one's parents." The Mahāyānists held that it has a long period of gestation as the "seed of Buddhahood" (*tathāgata-garbha*), and that it develops as the Bodhisattva traverses the long and arduous path leading to the development of the perfections (*pāramitās*) of Buddhahood.

The Abhisamayālaṃkāra (AA) gives a fairly extended description of the *dharma-kāya*. The *dharma-kāya*, it is said, comprises the sublime functions carried out by the Buddha in his *nirvāṇic* state for the salvation of others. Thus, it is said to consist of the six super-knowledges (*abhijñās*), the ten powers, the great compassion, the eighteen *dharmas* which are said to be special to the Buddha, the four kinds of purity, the uprooting of all the residues of defilement, the knowledge of all the modes (*sarvākāra-jñāna*) etc. The AA ends with a description of the 27 functions of the *dharma-kāya*. These include the activity which appeases the suffering of the places of rebirth in all the worlds, the Buddha's work for the welfare of beings, the practice of the six perfections, the path of the Bodhisattva, the pure Buddha-fields, and a state of complete purity. The *dharma-kāya* was said to be completely pure (*anāsrava*), to be full of infinite qualities, and to "fill all space in the six directions without measure or limit." Thus, in the Abhisamayālaṃkāra, too, there is a blurring (or confusion) of the properties of the uncompounded and compounded realms, for the AA accepts the notion of an *anāsrava-saṃskṛta* (pure-compounded). However, even the AA's conception of the *dharma-kāya* must be distinguished from the *vimukti-kāya* as it is defined in the citations in (c) above (pp. 74-75), for these passages state unequivocally that the *vimukti-kāya* is *asaṃskṛta*.

One of the problems raised by Triṃś. 29-30 is that, like the AA, these verses appear to define Buddhahood as consisting simultaneously of both the liberation body (*vimukti-kāya*) and the *dharma* body (*dharma-kāya*), although the foregoing citations from the Buddhist texts show that these terms generally refer to different things. Since the *dharma* body does not always exist, and is in a sense "produced," it must be distinguished from the *vimukti-kāya* which, since it is identical with suchness, emptiness etc., is neither a cause nor an effect of anything. The liberation body, in fact, appears to be merely a different name for the *nirupadhi-śeṣa-nirvāṇa*, because it is entirely pure (*anāsrava*) in the sense of being unconditioned and uncompounded. The *dharma-kāya*, on the other hand, consists of a stream of pure compounded *dharmas*. And this again is just the problem, for in the canonical Buddhist teachings, the compounded and the uncompounded, the impure and the pure, the impermanent and the permanent, the *saṃsāric* and the *nirvāṇic*, and the conditioned and the unconditioned *must* be two different things.

The Triṃśikā is very brief, and unfortunately we have no auto-commentary on it. Vasubandhu has simply left us these verses and the interpretational and doctrinal problems to which they give rise, and we can get no assistance from him. We do not even know if these problems troubled him, as they do his principal commentator Xuan Zang. Nor do we have any passage from Vasubandhu's writings which *explicitly* favors one or another of the five different views outlined above about the relationship between the *nirvāṇa* of the Arhat and the *apratiṣṭhita-nirvāṇa* of the Buddha. Nevertheless, some progress can be made in interpreting the Triṃśikā by noting that all but two of the five accounts of the *apratiṣṭhita-nirvāṇa* can probably be excluded as possible interpretations of the Triṃśikā on the basis of indirect evidence.

For example, Vasubandhu almost certainly did not endorse the "one vehicle" (*ekayāna*) view. The state of the Arhat is certainly not his main concern, but there is nothing in the Triṃśikā or in the Viṃśatikā which denies that there is such a thing.[12] Nor could he have shared the views of the Mādhyamikas on this question. Nor does he endorse the view that the *nirvāṇa* of the Buddha is incomplete or partial, for he never suggests that the state of Buddhahood is inferior to the *nirvāṇa* of the Arhat in any respect. In fact, all the attributes which one would expect to find in the description of the *nirupadhi-śeṣa-nirvāṇa* (e.g. "*acitta*," "*anupalambha*," "*āśraya-parāvṛtti*," "*dvidhā dauṣṭhulya-hānita*," "*anāsrava-dhātu*," "*dhruva*," and "*vimukti-kāya*") are found in Vasubandhu's description of *Buddhahood* in Triṃś. 29-30.

Consequently, we are left with either the fourth or the fifth of the views described above (pp. 66-67) concerning the relationship between Buddhahood and Arhatship. It is hard to say which of these two views Vasubandhu would have endorsed. As has already been noted, the problems facing the fourth interpretation — i.e. the "non-fixed" interpretation — are very great. The fifth view, which holds that the *dharma-kāya* is in some sense just the phenomenal aspect of the underlying *vimukti-kāya,* attempts to deal with some of these problems, but it also raises problems of its own. These difficulties are so great, in fact, that there may not be any distinction to be drawn between the fourth and the fifth interpretations.

Xuan Zang's attempt to describe the relationship between the *dharma-kāya* and the *vimukti-kāya* is embodied in his theory of the self nature body (*svābhāvika-kāya).* The term "*svābhāvika-kāya*" (which is not found in the Viṃśatikā or Triṃśikā) was used in some of the later Buddhist texts to refer to the unconditioned aspect of Buddhahood. In his commentary on Triṃś. 30, Xuan Zang uses this term to refer primarily to that aspect of the *dharma-kāya* that is devoid of all the compounded and conditioned *dharmas* (even the "pure" ones) and which is therefore identical with the liberation body or *vimukti-kāya*. At the same time, the *svābhāvika-kāya* is said to be the basis (*āśraya*) of the conditioned or phenomenal qualities of the active aspect of Buddhahood. Thus, Xuan Zang begins his analysis of the *dharma-kāya* with the following words:

The Lord Buddha, being replete with the supreme qualities of the silent sage, is called the great silent one (*mahā-muni*). The two fruits attained by this sage, being completely dissociated from the veilings (*āvaraṇas*), are designated not only by the word 'liberation body' but also by the word 'dharma body'; they are in effect adorned with the *dharmas* of the great qualities (*mahā-guṇa-dharmas*), without cause and infinite, e.g. the powers, the intrepidities (*vaiśāradyas*) etc.

The word 'body' (*kāya*) has the three-fold sense of 'nature' (*svabhāva*), support (*āśraya*) and accumulation (*saṃcaya*).

Therefore the *dharma-kāya* consists of five things: the pure *dharma-dhātu* and the four super-wisdoms (*jñānas*) of the Buddha. It is not only the pure *dharma-dhātu* which is called the *dharma-kāya*, because the fruits of the two 'revolutions of the basis' (*āśraya-parāvṛtti*) are included in the *dharma-kāya*.

The *dharma-kāya* is actually three-fold, consisting of three bodies: the *svābhāvika-kāya*, the *saṃbhoga-kāya* and the *nirmāṇa-kāya*.

The *svābhāvika-kāya* is the pure *dharma-dhātu* of the Tathāgatas, the immovable support (*āśraya*) of the *saṃbhoga-kāya* and the *nirmāṇa-kāya*, signless, at peace (*śānta*), beyond words and concepts (*prapañcātīta*), endowed with infinite qualities, real and eternal. It is the unchanging and identical nature of all the *dharmas*.[13]

Xuan Zang mentions several theories about the triple *dharma-kāya* (p. 706-713). According to one theory, the *svābhāvika-kāya* includes both the pure *dharma-dhātu* and the transcendental wisdoms (*jñānas*) of the Buddha. Xuan Zang rejects this view. His reasons for limiting the term "*svābhāvika-kāya*" to the absolutely pure, unconditioned and uncompounded *dharma-dhātu* (i.e. the *vimukti-kāya*) are as follows:

(1) There are texts, like the Mahāyāna-sūtrālaṃkāra and the Buddha-bhūmi-śāstra, which state that the *svābhāvika-kāya* is by nature eternal (*prakṛti-nitya*). Similarly, there are texts, like the Buddha-bhūmi-śāstra, the Yoga-śāstra and the Saṃdhi-nirmocana-

sūtra, which say that the *dharma-kāya* (= *svābhāvika-kāya*) of the Buddha is exempt from birth and destruction.

(2) Vasubandhu states in his Vajra-cchedikā-prajñā-pāramitā-śāstra that the *svābhāvika-kāya* is obtained by causes which enable one to attain it, not by causes which actually produce it.

(3) The *svābhāvika-kāya* must be utterly unconditioned because there are a number of texts which say that this body is common to all the Tathāgatas, that it penetrates all *dharmas*, that it is similar to space, that it is without definite marks (*animitta*), that it is uncaused (*asaṃskṛta*), and that it is neither form (*rūpa*) nor mind (*citta*).

(4) Although the *svābhāvika-kāya* is said to be replete with infinite qualities, it is different from the other two bodies because it is eternal, sublime, sovereign, free from all impurity, the support of the good (*kuśala*), and because it consists of unconditioned and uncaused qualities. Therefore it has neither the nature nor the activity of body, mind or mental qualities (*rūpa*, *citta*, or *caittas*).

(5) The *svābhāvika-kāya* is the self nature or essence of the nature of things (*dharmatā*), whereas the other two bodies of the *dharma-kāya* are the manifestation (*lakṣaṇa*) of the *dharmatā*.

(6) The *svābhāvika-kāya* and its associated realm are realized in an identical manner by all the Tathāgatas. There is therefore no distinction whatever between the *svābhāvika-kāya* of one Buddha and that of another.

According to fundamental Buddhist principles, it follows from all of the above descriptions that the *svābhāvika-kāya* must be absolutely pure, uncompounded and unconditioned.

Although Vasubandhu does not actually use the term "*svābhāvika-kāya*" in the Triṃśikā, there is support for Xuan Zang's interpretation of Triṃś. 29 and 30, for these two verses were clearly intended by Vasubandhu to describe one thing, not two different things. The *svābhāvika-kāya* appears to be something like a theoretical construct designed to connect these two different kinds of things, i.e. the *vimukti-kāya* and the *dharma-kāya*, or the *nirupadhi-śeṣa-nirvāṇa* of the Arhat and the *apratiṣṭhita-nirvāṇa* of the Buddha. According to Xuan Zang's interpretation, the *svābhāvika-kāya* is what the *dharma-kāya* really is, i.e. unchanging, immutable, pure, uncompounded, unconditioned etc. However, it is also the basis of the phenomenal properties of Buddhahood. These properties are actually contained in the other bodies of the Buddha, called the *saṃbhoga-kāya* and the *nirmāṇa-kāya*.

Additional support for Xuan Zang's interpretation is found in Triṃś. 30, which says "That (*asau*) is the liberation body, this (*ayam*) is the *dharma* body, so-called, of the great sage." Here "that" and "this" may very well refer to two different *aspects* of Buddhahood. Furthermore, it may be more than just the exigencies of metre which led Vasubandhu to refer to the *dharma-kāya* rather obliquely or elliptically as the "*dharma*(body)-so-called" (*dharmākhya*). His view may have been that the *vimukti-kāya* is what the Buddha *really* is, and that the *dharma-kāya* (or the *saṃbhoga-kāya* and the *nirmāṇa-kāya*) are merely what he appears to be to the saints who are able to see him.

It is also possible to find some textual support for Xuan Zang's interpretation in the terms "abandonment of the two-fold faults" (*dvidhā dauṣṭhulya-hānita*) and "revulsion of the basis" (*āśraya-parāvṛtti*) in Triṃś. 29. According to the Mahāyāna, the Arhats of the Lesser Vehicle realize only the voidness of the self or person (*pudgala-śūnyatā*), whereas the Bodhisattva who traverses the more arduous path leading to supreme enlightenment (*mahā-bodhi*) and Buddhahood realizes in addition the voidness of all the *dharmas* (*sarva-dharma-śūnyatā*). If the realization of the voidness of self is attained without the realization that all *dharmas* are void, then one enters the *nirupadhi-śeṣa-nirvāṇa*. On the other hand, if one sees that *both* self and *dharmas* are void, one attains supreme enlightenment and the *apratiṣṭhita-nirvāṇa* of the Buddha.

The fact that Triṃś. 29 speaks of the *two-fold* revolution of the basis is probably important. According to the Mahāyāna there is only one kind of revolution of the basis in the case of the Arhat, and this means that Triṃś. 29 and 30 are devoted exclusively to a description of Buddhahood. Furthermore, Triṃś. 5 refers to a "turning away" (*vy-āvṛtti*) from the store consciousness in the case of the Arhat, whereas Triṃś. 29 uses the term "*par(ā)-āvṛtti*," in the case of the Buddha. These two Sanskrit terms are closely related in meaning, but it may be significant that the latter is used to describe the attainment of enlightenment by the Buddha and that the former is used to describe the attainment of the Arhat, for the "*par(ā)*" of "*par(ā)-āvṛtti*," unlike the "*vy-āvṛtti*" of Triṃś. 5, may also mean "going beyond" or "transcending," rather than "turning away from" or "destroying."

This interpretation of the term "*par(ā)-āvṛtti*" can also be supported by some general considerations. If one is to take seriously the Mahāyānist distinction between the *nirvāṇa* of total extinction, on the one hand, and *mahā-bodhi*, *apratiṣṭhita-nirvāṇa*, Buddha-hood etc., on the other, then one must suppose that the two-fold *par(ā)-āvṛtti* of the Mahāyāna must lead, not to the destruction of or simple turning away from the mind, but to its transcendence, for the Buddha continues to be active for the welfare of others. On this view, all the *dharmas* get transformed and become the glorious qualities (*mahā-guṇa-dharmas*) of the transfigured Buddha.

Xuan Zang's interpretation is an attractive one on textual grounds, but it is not clear that it really does solve any of the problems which it was designed to address. These include the following:

(1) From the Buddhist point of view, the notion that one thing can be the support (*āśraya*) of another is suspect for doctrinal reasons. The later Buddhist scholastics frequently rejected the substance/attribute distinction as a "substantialist" or "eternalist" heresy. They were antipathetic to such doctrines since the view that there is something immutable underlying a thing's changing properties was a Vedāntist view. All such views would appear to be quite incompatible with both the letter and the spirit of the *pratītya-samutpāda-vāda*.

(2) In so far as the *svābhāvika-kāya* is said to be unconditioned (*asaṃskṛta*) it must be void (*śūnya*). But then the question arises: how can *śūnyatā* be the basis of the *mahā-guṇa-dharmas* of the Buddha?

(3) According to Xuan Zang's interpretation, the *svābhāvika-kāya* is unconditioned and therefore qualityless (*nirguṇa*). As such it is, among other things, devoid of mind (*acitta*). However, the *svābhāvika-kāya* is said to be the support of the supernatural wisdoms (*jñāna*) of the Buddha, which are powers or functions of

the Buddha mind. How can it be said that something which is both devoid of mind and unconditioned is the support of mind?

Let us consider each of these problems in more detail.

(1) The later Buddhist scholastics tended to use the *dharma* theory as a substitute for the metaphysical distinction between substances and properties. It is sometimes useful to think of the Buddhist *dharmas*, not as entities, but as qualities. (This is actually one of the possible meanings of the word "*dharma.*"). However, this is not *strictly* accurate, since properties are usually regarded as properties of substances, and the later Mahāyānist scholastics, at any rate, did not believe in substances. Perhaps the best way of conceptualizing the Buddhist *dharmas* is to say that they are what properties become when they are regarded as momentary and when they are not regarded as inhering in some underlying substance, either mental or physical.

It is not at all clear that Xuan Zang's interpretation of Triṃś. 29 and 30 is consistent with this kind of anti-metaphysical orientation. Xuan Zang attempts to explain the relationship between the *vimukti-kāya* and the *dharma-kāya* by saying that the former is the basis (*āśraya*) of the latter, but the notion of a *basis* is a questionable concept from the Buddhist point of view. Even the term "*svābhāvika-kāya*" would appear to be somewhat suspect, for the Mahāyānists tended to reject the notion of essences or self natures (as Nāgārjuna does, for example, in the *svabhāva-parīkṣā* of the Mūla-madhyamaka-kārikās). If it is permissible to say that the *svābhāvika-kāya* is the self nature or the basis of the *saṃbhoga-kāya* and the *nirmāṇa-kāya*, then why not say that there are qualities like heat, weight etc. which inhere in material substances, or that sensations, volitions, impressions etc. are the properties of selves? Is there a principled way of excluding such metaphysical views if one admits the notion that there is a *svābhāvika-kāya* which is the basis of the phenomenal properties of *Buddhahood*?

(2) Given the way the *svābhāvika-kāya* is defined in the texts that Xuan Zang cites, it would seem to be a particularly unlikely candidate for being the basis (*āśraya*) of anything. First of all, the *svābhāvika-kāya* is said to be identical with the *vimukti-kāya*, and this in turn seems to be just a synonym for the *nirupadhi-śeṣa-*

nirvāṇa of the Arhat, which is devoid of qualities (*nirguṇa*), devoid of mind (*acitta*), and the cessation of all the factors of existence (*saṃsāra-nirodha*). How, then, could it be the basis of the *mahā-guṇa-dharmas* of Buddhahood? Similarly, the *svābhāvika-kāya*, since it is absolutely immutable and uncompounded, must be identical with what the Buddhist texts call emptiness (*śūnyatā*). But as was argued previously in chapters 1-3, the Buddhist concept of *śūnyatā* appears to be a mere negation, and therefore *śūnyatā* could not be the basis for anything either.

Any effort to avoid this particular difficulty by interpreting the Vijñānavādins' use of the term "*śūnyatā*" as referring somehow or other to a positive entity would encounter a number of difficulties of its own. As was pointed out in the chapters of Part I, the texts themselves show that the Vijñānavādins used terms like "*śūnya*" and "*śūnyatā*" in the purely negative senses that they had in ordinary language. Moreover, the polemics of the Vijñānavādins and other Buddhists against their philosophical opponents show clearly that they could not have interpreted "*śūnya*" or "*śūnyatā*" in a positive way. We know, for example, that they would undoubtedly have rejected the suggestion that the liberation body of the Buddha is the basis (*āśraya*) of the *dharma* body in the sense in which, for example, mud is the material basis of the pots out of which it is made, or the sea is the basis of the waves that play on its surface.[14] The view that the world is the manifestation of an Absolute in this sense was a Vedāntic view, and it was regarded by all of the Buddhist schools as a heresy (*tīrthika-dṛṣṭi*). But the question then arises: if the unconditioned liberation body is not the basis of the conditioned *dharma* body in this sense, in what sense is it the basis of the latter? In other words, how *is* the *svābhāvika-kāya* of the Vijñānavāda different from the *brahman* or *ātman* of the Vedānta?[15]

(3) According to Triṃś. 29, the state of Buddhahood which results from the "two-fold revolution of the basis" is devoid of mind (*acitta*). Vasubandhu's description of Buddhahood as *acitta* is in this respect no different from the description of the knowledge devoid of imagination (*nirvikalpa-jñāna*), the temporary trance state of "deliberate cessation" (*pratisaṃkhyā-nirodha*), or the *nirupadhi-*

śeṣa-nirvāṇa of the Arhat. In fact, Xuan Zang is so adamant about identifying the world-transcending knowledge of Triṃś. 29 with the *nirvikalpa-jñāna*, and so insistent that this state is devoid of mind, that he insists that the *nirvikalpa-jñāna* of the Buddha cannot even be said to be omniscient, for omnscience — sublime as it is — is entirely mental. Even the omniscience of the Buddha, he says categorically, is impermanent and will eventually be destroyed, for "there is no form (*rūpa*) and no mind (*citta*) which is not impermanent".[16]

According to Xuan Zang's interpretation, then, the *dharma* body of the Buddha cannot be said to be *acitta* because the *dharma* body includes the four supernatural wisdoms (*abhijñās*) and the Buddha's omniscience. Therefore, Xuan Zang interprets Triṃś. 29 to mean that the Buddha in his active, phenomenal aspect is omniscient, possesses the four super-wisdoms etc., but that the *vimukti-kāya*, the basis of the other two bodies of the Buddha, is devoid of mind. Since the *svābhāvika-kāya* (= *vimukti-kāya*) is qualityless (*nirguṇa*) and essentially uncompounded (*asaṃskṛta*), one says that it is devoid of body and mind; however, it may be said to *possess* infinite qualities, real bodies and real minds because it is the support of these things.

Here, however, one encounters once again the problem of reconciling the idea that something can be the basis (*āśraya*) of something else with the fundamental principles of Mahāyānist philosophy. Furthermore, since the *nirvikalpa-jñāna* is said to be devoid of mind, it is not clear how it can be the basis of the supernatural wisdoms of the Buddha. One would be more inclined to suppose instead that the *nirvikalpa-jñāna* would involve the cessation (*nirodha*) of the mind — which is exactly how it is interpreted in the older texts.

Similar problems — as well as some additional ones — arise in the case of the Tri-svabhāva-nirdeśa's description of Buddhood, which is given in TSN 31-38. These verses describe the various stages of attainment for the aspirant who follows the path to supreme enlightenment (*anuttarā-bodhi*). Like the Triṃśikā, the TSN ascribes characteristics to the highest state of attainment which are difficult to reconcile with the traditional Buddhist *sūtras* and Abhidharma teachings.

TSN 31 says that as soon as one understands the doctrine of the three natures and the true nature of things (*artha-tattva*), there occurs knowledge, abandonment and attainment. The next verse specifies that in TSN 31 "knowledge" is non-perception,"abandonment" is non-appearance, and "attainment" is perception without any object as cause. TSN 33 says that duality (i.e. the purported external object) disappears when it is seen that everything is nothing but mind, and that the perfected nature (i.e. the non-existence of duality) is understood through the attainment of the perception that everything is mind only.

TSN 35 is not a complete sentence, but rather a list of four different things. All four items that are mentioned are in the ablative case and are to be regarded as instruments or stages for the attainment of even higher states. The four things mentioned are: the restraint of thought, the perception that discriminative intelligence is useless, the adherence to the three-fold knowledge, and the effortless attainment of liberation (*mokṣa*).

Note that the text says "*mokṣāpatteḥ*," i.e. "from or through the attainment of *mokṣa*." Here liberation, which in the oldest Buddhist teachings is regarded as an end in itself, is taken to be only a means to an even higher state. This higher state, as the concluding verse will tell us, is the supreme enlightenment (*anuttarā bodhi*) of the Buddhas. In the TSN, therefore, the *apratiṣṭhita-nirvāṇa*, or Buddhahood, is not regarded as the "incomplete" or "partial" *nirvāṇa* of the early texts, which involves the great renunciation of the full and complete *nirvāṇa* (*nirupadhi-śeṣa-nirvāṇa*). Nor is there anything in TSN 35 that implies that liberation (or the liberation body) is the basis (*āśraya*) of the glorious qualities of the Buddha in his active aspect, as it is in Xuan Zang's interpretation of Triṃś. 29 and 30. Nor is the *nirvāṇa* of the Arhats denied altogether, as it was in the "one vehicle" (*ekayāna*) teachings of the Tathāgata-garbha texts. TSN 35 seems to represent yet another view, according to which the *nirupadhi-śeṣa-nirvāṇa* is regarded as merely the partial or incomplete attainment of Buddhahood! Note that this is diametrically opposed to the way that Buddhahood is described in the earliest Mahāyāna texts, which emphasize the Buddha's renunciation and compassion when he declined to enter the *nirupadhi-śeṣa-nirvāṇa* in order to work for the salvation of all sentient beings (*apratiṣṭhita-nirvāṇa*).

TSN 36 says that the external object ceases to be perceived when the fact that everything is mind only (*citta-mātra*) is known, and that there is non-perception of mind (*cittānaupalambhatā*) when the perception of external objects ceases. This assertion, which is also found in Triṃś. 28 and 29 and in MV 1.6, is fundamental to the Vijñānavāda, and, so far as I know, distinguishes it from all other forms of idealism, Eastern or Western. Although the Vijñānavādins held that everything is nothing but mind, they were not interested in mind as such. As was pointed out in the Introduction, this is due to the fact that mind, according to fundamental Buddhist teachings, is essentially impermanent, conditioned, compounded and implicated in suffering. As such it is simply one of the links — perhaps the most important link — in the cycle of rebirth and suffering. What the Buddhist wants to attain, therefore, is something which is *not* mind.

Of course, the problem that this raises for an idealist philosophy like the Vijñānavāda is how this soteriological doctrine can be reconciled with the metaphysical and epistemological doctrine that everything is mind only, for unless Buddhahood is simply a state of extinction, the very doctrine that everything is mind only would be contradicted by the soteriological doctrine that Buddhahood is devoid of mind (*acitta*). This is the same problem that we encountered in the last chapter in the discussion of Triṃś. 29-30, but it is compounded in the TSN because TSN 37 and 38 speak of states that are subsequent to and even higher than the mindless (*acitta)* state.

TSN 37 says that *from* the non-perception of the external object and the non-perception of mind, there is the perception of the fundamental nature of things (*dharma-dhātu*), and that *through* the perception of the *dharma-dhātu* there is the perception of the all-pervading. Thus, TSN 37 takes the *dharma-dhātu* to be attained *by means of* the non-perception of mind, whereas Triṃś. 29 and 30 identify the state that is devoid of mind and objects with the *dharma-dhātu* itself (i.e. the *anāsrava dhātu*). Furthermore, TSN 37 refers (though the Triṃśikā does not) to a state of all-pervadingness which is higher than that of the *dharma-dhātu*. TSN 37 raises the following problem as well: how can there be perception of anything, or a knowledge (*jñāna*) of anything, without mind? Even if it could be shown that there is mind only and that the supposed external objects are unreal, what would follow, presumably, is that the perception of the true nature of things is the perception of the *non-dual* mind by the *nondual* mind. What we find in the TSN instead is that the highest perception is devoid of mind.

The 38th *kārikā* concludes the TSN's description of the various stages of attainment. It says that, having perceived the all-pervading and having attained the good of oneself and others, the sage attains the supreme enlightenment which consists of the three bodies of the Buddha. Note that the *kārikā* says that the Buddha attains a state that is all-pervading (*vibhutva*). The Triṃśikā *implies* that Buddhahood is all-pervading, because 1) the liberation body is included in the state of Buddhahood and 2) because the Mahāyāna texts describe the liberation body (*vimukti-kāya*) as all-pervading (*vibhu*). The all-pervadingness of the state of Buddhahood, which is merely entailed or implied by Triṃś. 30, is made explicit in TSN 38.

A state which is said to be all-pervading (or which at least involves the perception of something that is all-pervading) and which consists of the three bodies of Buddhahood must necessarily be a state of *existence*, and must therefore be a phenomenal and *saṃsāric* state according to traditional Buddhist teachings.[17] To deny this would be tantamount to contradicting the four-fold noble truths, which is perhaps the earliest and most fundamental teaching of the Buddhist *dharma*. According to these four-fold truths, escape from suffering ensues only when *saṃsāra* has been entirely destroyed (*nirodha-satya*).

It is true that the Mahāyānists did not accept this way of thinking of *saṃsāra* and *nirvāṇa*. For them, things were *already* void (*śūnya*). On this view, emptiness is not something to be attained, but rather something that already characterizes the essence of things even now. But if emptiness (*śūnyatā*) means what it does in ordinary language and in the traditional Buddhist teachings, this doctrine would entail that everything is just non-existent.

In conclusion, it appears that those scholars who have argued that the Vijñānavādins, as Mahāyānists, departed from the traditional Buddhist teachings by positing an Absolute are partly right and partly wrong. They are partly wrong, because in the Mahāyāna all things are said to be empty (*sarva-dharma-śūnyatā*), and emptiness cannot logically be construed as an Absolute. However, they are partly right, too, because the Vijñānavādins evidently thought of emptiness in just this way.

PART III:

THE EXISTENCE OF OTHER MINDS

AND

THE OMNISCIENCE OF THE BUDDHA

According to our ordinary way of thinking, sensory perception gives us knowledge of a world that is external to ourselves. According to the Vijñānavāda, this ordinary way of thinking is a serious error, and is the primary cause of our continued suffering in *saṃsāra*. According to the Vijñānavāda, what we *call* sensory impressions (*vijñapti*) cognize only *themselves*. All that people ever perceive are their own percepts.[1]

Such statements may sound somewhat solipsistic, but there are a number of doctrinal reasons why the Vijñānavādins would have wanted to avoid solipsism:

(1) The Buddhist *sūtras* clearly refer to a multitude of *saṃsāric* sentient beings. The Mahāyāna *sūtras* in particular exhort the Bodhisattva to dedicate himself to working for their release from *saṃsāra*. A doctrine of solipsism would contradict the very plain meaning of these scriptures.

(2) It is virtually inconceivable that any Buddhist would be a solipsist. The no-soul (*anātman*) doctrine is a fundamental doctrine of Buddhism. It is not at all obvious how this philosophy could be reconciled with the doctrine of solipsism, according to which I alone exist. From the Buddhist perspective, in fact, the doctrine of solipsism would appear to represent a particularly grotesque form of the belief in one's own self (*ātma-dṛṣṭi*).

(3) The Vijñānavādins believed in the existence of *yogins* who had developed the power to directly know other people's minds (*para-citta-jñāna*), and this belief does not make any sense if my mind is the only mind that there is. Furthermore, the Vijñānavādins believed in the omniscience (*sarvajñatva)* of the Buddha.[2] This doctrine effectively rules out the possibility of solipsism, even if one were to argue (as some Buddhists did) that the Buddha's omniscience only applies to the phenomenal level (*saṃvṛti-satya*) rather than the absolute level (*paramārtha-satya*). For while it might be argued that the Buddha's omniscience is true at the phenomenal level and that *monism* is true at the absolute level, it would make no

sense for *me* to say that the Buddha is omniscient at the relative level but that *solipsism* is true at the absolute level.

These considerations show very clearly that the Vijñānavādins could not have been solipsists. Did they, then, believe in a multiplicity of independent minds? There are, in fact, many passages in the Vijñānavāda writings which clearly refer to the existence of other minds. (There are, as we shall see, many verses in the Viṃśatikā of Vasubandhu which clearly refer to them.) However, the view that there are *other* minds was problematic in the Vijñānavāda. The Vijñānavādins felt that it was problematic to say, for example, that other minds are objects (*artha*) which are *inferred* on the basis of one's perception of another person's body, speech and actions, for this would implicitly assume the existence of an external object. If an inference to another mind stream outside one's own mind stream is legitimate, why isn't the inference to a physical object outside one's own mind stream an equally legitimate inference?

The third alternative to be considered is monism (*advaita, advaya*). If the Vijñānavādins were not solipsists, and if they had trouble accepting the existence of *other* minds, were they monists? There were, as I shall presently argue, very strong tendencies in this direction within the Vijñānavāda. However, monism was not a view that the Vijñānavādins could have endorsed explicitly, for the view that the world exists in one mind (*eka-citta*) was a Vedāntist and heretical view.

The result is that it is very hard to see how the Vijñānavādins could have endorsed any one of the three alternatives: solipsism, the denial of solipsism (i.e. the view that many minds exist), or monism. Within the context of idealism, these would appear to be mutually exhaustive and exclusive alternatives. Since the Vijñānavādins were apparently unable to unequivocally accept any one of them, it is very difficult to give a clear, coherent and consistent philosophical analysis of the views of the Vijñānavādins on these questions. The most that can be done is to show how and where the difficulties and dilemmas emerge, and to show how different writers of the school attempted to deal with them.

The most conservative of the well-known Vijñānavādins on these questions was perhaps Xuan Zang, for in his case there can be no doubt about the existence of other minds. In Cheng wei shilun (*k*. 17: 430-431) a doubt is raised on this point by the opponent, but it is dealt with peremptorily:

> [Opponent]: But how can the doctrine that everything is mind only (*vijñaptimātratā*) be reconciled with the existence of an object of thought — i.e. the thought of another person — distinct from one's own thought?
>
> [Xuan Zang]: How wise of you to be so sceptical! The doctrine of mind only does not teach the existence of a single *vijñāna*, i.e. of *my* mind. If only my mind existed, the variety of ordinary men and Āryas, of the good and the bad, of the causes and fruits of the ten cardinal directions, would disappear. What Buddha would teach me? To whom would he teach? What teaching (*dharma*) would he give in order to attain what fruit?
>
> ...
>
> The *dharmas*, such as they are, are not distinct from mind (*vijñāna*): one says, therefore, that all *dharmas* are mind (*vijñapti*), and one adds the suffix *-mātra* in order to deny the real existence of material form (*rūpa*) etc. distinct from mind, such as are admitted by the ignorant people.
>
> The man who understands the teaching of mind only in this fashion is able, without error, to penetrate the voidness of all the *dharmas* (*dharma-śūnyatā*), to realize the supreme enlightenment (*bodhi*), and to save beings who are embroiled in *saṃsāra*. But the total nihilist, who understands emptiness (*śūnyatā*), the scriptures and reason incorrectly, is incapable of attaining this.

In this passage, clearly, Xuan Zang rejects both monism and solipsism unequivocally.

Furthermore, Xuan Zang insists that the *nirvikalpa-jñāna* is devoid of the subject-object distinction; consequently, the person who possesses this kind of knowledge cannot be said to be omniscient. In CWSL ad Triṃś. 29 and 30 (pp. 681-701), for example,

Xuan Zang insists that the omniscience of the Buddha — sublime as it is — is simply a mental associate (*caitta*) of the mind of the Buddha. As such, he says, it belongs to the subject-object distinction, is conditioned (*saṃskṛta*), and is itself destined to be destroyed or to disappear in the final *nirvāṇa*, for "it is the categorical declaration of the Buddha that 'whatever is born is destined to destruction,' and there is no form (*rūpa*) and no mind (*citta*) that is not impermanent" (CWSL 30: 701). According to Xuan Zang, the omniscience of the Buddha belongs to the "subsequent wisdom" (*pṛṣṭha-labdha-jñāna*) which in some sense is the "product" or "outflow" of the *nirvikalpa-jñāna*.[3]

Xuan Zang's view can accommodate the doctrine that the Buddha is omniscient, that the Buddha's knowledge is nondual (*advaya, a-grāhya-grāhaka*), and that there are many minds, but only by drawing a sharp distinction between two kinds of "Buddha-knowledge" (*buddha-jñāna*). On his view, the "subsequent wisdom" (*pṛṣṭha-labdha-jñāna*) is omniscient, but it is not nondual; on the other hand, the *nirvikalpa-jñāna* is nondual, but it cannot be said to be omniscient (*sarvajña*).

One of the advantages of Xuan Zang's conservatism on this point is that he is able to avoid the monistic implications of accepting both the proposition that the Buddha is omniscient and the proposition that his knowledge is nondual. His doctrine, however, appears to imply that the Buddha alternates between two different kinds of knowledge. This is an unattractive consequence doctrinally and one that would be hard to justify textually by the *sūtras*. In any case, it would appear that Xuan Zang's conservatism on these points was not the prevailing view within the Vijñānavāda, for there is evidence in Dharmakīrti's Saṃtānāntara-siddhi, Śāntarakṣita's Tattva-saṃgraha and Ratnakīrti's Saṃtānāntara-dūṣaṇa that most of the Vijñānavādins held that the Buddha's knowledge was both omniscient *and* nondual. Indeed, the evidence in the Viṃśatikā (given below) indicates that this was Vasubandhu's view as well.

THE TWENTY VERSES (VIṂŚATIKĀ)

1. Everything is mind or representation only (*vijñapti-mātram-evaitat*), because there is the appearance of non-existent (*asat*) objects, just as a person suffering from an ophthalmological disorder sees things like hairs, the moon etc. which do not really exist.

   [vijñaptimātram-evaitad-asad-arthāvabhāsanāt /
   yathā taimirikasyāsat-keśa-candrādi-darśanam //

2. [Objection:] If representations were without an object (*an-artha*), then there would be no determination (*niyama*) of space and time, no indetermination (*aniyama*) of the various mind streams, and no efficacity (*kṛtya-kriyā*) corresponding to various actions.

   yadi vijñaptir-anarthā niyamo deśa-kālayoḥ /
   saṃtānasyāniyamaś-ca yuktā kṛtya-kriyā na ca //]

3. [Answer:] Space etc. are determined just as in dreams; furthermore, the indetermination of the mind streams is just as it is in the case of ghosts (*pretas*), who all see the rivers of pus etc. in hell.

   deśādi-niyamaḥ siddhaḥ svapnavat pretavat-punaḥ /
   saṃtānāniyamaḥ sarvaiḥ pūya-nadyādi-darśane //

4. The efficacity of actions is like the the nocturnal emission of semen by a dreamer. All these things (i.e. determination of space, determination of time, indetermination of the mind streams, and the efficacity of actions) is just as in hell, for in hell everyone sees the same hell guardians etc. and are tormented by them.

   svapnopaghātavat kṛtya-kriyā narakavat-punaḥ /
   sarvaṃ naraka-pālādi-darśane taiś-ca bādhane //

5. Just as animals are not born in either heaven or hell, so the ghosts (*pretas*) are not born in heaven or hell. For similar reasons, we say that the hell guardians do not even experience the sufferings of hell.

tiraścāṃ saṃbhavaḥ svarge yathā na narake tathā /
na pretānāṃ yatas-taj-jaṃ duḥkhaṃ nānubhavanti te //

6. If your view is that elements (*bhūtas*) are born from the force of *karma*, why don't you say that the hell guardians are just the transformations of consciousness (*vijñāna-pariṇāma*)?

yadi tat-karmabhis-tatra bhūtānāṃ saṃbhavas-tathā /
iṣyate pariṇāmaś-ca kiṃ vijñānasya neṣyate //

7. Instead of saying that the impression (*vāsanā*) of a deed (*karma*) is in one place and the fruit of the deed is in another place, why don't you just say that the cause (*kāraṇa*) and the impression of a deed are in the same place?

karmaṇo vāsanānyatra phalam-anyatra kalpyate /
tatraiva neṣyate yatra vāsanā kiṃ nu kāraṇam //

8. Just as the Buddha spoke with a secret intention about apparitional beings in the intermediate state (*upapāduka*), so he spoke also with a secret intention about the existence (*astitva*) of the bases of cognition (*āyatanas*) like form etc.

rūpādy-āyatanāstitvaṃ tad-vineya-janaṃ prati /
abhiprāya-vaśād-uktam-upapāduka-sattvavat //

9. Impressions, which are mere appearances, arise from their own seeds (*sva-bījāt*) as the two-fold bases of cognition. It was in this context that the Buddha spoke of the "bases of cognition."

yataḥ svabījād-vijñaptir-yad-ābhāsā pravartate /
dvividhāyatanatvena te tasyā munir-abravīt //

10. In virtue of the provisional teachings one enters into the selflessness (*nairātmya*) of the person (*pudgala*); by means of the mind only teachings one enters the selflessness of the *dharmas*.

tathā pudgala-nairātmya-praveśo hy-anyathā punaḥ /
deśanā dharma-nairātmya-praveśaḥ kalpitātmanā //

11. The perceptual object is neither a unity, nor a multiplicity, nor an aggregate (*saṃhatā*) of atoms, because the existence of the atom (*paramāṇu*) is not proved.

na tad-ekaṃ na cānekaṃ viṣayaḥ paramāṇuśaḥ /
na ca te saṃhatā yasmāt paramāṇur-na sidhyati //

12. An atom (*paramāṇu*) which is joined simultaneously on six sides with other atoms must consist of six parts (*aṃśa*). On the other hand, if an atom is in one place with six others, then the aggregate (*piṇḍa*) would be as one atom.

ṣaṭ-kena yugapad-yogāt paramāṇoḥ ṣaḍ-aṃśatā /
ṣaṇṇāṃ samāna-deśatvāt piṇḍaḥ syād-aṇumātrakaḥ //

13. Since there is no joining (*saṃyoga*) of atoms, what is the thing which is supposed to consist of the joined atoms? That joining (*saṃ-yoga*) of the supposed aggregate of atoms is not proved, and not just because of its partlessness (*anavayavatva*).

paramāṇor-asaṃyoge tat-saṃghāte 'sti kasya saḥ /
na cānavayavatvena tat-saṃyogo na sidhyati //

14. Wherever there is a distinction of spatial divisions, unity (*ekatva*) is not possible. How, on the other hand, can

shadows and occultation (*āvṛti*) of objects be possible for something that has no spatial divisions? If you say that the aggregate is not different from the atoms, then shadows and occultation cannot be caused by the aggregate.

dig-bhāga-bhedo yasyāsti tasyaikatvaṃ na yujyate /
chāyāvṛtī kathaṃ vānyo na piṇḍaś-cen-na tasya te //

15. If everything were a unity, then there could be no movement by stages, no grasping and non-grasping simultaneously, no multiple, differentiated conditions, and no subtle and imperceptible things.

ekatve na krameṇetir-yugapan-na grahāgrahau /
vicchinnāneka-vṛttiś-ca sūkṣmānīkṣā ca no bhavet //

16. The discrimination of perception (*pratyakṣa-buddhi*) is as in dreams. When it exists, the object of the perception does not exist. How, then, can perception (*pratyakṣatva*) be conceived?

pratyakṣa-buddhiḥ svapnādau yathā sā ca yadā tadā /
na so 'rtho dṛśyate tasya pratyakṣatvaṃ kathaṃ matam //

17. As has already been said, the appearance of an object (*tad-ābhāsā*) is a representation. Memory arises from it. As long as we have not awakened, we do not realize that the objects which are seen in dreams do not exist.

uktaṃ yathā tad-ābhāsā vijñaptiḥ smaraṇaṃ tataḥ /
svapne dṛg-viṣayābhāvaṃ nāprabuddho 'vagacchati //

18. The determination of the representations of consciousness is reciprocal by means of the "superordinate cause" (*adhipatitva*) of the mind of one sentient being acting on another. In sleep the mind is overcome with dullness; as a result, the consequences of actions done in the dreaming state are

different from the consequences of actions done in the waking state.

anyonyādhipatitvena vijñapti-niyamo mithaḥ /
middhenopahataṃ cittaṃ svapne tenāsamaṃ phalam //

19. Killing and injury are the modification (*vikriyā*) of the mental representations of another person, just as the minds of demons (*piśācas*) and others are able to cause the loss of memory etc. in other beings.

maraṇaṃ para-vijñapti-viśeṣād-vikriyā yathā /
smṛti-lopādikānyeṣām piśācādi-mano-vaśāt //

20. How else, indeed, did the wrath of the *ṛṣi* bring about the desolation (*śūnyatva*) of the Daṇḍaka forest? How else, indeed, could that legend prove the great blameworthiness of mental punishment?

kathaṃ vā daṇḍakāraṇya-śūnyatvam-ṛṣi-kopataḥ /
mano-daṇḍo mahāvadyaḥ kathaṃ vā tena sidhyati //

21. How is it that the knowledge of those who know other minds (*para-citta*) is not the knowledge of things as they really are (*anyathārtham*)? [Answer:] Because their knowledge is like the knowledge which unenlightened people have of their own minds (*sva-citta*). This kind of knowledge is in fact non-knowledge (*ajñāna*). This is what the Buddhas see, and it is the domain of their knowledge (*yathā buddhasya gocaraḥ*).

para-citta-vidāṃ jñānam-ayathārthaṃ kathaṃ yathā /
sva-citta-jñānam-ajñānād-yathā buddhasya gocaraḥ //

22. This "Vijñaptimātratā Siddhi" (Treatise on Mind Only) has been completed according to the best of my abilities. The

fact that things are mind only, however, is beyond thought (*acintya*), and pertains to the domain of the Buddhas.[4]

vijñaptimātratā-siddhiḥ svaśakti-sadṛśī mayā /
kṛteyaṃ sarvathā sā tu na cintyā buddha-gocaraḥ //

The problems discussed earlier in this chapter emerge clearly in Viṃś. 21, for this passage implies that the Buddha has a *nondual* awareness of the representations of consciousness in the mind streams of "other" individuals.

The autocommentary (VV) introduces Viṃś. 21 with a question by the opponent, who asks: "If representations (*vijñapti*) alone exist, does knowledge of another's mind really know another's mind or not?" Vasubandhu replies: "Suppose we assent either way? What difference does it make?" The opponent then presents the following dilemma. If the power which the *yogins* have of knowing another's mind does not really know other minds, then the power is misnamed and the scriptures do not really speak the truth; on the other hand, if they do know other minds directly, then the doctrine of mind only is contradicted. Vasubandhu's reply to this dilemma is as follows:

> How is the knowledge which the *yogins* have of other minds not true knowledge? It is like knowledge of one's own mind, because [even the latter is covered over] with ignorance (*ajñāna*), because, with regard to the Buddha's cognition (*buddhasya gocara*) it is ignorance (*ajñāna*).

Vasubandhu's autocommentary (VV 21) specifies that this verse means that even the knowledge of one's own mind is defiled by the distinction between subject and object (*grāhya-grāhaka-vikalpa*), and what this implies is that the Buddha's cognition is nondual (*agrāhya-grāhaka*). But if the Buddha is omniscient (the standard Mahāyāna view) and if the Buddha's cognitions are nondual, how could there be more than one mind?

Note that the dilemma arises in the case of other minds just as much as it does in the case of external objects. In VV 10, for example, Vasubandhu says categorically that in mind only one mind cannot take even another mind as an object. Viṃś. 10 says: "By means of the mind only teachings one enters the teaching of the selflessness of the *dharmas* (*dharma-nairātmya*)." The auto-commentary explains this verse in the following way:

> How does the mind only teaching lead one to the selflessness of the *dharmas*? Because according to this teaching everything is mind only and arises as the mere appearance of the *dharmas* of material form etc., though there is no *dharma* which actually has the characteristic of material form etc. If there were no *dharmas* at all (*yadi tarhi sarvathā dharmo nāsti*), then mind only would not exist either (*tad-api vijñaptimātraṃ nāsti*); how then could the mind only teaching be established? The entry into the selflessness of the *dharmas* is certainly not a matter of the absolute non-existence of the *dharmas* (*na khalu sarvathā dharmo nāstīti*).
>
> The 'selflessness' of the *dharmas* refers to the self nature (*svabhāva*) of the *dharmas* which belongs to the subject-object distinction (*grāhya-grāhakādi*) and which is falsely imagined by ignorant people; it does not refer to the ineffable nature which is the object of the Buddha's cognition (*na tv-anabhilāpyenātmanā yo buddhānāṃ viṣaya iti*). Thus, for example, the view of 'mind only' which is falsely imagined by another representation of consciousness is also 'selfless' (*nairātmya*). By means of the teaching that everything is mind only one enters the selflessness of all the *dharmas*, not by denying their existence completely (*na tu tad-astitvāpavādāt*). Otherwise one representation of consciousness would be an object of another representation of consciousness (*itarathā hi vijñapter-api vijñapty-antaram-arthaḥ syād-iti*), and if a representation of consciousness were itself an object, 'mind only' could not be established (*vijñaptimātratvaṃ na sidhyetārtha-vatītvād-vijñaptīnām*).

Vasubandhu makes at least three points in this passage that are worth noting:

(i) He argues (against the Mādhyamikas) that *dharmas* are not entirely non-existent.

(ii) He contends that the *dharmas* have an ineffable nature (*anabhilāpyātman*) which is the object of the Buddha's cognition (*buddhānāṃ viṣaya*). This ineffable self nature is devoid of the subject-object distinction.

(iii) He says that one representation of consciousness (*vijñapti*) cannot be an object (*artha*) of another representation of consciousness.

These three assertions would appear to imply that the Buddha's knowledge of other minds is *nondual*, for (i) says that *dharmas* are real (at least as mental appearances), (ii) says that the essence of these *dharmas*, which is nondual, is grasped by the Buddha's cognition, and (iii) implies that the Buddha's cognition does not take another *vijñapti* as an object (*artha*).

If one combines Viṃś.-VV 10 with Viṃś.-VV 21, one gets a view about the existence of other minds and the nondual knowledge of the Buddha which may be summarized as follows:

> The "ordinary" *yogin* has a knowledge of *other* minds, i.e. he has developed a power whereby he has representations (*vijñapti*) of the representations occurring in another person's mind stream. But this is not mind only, for in mind only one representation (*vijñapti*) cannot be the object (*artha*) of another representation.
>
> In pure mind only, everything is completely nondual (*a-grāhya-grāhaka*). This is the domain of the Buddha's knowledge. The ineffable knowledge of the Buddha differs from that of the "ordinary" *yogin* not only because the Buddha is actually omniscient, but also because the Buddha's cognition does not involve his representations "grasping" those of another mind stream. In the case of the Buddha's knowledge, the distinction between that which apprehends and that which is apprehended breaks down. The Buddha's knowledge is nondual.

This difference between the Buddha's cognition and the "ordinary" *yogin's* knowledge of other minds might be put this way. What happens when an ordinary *yogin* (call him A) knows telepathically, for example, that another individual (call him B) is in pain, is that A has an impression I_A which has the same form or aspect (*ākāra*) as B's pain (I_B). However, this only means that A has an impression which is *similar* to B's pain; it is not a matter of A's actually perceiving B's pain. In the case of the Buddha, however, this distinction must break down, for the Buddha's cognition has transcended the subject-object distinction completely. The *yogin*, in other words, has knowledge of other minds in the sense that he is able to know, without the intermediation of the body or the senses, when someone else, for example, is in pain. The Buddha, however, has a different kind of knowledge, for in the Buddha's case the thing that is known is not really outside the Buddha's mind stream at all.

The Saṃtānāntara-siddhi (SS), as its title indicates, is a proof of the existence of other minds. The work was originally in Sanskrit, but there is no extant Sanskrit text. There is, however, a Tibetan translation of the work in the Bstan-'gyur, along with commentaries (also in Tibetan) by the Indian commentator Vinītadeva and the Mongolian monk Ṅag-dbaṅ bstan-dar. The commentary by Vinītadeva ascribes the work to Dharmakīrti [Stcherbatsky (1922: 345)].

The Saṃtānāntara-siddhi has been translated into English by Hidenori Kitagawa (1955) and by Harish C. Gupta (1969) from Th. Stcherbatsky's translation (1922) of this text into Russian. The discussion of the text in this chapter, and the comprehensive synopsis of the text which is given in Appendix II, is based on a comparison of these two English translations.

The SS is a Vijñānavāda work which attempts to show that the idealist can infer the existence of other minds just as well as the realist can. This raises the following question: if matter does not exist, and if other minds are real, how do the perceptions of a multiplicity of minds get coordinated? In the SS the answer is unmistakable. They are coordinated, Dharmakīrti says, through the power of telepathy (*adhipati-pratyaya*). According to Dharmakīrti, it is this notion of a telepathic force directly connecting the different mind streams which absolves the Vijñānavādin of the charge of solipsism.

Dharmakīrti begins his treatise by attempting to defend the idealist (i.e. the Vijñānavādin) against two objections.

(1) First Objection. The opponent argues that the Vijñānavādin is in no position to infer the existence of other minds, because there is no place in his system for the existence of the bodies, action and speech of others. According to the opponent, the only evidence we have for the existence of other minds is our perception of the intelligent speech and behavior of the *bodies* of sentient beings. If, as the Vijñānavādin holds, we cannot be said to perceive the real bodies of other sentient beings, then we have no basis for thinking that there

are other minds than our own. The ultimate consequence of the Vijñānavāda doctrine, therefore, is solipsism.

Dharmakīrti's reply to this objection is that the Vijñānavādin is in just as good a position to infer the existence of other minds as is the realist. Dharmakīrti contends that the realist infers the existence of other minds on the basis of his own impressions, just as the idealist does. The only difference between the realist and the idealist, according to Dharmakīrti, is that the realist makes three inferences whereas the idealist makes only one.

(i) The first inference that the realist makes is to infer from his private mental impressions of the bodies, speech and actions of others that these impressions were caused directly by real, physical bodily actions and speech existing outside his own mind. Dharmakīrti does not recognize the validity of this inference.

(ii) The second inference the realist makes is to infer that these real and external bodily actions and speech were caused by the *mind* of some other person. Since Dharmakīrti does not recognize the validity of the first inference, he rejects this part of the inference as well.

(iii) The realist's second inference is in turn based on a third one, which is as follows:

First, we observe in our own case that our intelligent speech and actions are invariably preceded by a movement of our own minds (*anvaya-vyatireka* form of proof). Next, we observe intelligent bodily speech and actions which are *not* preceded by a movement of our own minds. We then infer from our own case that even these instances of intelligent speech and action must have been preceded by *some* mind or other. However, we know from our own experience that they were not preceded by any movement of our own minds. Hence we conclude that these instances of intelligent behavior and speech must have been caused by some other mind.

Dharmakīrti acknowledges the third part of the inference to other minds, but rejects the first two. According to Dharmakīrti, we do not use our immediate and direct impressions (*vijñapti*, *jñāna*) of the intelligent speech and behavior of some other person to infer the existence of external or material physical bodies and actions existing outside our own minds. Instead, we infer that these impressions are caused *directly* by these other minds, without the intermediation of matter. In other words, all that people ever directly perceive is the representations in their own minds. Some of these representations show signs of intelligence. Some of these latter representations are preceded by a movement of our own minds; these are own "bodily" speech and actions. Others are not preceded by the activity of our own minds. These, we conclude, are caused by the actions of *other* minds.

On the realist's view, the direct cause (*nimitta-kāraṇa*) of our impressions of the intelligent speech and actions of others is the physical actions of others, which in turn are directly caused by the actions of the other person's mind. On Dharmakīrti's view, the direct cause of our impressions of the intelligent speech and actions of others is the *minds* of those other persons. The inference to other minds, therefore, is based ultimately on impressions; this is as true for the realist as it is for the idealist. The idealists' inference to the existence of other minds is therefore just as good — in fact better — than the realist's inference to the existence of other minds.

(2) Second Objection. According to this objection, the inference to *other* minds is inconsistent with the fundamental principles of the Vijñānavāda. For if the inference to other minds is valid, then it must inform us of the existence of something which exists outside the mind of the one who makes the inference. The opponent takes this to be a violation of the mind only principle, for in this case the mind of the person making the inference would be taking the mind of another person as its object (*artha*). If this inference is legitimate, then the inference to external objects should also be legitimate. Conversely, if the inference does *not* inform us of the mind of another person as a real entity (*svabhāva*), then it is not a valid inference.

Dharmakīrti's answer to this dilemma is that the inference to other minds is valid, but that it does *not* inform us of the existence of the mind of another person as a real entity (*svabhāva*). According to Dharmakīrti, the inference to the mind of another person does not 'give' us that other mind as a particular (*svalakṣaṇa*); what it 'gives' us is a universal (*sāmānya*). This kind of knowledge cannot be said to be real knowledge, at least from the point of view of absolute truth (*paramārtha-satya*), though it is valid in the sense that it does not betray us for the ordinary purposes of our everyday lives (*vyavahārya-satya*). Note that this distinction between phenomenal and absolute truth makes Dharmakīrti's inferential "proof" of the existence of other minds rather ambiguous. It can be read either as a proof that other minds exist from the phenomenal level, or as a denial that inference provides a valid proof of the existence of other minds at the absolute level.

After discussing the use of inference to establish the existence of other minds, Dharmakīrti takes up the question whether *yogic* perception (*yogi-pratyakṣa*) provides a means of establishing the existence of other minds. Here Dharmakīrti cannot appeal to the distinction between the real particular (*svalakṣaṇa*) and the unreal generality or universal (*sāmānya*), as he does in discussing the *inference* to other minds, for Dharmakīrti and the other Vijñānavādins of his school held that valid perception is perception of a real *particular* (*sva-lakṣaṇa*).

In considering Dharmakīrti's views on the question whether perception can give us knowledge of other minds, it is important to distinguish between three different kinds of percipients: (1) the ordinary person, (2) the *yogin*, who has developed the power of supersensory perception (*atīndriyārtha-jñāna, para-citta-jñāna*), and (3) the Buddha.

(1) So far as the ordinary person is concerned, both Dharmakīrti and his opponent are in agreement that (i) the ordinary person does not perceive other minds, and (ii) that the ordinary person's belief in the existence of other minds therefore rests on inference.

(2) According to Dharmakīrti, even the *yogin* who has supersensory perception does not have the same kind of knowledge of other minds that the Buddha has. The most that can be said about "*yogic* perception" (*yogi-pratyakṣa*) is that the *yogin* has impressions which are similar to those of the other person. It is only on the basis of the similarity between the impressions of the *yogin* and the impressions of the other person that we say that the *yogin perceives* the mind of the other person. This way of speaking is acceptable in

ordinary linguistic usage, though from a philosophical point of view it is not accurate.

(3) Dharmakīrti is as reticent about the knowledge of the Buddha (*buddha-jñāna*) as Vasubandhu is in the Viṃśatikā. He simply closes the treatise with the following remark: "The Buddha cognizes everything, but his cognition cannot be grasped by analytical thinking."

Nearly all of the points made by Dharmakīrti in his short treatise on the existence of other minds raise questions:

(a) Is the assertion that inference is valid compatible with the assertion that the object of inference is unreal?

(b) What is the philosophical implication of the claim that *yogins* have direct perception of other minds?

(c) Are other minds external to the *Buddha's* cognition?

I shall discuss these questions individually, taking them up in the order in which they are presented in the text.

(a) Dharmakīrti addresses the first question in SS 66-87. The prima facie meaning of these verses is that the (purely phenomenal) validity of the inference to other minds does not entail that there are external objects, because the *object* of inference (*anumeya*) is a universal or general concept (*jāti, sāmānya*) rather than a real particular. Since the object of inference is therefore not a real entity (*niḥsvabhāva, niḥsvalakṣaṇa*), inference does not give us knowledge of minds as external objects. Inference only gives us knowledge that does not betray us for the practical, everyday purposes of our ordinary lives (*vyavahārya-satya, saṃvṛti-satya*).

According to the prima facie reading of the SS, one may use one's perception (*vijñapti*) of intelligent speech and actions that are not one's own to infer the existence of other minds. On this basis one may make predictions about what one will experience if one speaks and behaves towards "other" minds in certain ways. All of our ordinary intercourse with "other" sentient beings is accounted for in this way. For the ordinary purposes of our lives there is nothing wrong with this way of thinking. However, this way of thinking is not valid at the level of absolute truth. At this level, Dharmakīrti seems to be saying, the inference to other minds is invalid.

This reading of the SS, which is based on the view that the object of any inference is unreal, invokes what might be called the "two objects" view of cognition. This view draws a rigid distinction between the object (*prameya*) of perception, on the one hand, and the object of inference on the other. The object of perception is a real particular (*sva-lakṣaṇa*); the object of inference is an unreal universal (*sāmānya*).

In a work which has become the standard for the theory of perception of Dharmakīrti's predecessor, Diṅnāga, Masaaki Hattori described the "two objects" view of cognition as follows (1968: 79-80, n. 1.14):

> [Dignāga] makes an essential distinction between *sva-lakṣaṇa* and *sāmānya-lakṣaṇa*, the former being the particular individuality which can never be generalized or conceptualized and the latter being the universal which is conceptually constructed by the mind through generalizing from many individuals without regard for their particularity. As each is incompatible with the other, there cannot be anything which possesses both *sva-lakṣaṇa* and *sāmānya-lakṣaṇa* at the same time. Corresponding to this essential distinction between two kinds of *prameya*, there is a radical distinction between the two means of cognition (*pramāṇa-vyavasthā*): *pratyakṣa* which grasps *sva-lakṣaṇa* exclusively and *anumāna* which grasps *sāmānya-lakṣaṇa* exclusively. This theory is evidently set up in opposition to the Nyāya view of the coalescence of different means of cognition (*pramāṇa-samplava*)...

Stcherbatsky held a similar view about Diṅnāga. In his *Buddhist Logic* Stcherbatsky said (1962: 301):

> We have thus in [Dignāga's] system pure sensation and pure conception and the corresponding distinctions of pure object, which is identified with reality itself, or the thing in itself, and pure Universals... Dignāga [upheld] a sharp distinction between two sources [of knowledge] corresponding to two kinds of objectivity. The objects are either Particulars or Universals and the sources of knowledge are, accordingly, either Sensation or Conception.

The "two objects" interpretation of the epistemology of Diṅnāga and Dharmakīrti yields the conclusion that inference does not give us knowledge of real things when it is conjoined with the Diṅnāgian *apoha* theory of universals. According to this theory, properties or universals (*sāmānya, jāti*) of things do not exist. Saying that *x* is a cow, for example, does not establish any kind of relation between *x* and a universal or property "cowness." This theory of universals — at least on the prevailing interpretation — holds that there is no such thing as the property "cowness" etc., for when we assert that *x* is a cow we are only saying that *x* is not a rose, a book, a chair, a tree, a number etc. Any entity *x* is in fact only a discrete, unique particular. Ascribing properties to *x*, or placing *x* into any general category, is a function of the constructive faculty (*vikalpa*) of the mind. In short, on this interpretation Diṅnāga and Dharmakīrti advocated a version of nominalism, according to which there are no universal properties of things. Such things are not real entities (*svabhāvas*) in their own right; they are merely mental constructions (*kalpanā*). If this view is conjoined with the view that the proper object of inference is a universal, one immediately gets the result that the object of inference is unreal.[1]

Step by step, the argument that leads to the conclusion that the object of even a valid inference is an unreal universal goes as follows:

(1) The object which is perceived is not the same thing as the object which is inferred.

(2) The object which is perceived is the real, unique particular (*svalakṣaṇa*).

(3) The object which is inferred is not a particular (*svalakṣaṇa*); it is a universal (*sāmānya*).

(4) The universal as such does not exist; it is merely a mental construction.

(5) Hence the object which is inferred (*anumeya*) in the inference to other minds is not a real entity. It is only a mental construction. The inference to other minds is valid at the level of phenomenal or relative truth, for it never leads us into error at the level of practical action (*saṃvṛti-satya*). However, it is not valid at the level of absolute truth.

This is what the Saṃtānāntara-siddhi *seems* to be saying on a first reading. It is also the interpretation of the text that is endorsed by Stcherbatsky and Kitagawa. In fact, it is in all likelihood the correct interpretation of the text. Nevertheless, it seems to me that this prima facie interpretation of the SS raises some very serious philosophical and textual problems.

(a) That there is *some* kind of philosophical distinction to be drawn between perception and inference cannot be doubted — nor were the Buddhist epistemologists (*bauddha-pramāṇa-vādins*) the only philosophers to draw such a distinction. In fact, the remarks by Dharmakīrti and Diṅnāga on the difference between perception and inference appear to have much in common with Bertrand Russell's (1959: 146-59) distinction between knowledge by acquaintance and knowledge by description. Russell thought it was important to distinguish between, say, one's perception of a table and the knowledge one can have of the table through propositions that truly describe it; the former mode of cognition, unlike the latter, is sensory, immediate and direct. Although Russell stressed this distinction just as forcefully as Diṅnāga and Dharmakīrti did, and in a very similar way, Russell did *not* believe that in every case there is more than one object of cognition; nor is there any reason to think that this particular distinction entails this conclusion.[2]

This kind of distinction appears to be a very commonsensical one. If there is a fire on a mountain, and if I am *told* that there is a fire on that mountain, or if I *infer* that there is a fire on the mountain from the fact that there is smoke on the mountain, I certainly have knowledge of *that* particular fire. But this kind of knowledge is rather indefinite in nature; one might say that it does not provide me with a direct *acquaintance* with the fire in question. Thus, inferring or being told that there is a fire on the mountain would not enable me to draw a very good picture of the fire, for I do not know the size of the fire, what it is burning etc. However, the assertion that there is some fire at a place is true (if it is true) if and only if there is a *particular* fire with all kinds of very specific attributes there, even though I may not know what they are. This would appear to be the point that Dharmakīrti makes in PV 2.53 (*pratyakṣa-pariccheda*), where he says that the *sva-lakṣaṇa* is the only thing that is known (*meyaṃ tv-ekaṃ svalakṣaṇam*), and also in the following verse (PV 2.54), where he says that the thing that is known is two-fold in the sense that the *sva-lakṣaṇa* is the object's self-nature, whereas the *sāmānya-lakṣaṇa* is its other nature (*tasya sva-para-rūpābhyāṃ gater-meya-dvayaṃ matam*). At least one rationale for these assertions is that if I actually see the fire in question, I know everything that I know through inference *and more*. Even more importantly, whatever I know through inference is true, if it is true, only in virtue of the concrete, specific fire that can be perceived through perception. Thus, even though inference and perception have the same object, there is an important difference of what might be called "scope" or definiteness between them.

The "two objects" view of cognition appears to hold that since inference is more indefinite than perception, perception must have a real object and inference must have only an intentional object (i.e. a universal, which is only a thought-construction). This is, surely, a non sequitur. Valid knowledge obtained through inference or testimony is more indefinite than perceptual knowledge, perhaps, but it surely does not follow from this that it is knowledge of a different object from the one that is cognized through perception.

This can be shown more easily, perhaps, in cases where the person making an inferential judgement (e.g. "X is P") actually perceives (or has perceived) X, the subject of the inference. Consider the following trivial but perfectly relevant counter-example to the "two objects" theory of inference. Suppose that A sees X (whom we may suppose that A knows) walk behind a building holding a hammer. If A then hears the sound of hammering when X is out of view, A may very well infer that that it is X who is doing the hammering. Here it is perfectly clear that A is not inferring the existence of some universal or general concept. What A is inferring, obviously, is that it is the very person that A had previously seen who is doing the hammering.

Although the untenability of the "two objects" view of cognition may be intuitively somewhat clearer when A has had direct acquaintance with X, the "two objects" view is also untenable in all the other cases. When one makes an inference about something with which one has had no prior direct acquaintance, one is simply asserting that there *is* an x with a certain property, say P. In these cases, one certainly doesn't suppose that one is inferring a universal (i.e. the property P); what one is inferring, simply, is that there is a particular entity x which *is* P, i.e. that there is an x such that x is P. Furthermore, the connection between inference and perception is much more more direct than the "two objects" view suggests, for if A infers that there is a fire on a distant hill on the grounds that there is smoke on the hill, A's inference implies the counterfactual assertion that A would (in normal circumstances etc.) see the fire if A *were* on the hill.[3]

(b) The foregoing considerations have provided some obvious *philosophical* objections to the "two objects" theory of cognition which has been attributed to Diṅnāga and Dharmakīrti. Of course, such philosophical considerations (even if they were taken as probative) would not prove that Diṅnāga and Dharmakīrti did not hold these views. Nevertheless, they are weighty considerations, for the principle of charity should be used (ceteris paribus) to rule out any interpretation of a philosopher which is prima facie implausible. Furthermore, philosophical considerations are not the only kind of considerations to make one hesitate to ascribe the "two objects" view of cognition to Diṅnāga and Dharmakīrti.

The textual evidence *in favor* of the two objects interpretation of these two philosophers has been given in detail by Stcherbatsky (1962) and Hattori (1968). There appears to be a significant body of evidence to support this interpretation, both from the writings of Diṅnāga and Dharmakīrti themselves and from the commentarial literature on them. Nevertheless, I believe that the textual evidence is not unequivocal.

In many passages, it seems to me, it is unclear whether Diṅnāga and Dharmakīrti are claiming that perception and inference have two entirely different objects (*prameya*), or whether they are simply claiming that they have two different "scopes" (i.e. two different *intentional* objects). Although the argument in the SS requires the former interpretation if it is to be valid, there are textual reasons for favoring the weaker interpretation. On this weaker interpretation, Dharmakīrti's argument in the SS fails to show what he apparently wants it to show.

Perhaps the clearest instance of the "two objects" interpretation — at least as applied to Diṅnāga — is note 1.14, p. 79 of Hattori's work *Dignāga, On Perception*, part of which I have cited above. In this note what Hattori is giving, essentially, is his interpretation of the opening argument in the first chapter of Diṅnāga's Pramāṇa-samuccaya (PS) and Pramāṇa-samuccaya-vṛtti (PSV).

The (PS) and the PS(V) are extant only in two Tibetan translations. However, Hattori (ibid: 76-80; 239) has been able to reconstruct the original Sanskrit of this passage from fragments found in extant Sanskrit texts. His reconstruction goes as follows:

> *pratyakṣam anumānaṃ ca pramāṇe / ... / yasmād lakṣaṇa-dvayaṃ prameyaṃ / na hi sva-sāmānya-lakṣaṇābhyām-anyat-prameyam asti / sva-lakṣaṇa-viṣayaṃ hi pratyakṣaṃ sāmānya-lakṣaṇa-viṣayam-anumānam-iti pratipādayiṣyāmaḥ*

His translation of this passage goes as follows (p. 24):

k. 2a-b_1. The means of cognition are [immediate and mediate, namely,] perception (*pratyakṣa*) and inference (*anumāna*).

They are only two, because

k. $2b_2$-c_1. the object to be cognized has [only] two aspects.

Apart from the particular (*sva-lakṣaṇa*) and the universal (*sāmānya-lakṣaṇa*) there is no other object to be cognized, and we shall prove that perception has only the particular for its object and inference only the universal.

Hattori's translation attributes to Diṅnāga the view that there are actually two different objects of cognition, i.e. the particular (the object of perception) and the universal (the object of inference). Hattori's note to this passage, part of which I have already cited, underscores this point, for as we have seen (n. 1.14, p. 79), it specifies that the passage is to be understood to mean that there are two different *objects* (*prameya*) of cognition. That is, on Hattori's interpretation there is a radical distinction not only between the two *means* of cognition but also between the two kinds of *prameya*. This reading, in effect, equates the term "*prameya*," which is used in PS 1.2b_2-c_1, with the term "*viṣaya*," which is used in the PSV's commentary on that verse.

Another possibility, however, is that the term "*viṣaya*" in the passage of the Vṛtti refers, not to the object as such, but to the object as it is directly *known*; i.e. it may refer to a purely intentional object rather than the object per se. This is how the term "*viṣaya*" is used in many of the Buddhist texts, particularly in the Abhidharma. The Ābhidharmikas held, for example, that each of the five sensory modalities has its own specific kind of sensory object; i.e. the eye apprehends color, the ear apprehends sound etc. Each of these five kinds of sensory objects were called "*viṣayas*" or "*āyatanas*" (sense fields). Note that according to this use it should be possible to hold that there is one object that is grasped in different ways — i.e. that there is one *prameya* even when there is more that one *viṣaya*. (For example, when one hears and sees a bell it does not follow from the fact that one hears a sound-datum and sees a visual-datum that the two sense-data belong to different objects.) Indeed, Hattori seems to acknowledge this very possibility in his translation of *kārikā* k.2b_2-c_1, for there his translation speaks of the *prameya* as having two aspects (*lakṣaṇas*).[4]

It must be conceded, however, that there are grounds for a *non*-intentional reading of the term "*viṣaya*" in this passage of the Vṛtti, for Diṅnāga uses the term in this passage in connection with the term "*prameya*." This certainly suggests the possibility that Diṅnāga intended the two terms to be understood — at least in this passage — as coterminous and perhaps even as synonymous. In that case the term "*viṣaya*" in this passage would have to be understood as a non-intentional object.[5]

However, even if one were to read the term "*viṣaya*" in PSV 1.2b_2-c_1 in this way, it would still be possible to interpret the compounds "*sva-lakṣaṇa-viṣayam*" and "*sāmānya-lakṣaṇa-viṣayam*" as referring to a *single* object. According to this interpretation, the passage in question is to be read as follows:

> The means of cognition are perception and inference. [They are only two,] because the object to be known consists of a dyad of characteristics. Apart from the self-characteristic and the univer-

sal characteristic, there is no other object to be cognized. We shall prove later on that perception is of the self-characterized object and that inference is of the [same] universally characterized object.

Hattori's interpretation and the one I have just given differ over the grammatical analysis of the compounds "*sva-lakṣaṇa-viṣayam*" and "*sāmānya-lakṣaṇa-viṣayam.*" These compounds clearly mean that perception is a *sva-lakṣaṇa*-object-possessor and that inference is a *sāmānya-lakṣaṇa*-object-possessor — i.e. both compounds are clearly possessive (*bahuvrīhi*) compounds. But — assuming that Diṅnāga meant the term "*viṣaya*" to refer to a non-intentional object — what kind of *bahuvrīhi* compounds are they?

Here there are two possibilities. On the one hand, the compounds can be analyzed to mean that perception possesses an object which *is* a particular characteristic and that inference possesses an object which *is* a universal characteristic. On this analysis "*sva-lakṣaṇa-viṣayam*" and "*sāmānya-lakṣaṇa-viṣayam*" are appositional (*karmadhāraya*) compounds in which "*sva-lakṣaṇa*" and "*sāmānya-lakṣaṇa*" occur as nominals. On the other hand, the compounds can be analyzed to mean that perception possesses an object which is self-characterized (i.e. the object itself) and that inference possesses an object which is characterized by a universal. On this analysis, "*sva-lakṣaṇa-viṣayam*" and "*sāmānya-lakṣaṇa-viṣayam*" are *karmadhāraya* compounds in which "*sva-lakṣaṇa*" and "*sāmānya-lakṣaṇa*" are used adjectivally.[6, 7]

Since Diṅnāga says that there is no object to be known other than the two characteristics, the particular and the general (*na hi sva-sāmānya-lakṣaṇābhyām-anyat prameyam-asti*), there is some prima facie support for Hattori's interpretation of the passage. However, it seems to me that little or no philosophical weight can be put on this, because the immediately preceding statement tells us that the object to be known (*prameya*) has two *aspects*. What the statement "*na hi sva-sāmānya-lakṣaṇābhyām-anyat-prameyam asti*" probably means, therefore, is that there is no object to be known other than the object that *possesses* the particular and the general characteristics.

This interpretation is confirmed, not only by the fact that Diṅnāga speaks of one *prameya* consisting of two aspects rather than of two different *prameyas* (*dve prameye*), but also by the succeeding passage. This passage answers an objection to the claim that there are two entirely different modes and objects of cognition. The objection is that the view that these are entirely different would require us to invoke yet a third mode of cognition, which would be absurd. Take the sentence "Sound is non-eternal." The objection is that another means of cognition (*pramāṇa*) would be needed to combine (*saṃdhatte*) the cognition of sound and the cognition of non-eternality into a single cognition. Significantly, Diṅnāga's reply to the objection is that no third *pramāṇa* is needed, for the mind is able to draw the necessary conclusion. (This is done, presumably, through inference.) Diṅnāga's reply seems to takes it for granted that the true object of cognition (*prameya*) is a unitary entity (consisting, however, of different aspects), for his reply is expressly designed to explain how there can be a cognition of a single object which is both sonant and impermanent without invoking a third *pramāṇa*.

Additional counterevidence against the "two objects" interpretation of Diṅnāga can be found in the second chapter (*svārthānumāna-pariccheda*) of the PS(V). At the end of PSV 1.2b_2-c_1, Diṅnāga says: "We shall prove [later on in the present work] that perception is of the 'own-marked object' and inference of the 'universally-marked' object." This is presumably a reference to the second chapter of the PS(V) — especially PS(V) 2.8-11 — where Diṅnāga states his views about the nature of the inferred object (*anumeya*). This passage provides further evidence against the two objects interpretation of Diṅnāga's epistemology.

Most of the Sanskrit text of the PS(V) has been lost, but the text of this particular passage has been preserved in Vācaspatimiśra's Nyāya-vārttika-tātparya-ṭīkā. The Sanskrit of these verses and my translation of them are given below:

> [First *pūrvapakṣa*]: Some say that it is another property [e.g. fire] that is inferred because of its invariable connection (*avyabhicārataḥ*) with the reason [e.g. smoke]. [Second *pūrvapakṣa*]: Others affirm that since the property [e.g. fire] and the

property bearer [e.g. the mountain] are already established, it is the relation (*sambandha*) between the two that is inferred. //8//

kecid dharmāntaraṃ meyaṃ liṅgasyāvyabhicārataḥ /
saṃbandhaṃ kecid-icchanti siddhatvād dharma-dharmiṇoḥ //8//

[As for the first view], if the inferential mark (*liṅga*) is already established as being related to the property (*dharma*), what else is there to be inferred from it? Alternatively, if it is already established as being related to the property bearer (*dharmin*), why isn't it the *dharmin* that is inferred? //9//

liṅgaṃ dharme prasiddhaṃ cet kim-anyat tena mīyate /
atha dharmiṇi tasyaiva kim-arthaṃ nānumeyatā //9//

[As to the second view]: the property and the property bearer do not occur in the relation; [if they did] the genitive case-relation would be used in relation to the property possessor. [E.g. we would say "There is the relation of fire here," not "Fire is here."] [The relation itself] is something inexpressible (*avācya*), and only implied. It has no [explicit] relation (*saṃgata*) with the reason. //10//

saṃbandhe 'pi dvayaṃ nāsti ṣaṣṭhī śrūyeta tad-vati /
avācyo 'nugṛhītatvān-na cāsau liṅga-saṃgataḥ //10//

[However, the correct view is]: [When] the invariable connection of the reason [e.g. smoke] with the property [e.g. fire] is seen elsewhere, and when the reason has been established in other places, then one is led to infer the property [e.g. fire] in the property possessor [e.g. the mountain]. //11//

liṅgasyāvyabhicāras-tu dharmeṇānyatra dṛśyate /
tatra prasiddhaṃ tad-yuktaṃ dharmiṇaṃ gamayiṣyati //11//[8]

There are a number of things about this passage that are not as clear as one might like, but fortunately we need not enter into all of the details of Diṅnāga's views on this topic here. The point to be made in the present context is that Diṅnāga's view about the object of inference (*anumeya*) appears to be incompatible with the "two objects" view of cognition. According to that view, Diṅnāga held that perception and inference have different objects, i.e., perception has a particular (*sva-lakṣaṇa*) as an object and inference has a universal (*sāmānya-lakṣaṇa*) as an object. According to the two objects view, therefore, Diṅnāga should have held that the object of inference (*anumeya*) is a *property* (*sāmānya*). However, this is a view which Diṅnāga expressly rejects in PS(V) 2.8-11 in favor of the view that the *anumeya* is the object's (i.e. the *dharmin's*) *possession* of the property (*sādhya*). In short, the two objects view of cognition is not borne out by what Diṅnāga actually says about the inferred object in PS(V) 2.8-11. In this passage Diṅnāga appears to commit himself once again to the view that the object of cognition is a unitary one which only possesses different aspects.

There are also a number of passages in *Dharmakīrti's* writings which go to show that the "two objects" view of cognition must be rejected in his case as well. For example, Dharmakīrti largely echoes PS(V) 2.8-11 in NB 2.6, where he says that the object which is cognized in inference is the property *possessor* which is characterized by the thing which is desired to be known (*anumeyo 'tra jijñāsita-viśeṣo dharmī*). Dharmottara's gloss on this idea (Malvania, p. 21) is a simple one, and appears to be entirely straightforward. He says: "Inference points out a definite object because of the mark with which it is connected" (*anumānaṃ ca liṅga-sambaddhaṃ niyatam arthaṃ darśayati*). Presumably, the "definite object" (*artha*) of which Dharmottara speaks is the *dharmin*.

Passages like PS(V) 2.8-11 and NB(Ṭ) 2.6 would appear to raise serious problems for the "two objects" reading of Diṅnāga and Dharmakīrti no matter how they are interpreted. Two of the more obvious ways that one might try to fit the "two objects" interpretation to these passages, and the objections to them, are given below.

(1) According to Buddhist philosophy, everything is impermanent; hence what we ordinarily take to be an entity persisting through time is in fact a thought construction. Some of the later Buddhist writers regarded this thought-construction as a kind of universal. Accordingly, they drew a distinction between two different kinds of universals, i.e., an individual universal (*ūrdhvatā-lakṣaṇa-sāmānya*) and a class-concept universal (*tiryag-*

lakṣaṇa-sāmānya). The *ūrdhvatā-lakṣaṇa-sāmānya* was said to be constructed from the series of moments comprising an individual object like a jar (*sa-jātīya-vyāvṛttāyām-aneka-kṣaṇa-samudāyaḥ sāmānyam*); the latter was identified with a class concept (TB: 22).[9]

It might be thought that passages like PS(V) 2.8-11 and NB(Ṭ) 2.6 could be made to fit the "two objects" interpretation by interpreting the *dharmin* that is said to possess the *sādhya* as an *ūrdhvatā-lakṣaṇa-sāmānyam*. However, this way of dealing with the difficulty would be beside the point. If one were to apply the distinction between an individual universal and a class-concept universal to the problem at hand, the most that could be shown is that the *dharmin* (*anumeya*) of PS(V) 2.8-11 and NB 2.6 should be identified with the *dharmin* that possesses a given property (i.e. the *sādhya-sāmānya*) *at a given moment*. Thus, this refinement could not establish that the *dharmin* is a universal rather than a particular. The most that it could show is that the *dharmin* is a *momentary* particular.

Furthermore, any attempt to construe the *dharmin* of PS(V) 2.11 and NB 2.6 as a universal of *any* kind would entail the view that a universal can possess another universal, for these passages clearly state that the *dharmin* possesses its universal. It is, of course, more common to say that a given class that is determined by a given property is *subsumed* as a subset in a larger class. This standard way of relating one property to another would appear to be more congenial to a nominalist account of universals than the view that one property can actually possess another one. Moreover, I am not aware of any passage in the writings of Diṅnāga and Dharmakīrti that would legitimize speaking of one property as *possessing* another property.

(2) Any attempt to avoid the two foregoing difficulties by interpreting the *dharmin* (*anumeya*) of PS(V) 2.11 and NB 2.6 as a hybrid — i.e. as something that is *both* a universal and a particular — would be quite untenable. The whole point of the "two objects" view of cognition is to maintain a rigid distinction between the modes of cognition (*pramāṇa-vyavasthā*) and the objects of cognition (*prameya-vyavasthā*). On the "two objects" view, treating the *dharmin* (*anumeya*) as something that is both a universal and a

particular would be totally illegitimate. As Stcherbatsky observes, an entity of this sort would be "a *sāmānyavad-viśeṣaḥ,* a 'particular universal,' a *contradictio in adjecto*" (1962., vol. 2, p. 303, n. 1).

The foregoing considerations provide very strong reasons for questioning the "two objects" interpretation of Diṅnāga and Dharmakīrti. I am not prepared to say that they are probative, however, for countervailing evidence in favor of the two objects interpretation can be found. [See Stcherbatsky (1962) and Hattori (1968).] It is an interesting question whether a "one object" interpretation can be made to fit the writings of Diṅnāga and Dharmakīrti better than the prevailing interpretation, but this question is a difficult and complicated one that cannot be pursued here.

In any case, the *philosophical* objections to a "two objects" view of cognition are very strong. Since the Saṃtānāntara-siddhi, on its prima facie reading, appeals to the "two objects" view of cognition, these philosophical objections are also objections to the argument in the SS itself. If perception and inference do not necessarily have two different objects (*prameya*s), then Dharmakīrti has failed to deal with the opponent's objection.

The opponent argues that the idealist cannot avoid accepting the legitimacy of some kind of inference to entities outside his own mind stream. His objection is that the Vijñānavādin must accept the legitimacy of inferences to other minds in order to avoid the alternative of solipsism. This presents the following dilemma to the Vijñānavādin. On the one hand, if the inference to other minds fails to give us knowledge of real entities (*svabhāvas*), then the inference is not a valid inference. On the other hand, if the inference to other minds *is* a good inference, then it must by definition give us knowledge of other minds as real entities (*svabhāvas*). But in that case, why isn't the inference to material objects an equally legitimate inference?

In the SS, Dharmakīrti attempts to deal with this dilemma by denying that the two possibilities mentioned by the opponent exhaust all the possibilities. According to Dharmakīrti, there is a third possibility: that inference is valid but does *not* give us knowledge of real entities (*svabhāvas*). This line of defense involves appealing to the "two objects" view of cognition. Thus Dharmakīrti says:

SS 69 [Stcherbatsky:] ... what is cognized by inference is only the general concept and not an individual form.

[Kitagawa:] [... In so far as one cognizes another mind] through the medium of indicators [and not by direct perception,] his cognition is [by nature limited to] a generality. [It is understood,] therefore, [that] one cannot cognize the specific forms [of another mind through indicators].

SS 71 [Stcherbatsky:] It is only the general concept that is cognized and not the other mind itself. Consequently it (the other mind) cannot be cognized by inference.

[Kitagawa:] If [the generality] is not another mind itself, or if [the generality] is something which cannot be expressed by words, then what is grasped by that [inference] is no doubt a generality, but not the other mind [itself]. How [can you say that] one can cognize *another mind itself by such an inference*?

SS 74 [Stcherbatsky:] Inference (or thinking) does not cognize the real existence of objects; otherwise the rational cognition would not have differed from the sensual one, and its own special field of knowledge etc. would not have been there.

[Kitagawa:] [... inference cannot grasp the independent nature of things.] For, [if it did,] we would make the mistake [of supposing that by inference] one can cognize the same phenomena as by perception.

SS 75 [Stcherbatsky:] Inference is a source of true cognition, but not because it gives the knowledge of the real.

[Kitagawa:] The validity of *inference* does not lie *in the cognition of the independent nature of things*.

It is not entirely clear from these passages (or at least it is not entirely clear from the translated passages) whether Dharmakīrti is arguing that the *intentional* object of inference is an unreal universal or whether he is arguing that the *non*-intentional object of inference (i.e. the ultimate or "real" object) is an unreal universal.[10] The former interpretation, which does not invoke the "two objects" view of cognition, does not support the conclusion for which Dharmakīrti is arguing. If Dharmakīrti is claiming only that the object of inference understood *intentionally* is an unreal universal, then (as argued above) the inference does not show that other minds do not exist as real entities. On the other hand, if he is arguing that the object of any inference (understood non-intentionally) is eo ipso an unreal universal, then he needs to explain how and why the inferences to other minds are valid even at the "phenomenal" level.

According to the prevailing scholarly view — which seems to me to be correct — Diṅnāga and Dharmakīrti were idealists (Vijñānavādins) and epistemic monists (*a-grāhya-grāhaka-vādins*). We therefore need to ask: Is it possible to account for the phenomenal validity of the inference to other minds in a way that is consistent with this philosophical viewpoint?[11]

Stcherbatsky addressed this question in the introduction to his translation of the SS. There he said (1922: 340-341):

> The basis of everything is the indivisible consciousness accessible only to the penetration of the absolute mind, or rather not at all accessible to cognition. On its basis, the "biotic force" creates individual "currents," that is, individual personalities with limited cognition, conceiving everything in the double form of subject and object. These individual currents are like individual limited worlds. Each one has its own "biotic force," or force of "previous actions," force of "previous knowledge," its *karma*. The agreement between them, that is, the mutual understanding of individual personalities is thus something accidental, inexplicable, like the agreement of two persons suffering from the same eye disease, each one of which, independently of the other, sees two moons on the basis of his own illusion. This is reminiscent of the theory of the pre-established harmony of Leibnitz. Any individual stream of consciousness is developed from material which is the basic consciousness; it is the true source, the causa materialis of any course of representations comprising a

> personality. The mutual relation of individual streams of consciousness is expressed by a special term (*adhipati-pratyaya*) which we, for lack of a better word, have translated as 'some cause,' that is, the additional factor distinct from the material or basic cause.
>
> Vinītadeva explains to us that Dharmakīrti uses here alien terminology. For the Vaibhāṣikas, who acknowledge the existence of the mass of individual elements in each moment of life, this term denotes, in general, the relation of each element to all others existing at the time. In the case of Dharmakīrti, too, as we have seen, there is no mutual influence of individual streams of consciousness at all, and everything is explained by the interaction of basic consciousness and the power of transcendental illusion.

Although this passage shows that Stcherbatsky wanted to address the aforementioned problem, his analysis of the difficulty does not seem convincing. Indeed, it does not even seem very coherent.

First of all, the views of the SS are not really reminiscent of Leibnitz's parallelism at all. Leibnitz clearly did not believe that the mirroring of his monads was accidental or fortuitous. According to Leibnitz, the parallelism of the perceptions of his different monads is to be explained by the omnipotence and omniscience of God. The author of the SS, as a Buddhist, was precluded from offering this kind of solution to the problem.

Secondly, Stcherbatsky makes two different suggestions about how the author of the text dealt with this problem. One is that the parallelism of the separate mind streams is "something accidental" and "inexplicable." His second suggestion is that the parallelism is explained in terms of a transcendental power of illusion.

Neither suggestion appears to be supported by the text — not even by Stcherbatsky's own translation of the text. There is nothing in his translation that supports either the contention that the coordination of the various mind streams is fortuitous or that it is to be explained by a "transcendental power of illusion." What the text says quite explicitly (at least in the English translations) is that the coordination of the various mind streams is explained by a specific force (*adhipati-pratyaya*) which operates between each of the various mind streams. This means that Stcherbatksy's contention that "there is no mutual influence of individual streams of consciousness at all" (ibid., p. 341) is incorrect. (According to the SS, the relation is telepathic — i.e. of an idealist nature — but is nevertheless quite real.) Consequently, the author's attempt to avoid the alternatives of realism on the one hand and solipsism on the other requires that other minds be *real* entities, and this assertion is clearly inconsistent with the following conjunction: (1) the existence of other minds can be established only by inference, and (2) the object that is made known by this particular inference is an *unreal* universal.

It is reasonably clear that Dharmakīrti has not succeeded in meeting the objection raised by the realist opponent. When inference is valid, it *does* give us knowledge of real things — i.e. (to use Dharmakīrti's term) it gives us knowledge of *svabhāvas*, even if the kind of knowledge that it gives of the object is indefinite in nature. How else, in fact, can the validity of good inferences be accounted for? It will not do to say that such inferences are not valid at the absolute level, whereas they are valid at the phenomenal level, for what we want to know is: How and why are they valid even at the phenomenal level? The only apparent explanation of this validity is that good inferences give us knowledge of *real* things; otherwise, as the opponent points out, they would not be good inferences. But this means that Dharmakīrti must either argue that the inference to other minds is not a valid inference, or he must concede that it gives us knowledge of real entities.

The dilemma in question is in all likelihood an inescapable one as long as one takes it for granted that what we take to be other minds are in fact external to our own. Most philosophers, both in India and the West, have unhesitatingly made this assumption, but it may not be meaningless to question it. Thus, one way of avoiding the dilemma posed by the opponent in the SS might be to argue that I can deny that what I *take* to be other minds really are external to me, while claiming at the same time that this denial of their externality does not entail solipsism (i.e. the view that "my" mind is the only thing that exists). On this view, the "ordinary" inference to other minds actually has two components, one of which is legitimate, the other not.

The inference to other minds goes (roughly) as follows.[12] I first observe intelligent speech and behavior which do not seem to have been caused by "my" mind. Despite the fact that a) this intelligent speech and behavior do not seem to have been caused by *my* mind, and b) that the mental character of this speech and behavior cannot be said to be established through perception, I continue to believe 1) that this speech and behavior is in fact mental in character. I also conclude 2) that the (real) mental entity that caused this speech and behavior is *another* mind than my own. According to monistic idealism, 1) is legitimate, but 2) is not, because what we *take* to be the difference (*bheda*) between different minds is just an appearance (*ābhāsa*) in a single consciousness.

Ordinary hallucinations are judged to be the purely illusory mental creations of the hallucinator's mind because 1) the hallucinator's percepts are not publicly perceivable and 2) because we now believe — for reasons which are complicated but no longer particularly controversial — that in the case of hallucinations it is simply the unconscious mind of the hallucinator that is projecting non-veridical sensory (or quasi-sensory) imagery. It is important to note, however, that this is not the way hallucinations *appear* to the person who is subject to them. Phenomenologically, an hallucination appears as something external, and as something that is just as real as a veridical perception. If it did not, it would not be an hallucination.

Monistic idealism holds that all of our ordinary, veridical perceptions are also mind only. However, even on this view there are distinctions to be made between hallucinations and veridical perceptions. One difference, according to monistic idealism, is that the (unconscious) mind that projects *veridical* percepts (i.e. what we call "real objects," because they are publicly perceived) is not an individualized mind. It is not *in* anybody, nor can it be identified *with* a particular person or organism: all persons and organisms are in it, rather than vice-versa. This is, of course, a highly speculative metaphysical view, but there are arguments in its favor, and it may be a philosophically defensible view.

Despite the fact that monistic idealism is a Buddhist heresy (*tīrthika-dṛṣṭi, aupaniṣada-vāda*), some scholars have thought that the Vijñānavādins were absolute idealists.[13] Although I believe that most of the Vijñānavādins wanted very much to avoid this doctrine, some Buddhist writers do seem to have endorsed it. An interesting example is the Śaṃkarānanda who authored the lost text called Prajñālaṃkāra, who has been identified by Gnoli (1960) with the author of a commentary on the Pramāṇa-vārttika.[14]

According to Gnoli, Śaṃkarānanda "explicitly affirms that, without any infringement to the doctrine by him professed, one may well say that the world is but the body of a unique entity, devoid of parts" (*evam tarhi jagad ekasyaiva kasyacid anaṃśasya yathokta-vidhinā rūpam astu kiṃ naḥ kṣīyeta*) [Gnoli, 1960: xxiv-xxv, n. 3]. As Gnoli remarks (in connection with a related passage), this view upsets all the Buddhist gnoseology, although it is quite consistent with the position of monist Śaivism.

(b)-(c) Although the kind of view embraced by the author of the Prajñālaṃkāra was anathema to orthodox Buddhists, it is hard to see how Vijñānavādins could have avoided endorsing it. This can be seen even in Dharmakīrti's writings. Dharmakīrti's remarks on the subject of *yogic* perception (*yogi-pratyakṣa*) and the Buddha's cognition (Buddha-*jñāna*), which come at the end of the SS, are a case in point. These remarks provide additional support for the claim that the views of the Vijñānavādins really amounted to a kind of idealist monism, despite the fact that this view was a Buddhist heresy.

So far as the "ordinary" *yogin* is concerned, Dharmakīrti follows Vasubandhu in drawing a distinction between (i) a person directly apprehending the contents of another person's mind and (ii) a person having impressions in his own mind which are exactly *correlated* with the contents of another person's mind. Thus, the analysis of *yogic* perception (*yogi-pratyakṣa*) which is given by Dharmakīrti is identical with the one found in Vasubandhu's Viṃśatikā. As discussed previously in chapter 5, Vasubandhu analyzes A's *yogic* perception of the contents of B's mind as: (1) A has an impression

I_A; (2) B has an impression I_B at the same time; (3) I_A and I_B are exactly similar forms or appearances; and (4) I_A is correlated with I_B through telepathy (*paras-parataḥ*). According to this analysis, *yogic* perception is not a matter of directly apprehending another person's mind.

However, both Vasubandhu and Dharmakīrti refer to the nondual (*a-grāhya-grāhaka*) knowledge which pertains to the omniscience of the Buddha. This Buddha-knowledge is different from both ordinary worldly knowledge and the knowledge of the *yogins* because the Buddha has transcended the distinction between subject and object altogether. It is only this knowledge which sees things the way they really are. The erroneous distinction between subject and object is present even in the knowledge that ordinary, deluded people have of their own minds (*sva-citta*). However, the ultimate reality, according to Vasubandhu and Dharmakīrti, is free from the imagined duality of grasper and grasped (*na yathārthaṃ vitathā-pratibhāsa-tayā grāhya-grāhaka-vikalpa*); it is nondual (*advaya*), ineffable (*anabhilāpya*) and unthinkable (*acintya*).

It would appear, therefore, that the doctrine of a nondual, absolute consciousness is the only one that is consistent with the following three assertions which were apparently accepted by both Vasubandhu and Dharmakīrti:

(i) Everything is mind only (idealism).

(ii) "Other minds" are real, at least at the level of "relative" truth (denial of solipsism).

(iii) Knowledge of the way things really are is *nondual* knowledge (epistemic monism).

Chapter 23 (*bahir-artha-parīkṣā*) of the Tattva-saṃgraha of Śāntarakṣita (fl. 750) and the Tattva-saṃgraha-pañjikā (TSP) of Kamalaśīla (fl. 770) is a refutation of the view that there are external objects; included in it are some important statements about the existence of other minds as well.[1] Chapter 26 (*atīndriyārtha-darśi-parīkṣā*) of the same two works defends the doctrine of the Buddha's omniscience. The present chapter analyzes these two chapters of the TS(P) under the following three topics: (a) the denial that cognition (*saṃvedana, bodha, jñāna*) is cognition of external objects; (b) the *yogin's* knowledge of other minds; and (c) the nature of the Buddha's cognition.

(a) The following passages from the "Chapter on the External Object" (*bahir-artha-parīkṣā*) of the TS(P) assert that there is no perception of external objects:

TS 2001 [Hence] the self-cognition (*svavedana*) is of the very nature of consciousness (*bodha-rūpa*). How could there be cognition (*saṃvedana*) of any other thing in the form of an object?

tad-asya bodha-rūpatvād yuktaṃ tāvat svavedanam /
parasya tv-artha-rūpasya tena saṃvedanaṃ katham //200//

TS 2003 It is possible for a cognition (*jñāna*) to be cognized, because it arises as a form in consciousness (*bodha-rūpa*). But an external object (*artha*) does not arise in this way. How, then, can it be known?

bodha-rūpatayotpatter-jñānaṃ vedyaṃ hi yujyate /
na tv-artho bodha utpannas-tad-asau vedyate katham //2003//

TS 2004 According to the view that a cognition is a mere appearance, cognition (*jñāna*) and its object would in truth be different (*bheda*). Just as a reflection (*pratibimba*) has the same form (*tād-rūpa*) as the thing it reflects, so would a cognition [have the same form but actually be different from its object].

nirbhāsi-jñāna-pakṣe tu tayor-bhede 'pi tattvataḥ /
pratibimbasya tād-rūpyād bhāktaṃ syād-api vedanam //2004//

TS 2005 But for the person who holds that there is no appearance of the form of an object in consciousness there is not even the semblance of cognition of an external object.

yena tv-iṣṭaṃ na vijñānam-arthākāroparāgavat /
tasyāyam-api naivāsti prakāro bāhya-vedane //2005//

TS 2006 It might be thought: Just as a sword and a fire, even though not of the same form as an elephant and a combustible object, can do the cutting and burning of those things, so in the case of a cognition and the thing it cognizes.

syān-matiḥ:— danti-dāhyāder-yathā 'si-jvalanādayaḥ /
atād-rūpye 'pi kurvanti cheda-dāhādy-adas-tathā? //2006//

TS 2007 But the cases are not the same, because in the cases cited the sword and the fire are productive of things in that form and are known as such. Cognition (*jñāna*) does not arise in this way.

tad-idaṃ viṣamaṃ yasmāt te tathotpatti-hetavaḥ /
santas-tathā-vidhāḥ siddhā na jñānaṃ janakaṃ tathā //2007//

***

TS 2029 The cognition of something that is nothing but cognition is incorrigible (*dhruvam*). Therefore a cognition is undivided. Therefore there is nothing separate from it.

yat-saṃvedanam-eva syād yasya saṃvedanaṃ dhruvam /
tasmād-avyatiriktaṃ tat tato vā na vibhidyate //2029//

TS 2030 For example, consider the nature of consciousness of blue, or the second moon [seen by someone with an ophthalmological disorder]. Here the cognition of the consciousness of blue (*nīla-dhī-vedanam*) is the cognition of the form of blue (*nīlākārasya vedanam*).

yathā nīla-dhiyaḥ svātmā dvitīyo vā yathoḍupaḥ /
nīla-dhī-vedanaṃ cedaṃ nīlākārasya vedanam //2030//

TS 2031 How could there be awareness (*saṃvitti*) of the form of blue (*nīlākāra*) when there is cognition of the awareness of blue unless the nature of the cognition and the nature of the object are the same?

na jñānātmā parātmeti nīla-dhī-vedane katham /
nīlākārasya saṃvittis-tayor-no ced-abhinnatā //2031//

TS 2032 Everything (*sarvam idam*) is [just] cognition, not a domain of external objects (*arthāntara-gocara*). Because everything is of the nature of cognition, cognition is of itself alone (*svātma-saṃvedanaṃ yathā*).

saṃvedanam-idaṃ sarvaṃ na cārthāntara-gocaram /
saṃvedana-svabhāvatvāt svātma-saṃvedanaṃ yathā //2032//

TS 2033 According to the primary meanings of words, cognition (*saṃvedana*) does not grasp an object (*artha*), because it is always established in its own nature. And because it lacks the appearance of an external form, it is not divided [in itself].

mukhyato 'rthaṃ na gṛhṇāti sasvabhāva-vyavasthiteḥ /
arthākāroparāgeṇa viyogāc-ca na bhaktitaḥ //2033//[2]

The epistemology of the foregoing passages may be summarized in the following ways (all of which I take to be synonymous):

(i) Perceptions in themselves are objectless (*agrāhya, advaya*).
(ii) Perceptions, as such, are only perceptions of themselves.
(iii) Perceptions in themselves are purely self-referential.

In the following discussion it will help to have a convenient way of referring to this epistemology. I shall therefore refer to propositions like (i)-(iii) as the *sahopalambhādi* principle, after verse I.55b of Dharmakīrti's Pramāṇa-viniścaya:

There is no difference between the color blue and the cognition of blue, because they are always found together.

sahopalambha-niyamād abhedo nīla-tad-dhiyoḥ.

My formulations of the *sahopalambhādi* principle in (i)-(iii) above are somewhat ambiguous — intentionally so, because the epistemological view they try to formulate is itself somewhat ambiguous. Thus, (i) says that perceptions *in themselves* are objectless; (ii) says that perceptions *as such* are only perceptions of themselves; and (iii) says that perceptions *in themselves* are purely self-referential. The "as such" qualification etc. means that (i)-(iii) do not, in themselves, rule out the causal theory of perception, according to which perceptions are caused (ultimately) by something outside the perceptions themselves. The *sahopalambhādi* principle, in other words, emphasizes that immediate perception is objectless, but its actual formulation does not explicitly exclude a *mediated* cause of perception in the form of an external object.

This ambiguity is present in the corresponding passages of the TS(P). What the passages cited above amount to, for example, is the statement that all *perceptions*, like the perception of blue, are purely mental appearances, and as such are not perceptions — at least not *direct* perceptions — of anything existing outside of them. These assertions, if true, rule out naive realism, according to which real physical objects and real physical properties are directly perceived by the senses. However, they do not necessarily rule out "non-naive" or representative realism, according to which perceptions are essentially mental but are caused by external objects that impinge on the physical senses. In other words, the *sahopalambhādi* principle, in itself, does not settle the question whether external objects are 1) non-existent or 2) simply unperceived (at least "directly").

If the immediate object of perception is a purely mental appearance then presumably one cannot establish the existence of external objects through immediate perception alone. But does that mean that external objects do not exist at all? Here everything depends on whether external objects can be *inferred*. If they cannot, and if direct perception gives us only direct knowledge of the appearances in our own minds, and if perception and inference are the only two valid means of knowledge (*pramāṇa*), then one must conclude either that the external world does not exist, or that, if it does, we have no means whatever of knowing it.

It appears that the later (*nyāyānusārin*) Vijñānavādins were undecided about how to deal with this fundamental question. On the one hand, the later Vijñānavādins followed earlier Buddhist writers and accepted both perception and inference as valid means of knowledge (*pramāṇa*). Furthermore, the view that the object of inference (*anumeya*) is a real particular appears to permit — and perhaps even require — a Sautrāntika-like realism. On the other hand, there are a number of passages, like the ones above, which appear to reduce the means of cognition to perception only. Since the Vijñānavādins gave an idealist analysis of immediate perception, the resulting epistemology often seems exclusively idealist in orientation.

Note, in this connection, that the TS(P), when it presents and defends the *sahopalambhādi* principle, does not limit itself to the term "perception" (*pratyakṣa*). Instead, it uses terms that clearly refer to knowledge in general, e.g. "*saṃvedana*," "*bodha*," and "*jñāna*." It is legitimate to use these general terms as virtual synonyms of "*pratyakṣa*" only if perception is the *only* means of knowledge.[3] Since Śāntarakṣita and Kamalaśīla adhere to a consistently idealist account of perception, and systematically decline to appeal to inference as an independent means of cognition in their discussion of the existence of external objects, the analysis of cognition *in general* in the TS(P) is undeniably idealist.

It should also be noted that the *sahopalambhādi* principle is ambiguous as to whether the cognition of blue is just *my* cognition of blue (in which case Blue does not exist unless *I* am perceiving it), or whether the color Blue does not exist apart from its perception by some mind or other. The first alternative is the solipsistic one. The second alternative is compatible with subjective idealism (i.e. the view that the world exists in a multiplicity of minds), some forms of theism (e.g. Berkeleian idealism) and monism (e.g. the Advaita Vedānta).

As was pointed out in previous chapters, it is highly unlikely that any Buddhist would be a solipsist, and in any case a solipsistic interpretation of the TS(P) can be ruled out because the TS(P) accepts the doctrine of the Buddha's omniscience.[4] However, if one rejects naive realism (as Śāntarakṣita and Kamalaśīla do), one can avoid solipsism only if one allows the validity of *some* kind of inference beyond what is directly given in the sense data. Since Śāntarakṣita and Kamalaśīla accepted the validity of inference as a *pramāṇa*, and clearly were not solipsists, one might have supposed that they held the view that inference does give us knowledge of something that lies beyond the immediate sense data. But what *does* lie beyond the immediate impressions of the senses? Unfortunately, the TS(P) is conspicuously silent on this crucial question.

This silence is particularly disappointing, because it seems that all the available non-solipsistic alternatives would have been as unacceptable to Śāntarakṣita and Kamalaśīla as the solipsistic one. Note that two of the non-solipsistic alternatives — Berkeleian idealism and monism — are incompatible with fundamental Buddhist doctrines. Furthermore, anyone who rejects solipsism must somehow explain how the perceptions in a multiplicity of mind streams get coordinated with each other. The two obvious ways of doing this are to appeal to God (as Berkeley did) or to a world of matter. As idealists Śāntarakṣita and Kamalaśīla were precluded from solving the problem in the second way, and as Buddhists they were precluded from solving the problem in the first way.[5]

(b) As was pointed out in the previous chapter, the existence of *other* minds is somewhat problematic in the Vijñānavāda. The SS, it will be recalled, is somewhat ambivalent about the existence of other minds. While it does not want to deny the existence of other minds altogether, it consigns the *inference* to other minds to the realm of relative or pragmatic truth.

The question of *direct perception* of other minds (i.e. telepathy) was even more problematic for the Vijñānavādins. The Vijñānavādins held that all perception was, in a sense, telepathic; they also believed that *yogins* could have explicit knowledge of other minds. But if it is possible to have direct perception of other minds, then other minds must exist. This presents a dilemma. *How* does the "other" mind exist? The view that the other mind is not a *separate* entity would be incompatible with the fundamental pluralism of Buddhist philosophy. On the other hand, if the other mind is a held to be a separate entity, then *yogi-pratyakṣa* would be an example of a cognition of an *external* entity (albeit a mental one), and this would contradict the nondualist orientation of the *sahopalambhādi* principle.

Recall that the Viṃśatikā and the SS attempted to deal with this dilemma by analyzing *yogi-pratyakṣa* as a mere *correlation* between the mental contents of two different mind streams. On this view, to say that A (the *yogin*) directly perceives the contents of the mind stream of another individual B is just to say that (1) A has an impression I_A at time *t*; (2) that B has an impression I_B at time *t*; (3) that I_A has the same form (*ākāra*) as I_B; and (4) that I_A is correlated with I_B through telepathy. Interestingly, however, Śāntarakṣita and Kamalaśīla do not endorse this analysis of *yogi-pratyakṣa*.

The TS(P)'s own analysis of *yogi-pratyakṣa* is presented in TS(P) 3632-3633. This passage is a defense of the notion of *yogic* perception against the following objection. The *pūrvapakṣin* objects that a *yogin* does not have knowledge of the essence of things (*svarūpa*) because, according to the *śāstras*, the pure cognition of the *yogins* (*yoginām-anāśravaṃ jñānam*) pertains to universals only (*sāmānya-viṣayam-eva*) and not to particulars (*svalakṣaṇa-viṣayam*). Śāntarakṣita does not accept this view, and tries to explain away the testimony of these *śāstras*. In TS 3632-3633 he says explicitly that what is spoken of as a "universal" (*sāmānya*) in these texts is in fact a particular (*svalakṣaṇa*), and in TS 3634-3635 he says that what is apprehended by the consciousness of the *yogin* (*yogi-cetasā*) is not a universal or general property, for the consciousness of the *yogin* is free from conceptual construction (*avikalpam-avibhrāntaṃ tad-yogīśvara-mānasam*).

The TS(P) does not specify what *śāstras* taught that the "pure cognition of the *yogins* pertains to the universals only," but such a view is somewhat reminiscent of the Saṃtānāntara-siddhi, at least in the sense that the SS argues at some length that what the ordinary person calls "other minds" as the objects of inference are just unreal universals. Nevertheless, the view which Śāntarakṣita attacks — or rather tries to explain away — is not identical with the view of the SS. The SS does not maintain that the *yogin's* knowledge of other minds (*para-citta-jñāna*) is knowledge of a universal which is gained, for example, through inference. The SS seems to imply that the *yogin* has immediate, *non*-inferential knowledge of another mind, although this knowledge is still dualistic.[6] In this respect, the knowledge of the *yogin* and the knowledge of the Buddha are different in kind.

This view, however, is not accepted by the TS(P). According to the TS(P), apparently, the *only* difference between the ordinary *yogin* and the Buddha is that the *yogin* knows only *some* of the particulars of things, whereas the Buddha knows about everything. TS 3637, for example, says that the person who knows all actions (*karma*), all causes and all results with a supramundane knowledge that is born from *yogic* trance (*jñānenālaukikena samādhijena*) is said to be omniscient (*sarvajña*). On this view, the knowledge of the Buddha (who knows *all* things) is a more complete knowledge than the knowledge of the common *yogin* (who only knows *some* things through a supramundane knowledge that is born from *yogic* trance), but *yogi-pratyakṣa* and *buddha-jñāna* are not essentially different from each other.

(c) As P. S. Jaini (1974) has noted, it is rather surprising that the doctrine of omniscience, which is ordinarily thought to be a prerogative of a supreme being, was attributed by the Jainas and the Buddhists, who do not believe in a supreme being, to the historical founders of their religions, Vardhamāna Mahāvīra and Siddhārtha Gautama. As Jaini argued, the Buddhists probably adopted this view of the founder of their religion under the influence of (and in competition with) the slightly older sect of the Jainas. In any case, the doctrine that the Buddha was literally omniscient became, at a relatively early age, the prevailing, orthodox doctrine about the Buddha in the Buddhist schools.[7]

Chapter 26 (*atīndriyārtha-darśi-parīkṣā*) of the TS(P) is devoted to a defense of the doctrine of the Buddha's omniscience. The importance attached to the defense of this notion is undoubtedly attributable to Kumārila Bhaṭṭa (fl. 660), a writer of the Pūrva

Mīmāṃsā, who had launched in his Mīmāṃsā-śloka-vārttika a vigorous attack against what he regarded as the exaggerated pretensions of the Buddhists and Jainas in claiming omniscience for the founders of their religions. His attack was also motivated by the desire to establish all truths about religion (*dharma*) on the revealed word (*śabda*) of the Vedas alone, i.e. without making any appeal to human knowledge, either sensory or super-sensory.

In chapter 26 of the TS(P), the opponent (*pūrvapakṣin*) is a Mīmāṃsaka like Kumārila. The purpose of the chapter is two-fold: 1) to show that the opponent has not shown — and cannot show — that there is no omniscient person, and 2) to show that the belief in an omniscient being is reasonable. Śāntarakṣita-Kamalaśīla and the Mīmāṃsaka opponent are in agreement that the really important thing is to know what *dharma* is and not, for example, how many insects there are in the world. They disagree, however, over the question whether knowledge of the second type is possible. The TS(P) contends that it is possible, and that only the Buddhas have this omniscience.

The argument is based on the view that ignorance is the result of impediments or veilings (*āvaraṇa*). (This doctrine was also held by the Jainas, and may therefore represent Jaina influence on Buddhist doctrines.) What prevents us from having supernormal knowledge (*atīndriya-jñāna*), the TS(P) says, are the defilements of lust, greed, anger, self-love, hatred etc., all of which rest on the belief in the existence of a self (*ātman*). The Buddhas are the only ones who have realized that this self is actually non-existent, and therefore they are the only ones who have completely eradicated all the defilements that obstruct pure knowledge. When the individual removes all these defilements, he becomes an omniscient Buddha. According to TSP 3591, when a person aspires to Buddhahood he is aspiring, among other things, to this omniscience.[8]

Śāntarakṣita and Kamalaśīla contend that the opponent's argument against the doctrine of the omniscience of the Buddha simply comes down to this: there is no omniscient person because the opponent does not himself know of any omniscient person. They contend that this proves, not that there is no omniscient person, but only that the *opponent* does not know of such a person. They argue, furthermore, that the opponent could only assert that there is no omniscient person if he knew that all beings were *not* omniscient. This means that the opponent could only know that there is no omniscient being if he were himself omniscient, in which case his own thesis would be false.

As was noted in chapter 4, some Buddhists drew a sharp distinction between the *nirvikalpa-jñāna* of the Buddha and the *savikalpa-jñāna*. According to Xuan Zang, for example, the omniscience of the Buddha belongs only to the *savikalpa-jñāna*; absolute purity and nonduality (*agrāhya-grāhakatva*) belong solely to the *nirvikalpa-jñāna*. Śāntarakṣita and Kamalaśīla did not draw this distinction. Consequently, they were faced with the problem of explaining how the Buddha's knowledge could be both omniscient and pure without abandoning fundamental Buddhist principles. The following passages from the TS(P) address this problem:

> All thoughts of formlessness etc. are quite out of place in relation to omniscience. Just as your cognition (*jñāna*) is in regard to a certain object, so is omniscience. (TS 3645)
>
> *nirākārādi-cintā tu sarvajñe nopayujyate /*
> *yathā hi bhavatāṃ jñānaṃ kvacid-arthe tathā param //3645//*
>
> [It is not so.] In the case of the Buddha there is of course no defiled volition (*saṅkalpa*) for these have been utterly destroyed in his case. But who would prevent a desire that is pure (*kuśala*) and conducive to the worlds' welfare? (TS 3597)
>
> *naivam; kliṣṭo hi saṅkalpas-tasya nāsty-āvṛti-kṣayāt /*
> *jagad-dhitānukūlas-tu kuśalaḥ kena vāryate //3597//*
>
> The mind of the Buddha does not apprehend the thought moments of other mind streams, because the Buddha is far removed from all obscurations and is free from the defect of subject and object. Thus it has been said: 'For him there is no object, no apprehension, and no grasing of it by any other cognition; it is void (*śūnya*).' (TSP 2030)
>
> *na ca buddhasya bhagavataś-cittena para-santāna-vartti-niścitta-kṣaṇā avasīyante; tasya bhagavataḥ sarvāvaraṇa-vigamena*

grāhyāgrahaka-kalaṅkara-hitatvāt / yathoktam — "grāhyaṃ na tasya grahaṇaṃ na tena jñānāntara-grāhyatayāpi sūnyam"//2030//

Whether it is with form (*sākāra*) or without form (*nirākāra*), the Buddha's cognition does not apprehend anything outside it (*anya*). In the case of the Buddha's cognition, all such thoughts are irrelevant. (TS 2046)

sākāraṃ tan-nirākāraṃ yuktaṃ nānyasya vedakam /
iti bauddhe 'pi vijñāne na tu cintā pravarttate //2046//

On the view that the Buddha's cognition has an object (*aupalambha*), it would have real obscurations, because in that case it would have the same form (*sārūpya*) as desire etc. in the minds of others.(TS 2047)

anya-rāgādi-saṃvittau tat-sārūpya-samudbhavāt /
prāpnoty-āvṛti-sadbhāva aupalambhika-darśane //2047//

The Buddha's teachings proceed in spite of the fact that he does not experience anything (*anābhogenaiva*), for the stream of his cognitions is entirely devoid of the web of conceptual thought (*samasta-kalpanā-jāla-rahita-jñāna-santateḥ*). (TS 1855)

samasta-kalpanā-jāla-rahita-jñāna-santateḥ /
tathāgatasya vartante 'nābhogenaiva deśanāḥ //1855//

The Buddha does not have even the "pure worldly" cognition (TSP 1855)

bhagavatas-tu tathāgatasya śuddha-laukikam-api jñānaṃ nāsti //1855//

TS 3645 above is a reply to an objection raised by the Mīmāṃsaka opponent. The opponent asks how the Buddha can be omniscient if the mind does not apprehend any external object whatever. Śāntarakṣita's reply is that the Buddha's cognition, even though it is nondual, cognizes objects (*artha*), just as in the case of the perception of objects by ordinary people. TSP 2030 and TS 2046-7 are replies to Bhadanta Śubhagupta's criticisms of the

Vijñānavāda in his Bāhyārtha-siddhi-kārikās. [See Aiyaswami Shastri (1967).] Śubhagupta had argued that the doctrine of the Buddha's omniscience was inconsistent with the idealist view that the Buddha's cognitions were objectless. The TS(P)'s reply to this objection is that, while the Buddha is indeed omniscient, the Buddha's cognitions are formless (*nirākāra*) and objectless (*nirviṣaya*). The TS(P) contends that the Buddha's cognitions cannot have any object or form, either external or internal, because in that case the Buddha's cognitions would be similar to the defiled thoughts in the minds of others. In short, in order to deal with one kind of objection Śāntarakṣita and Kamalaśīla say that *buddha-jñāna* has an object, and to deal with another kind of objection they say that it doesn't.

TS 3597 tries to accommodate the compassion of the Buddha by allowing that the desire to promote the good of the world is pure (*kuśala*) and therefore does not pollute the mind stream of the Buddha. This is hard to reconcile with TSP 2030 and TS 2046-7, which deny that the Buddha's cognition apprehends anything outside itself. TS 1855 and TS(P) 1855 are even more radical in this respect than TSP 2030 and TS 2046-7, for these passages deny that the Buddha experiences anything at all (*anābhogenaiva*), on the grounds that the stream of his cognitions is entirely devoid of the web of conceptual thought.

The foregoing passages show that the problem of reconciling the doctrine of the Buddha's omniscience with the doctrine of the purity of the Buddha's cognitions arises even within the context of the mind only doctrine of the Vijñānavādins. The Buddhist realists (e.g. the Sautrāntikas and the Vaibhāṣikas) maintained that perception involves the cognition of an external object. The Vijñānavādins denied this, maintaining that what we call an external object is simply the mind itself having the form or appearance of an object. However, even in this case the aforementioned problem arises, for if the Buddha's mind takes the form (*ākāra, ābhāsa*) of a defiled object, isn't his own mind stream defiled as well? Some of the later Vijñānavādins — in part to escape this kind of difficulty, perhaps — held that cognitions are formless (*nirākāra*).[9] But if cognitions are completely formless, then it would seem to follow that the cognition of blue is not itself blue and the cognition of yellow is not itself yellow. In that case, how can one distinguish one cognition from another?

There are passages in the TS(P) which show that Śāntarakṣita and Kamalaśīla were aware of this difficulty and were concerned to find a way of disposing of it. Of these, TS 3598-3599, TSP 3362-3364 and TSP 3317 are particularly instructive:

> The Buddha does not regard the imaginary entity as a thing; he knows that it is baseless (*nirālamba*); he is like the magician.(TS 3598)
>
> *na ca tasya vikalpasya so 'rthavat-tām-avasyati /*
> *taṃ hi vetti nirālambaṃ māyākāra-samo hy-asau //3598//*
>
> [The Buddha] is like the magician, who knows that his magical horse is without an object (*nirviṣaya*), and who is therefore free from illusion. (TS 3599)
>
> *māyākāro yathā kaścin-niścitāśvādi-gocaram /*
> *ceto nirviṣayaṃ vetti tena bhrānto na jāyate //3599//*
>
> [The Buddha's cognitions would be illusory only if] the Buddha did not know the difference between the true form of a thing and its superimposed form. As it is, how can he be deluded, since he is not deluded about the external object which is a mere superimposed appearance of the imagination, and since he sees that the real (*tāttvikam*) pertains to the different realm of the knowledge devoid of imagination? (TSP 3362-3364)[10]
>
> *naitad-asti; yady-āropitasya tāttvikasya ca rūpasya vibhāgaṃ na jānīyāt, tadā bhrānto bhavet, yāvatā vikalpa-viṣayam-āropitākāraṃ niścinvan bāhyam ca vastu nirvikalpaka-jñāna-gocaraṃ pṛthag-eva tāttvikaṃ tāttvikātmanā paśyan kathaṃ viparyasto nāma*
>
> The person who cognizes taste etc. through the contact of the sensory organ with taste etc. is blameworthy according to the worldly truth (*loka-saṃvṛttyā*), but the Buddha does not know things in this way. How so? Because he knows things through the

mind, without coming into contact with the object; hence he is not regarded by people as blameworthy. ... But all these objections arise only if the external world exists. In the Vijñānavāda, however, this possibility does not even arise. Thus, in reality there is nothing unclean because there is no *rūpa-skandha*, nor any false impression (*parikalpyā-vāsanā*) arising from that, for everything arises as consciousness only (*bodha-mātra*). Such impressions, therefore, do not appear to the sight of those who have seen the true nature of things and shaken off the impression of all impurities, just as one who has been cured of an ophthalmological disorder does not see hairs in the sky etc. (TSP 3317-3318)

yo rasanādīndriya-saṃsargeṇa tān rasanādīn saṃvedayate sa loka-saṃvṛttyā nindyo bhavet, na tu bhagavāṃs-tathā saṃvedayate, kiṃ tarhi? manasā, tac-cāprāpta-viṣayam-iti na loke tat-kṛtaṃ nindyatvaṃ pratītam ... etac-ca sarvaṃ bāhyārtha-sambhave sati codyama-varati / vijñānavādanaye tu dūrīkṛtāvakāśam-etat / tathā hi — paramārthato rūpa-skandhāsambhavān-na santy-evāśucy-ādayas-teṣām, mā bhūt tat-parikalpyā vāsanā; bodha-mātra-samutthitatvāt / ato na sātmīkṛta-paramārtha-darśanānāṃ dūrībhūtāśeṣāśucyādi-pratibhāsānāṃ darśane pratibhāsante, yathā timirādi-doṣāpagame 'nupahata-cakṣuṣāṃ darśane, na keśādayaḥ

TSP 3362-3364 is a reply to the objection that if the Buddha's cognitions were conceptual (*vikalpa-pratyaya*) and therefore with form (*sākāra*), then the Buddha would be subject to illusion, for everything involving conception or imagination is illusory. Kamalaśīla's reply to the objection is that, while the Buddha's cognition does involve conception or imagination, the Buddha is not deceived by it because he knows that what is imagined is merely a superimposed form over the true nature of the thing. TSP 3317-3318 is a reply to the Mīmāṃsaka oppponent, who argues that if the omniscient person had direct perception (*sākṣāt-pratyakṣa-darśana*) of all things, then he would become impure by his perception of unclean things. Kamalaśīla replies that the whole question of whether the Buddha's mind is soiled by the perception of external objects cannot arise in the Vijñānavāda, for in this system of thought the external object is in fact unreal. The same point is made by Śāntarakṣita in TS 3598-3599. These verses state that the Buddha is not deluded by his perceptions because he sees that they are unreal and devoid of any basis in the external object, like a magical entity created by a magician.

The view expressed by these passages may be summarized as follows. According to Śāntarakṣita and Kamalaśīla,

(1) *Buddha-jñāna* can be both omniscient and pure because there is no external object (*bāhyārtha*)

and

(2) *Buddha-jñāna* can be both omniscient and pure because the Buddha *knows* that there is no external object.

According to the Vijñānavāda, of course, there is no external object even in the case of unenlightened beings. The main difference between the Buddha and ordinary, unenlightened beings is that the Buddha realizes this fact, whereas ordinary beings do not. This is why (2) plays an essential part in the TS(P)'s attempt to show that the Buddha's cognition can be both omniscient and pure.

Let us assume for the sake of argument that there is no external world and that the Buddha knows this. Assuming that (1) and (2) are true, can it be shown, as Śāntarakṣita and Kamalaśīla try to do, that there is no conflict or contradiction between saying that the Buddha is omniscient and saying that his cognitions are undefiled? It is doubtful that this can be done even if one grants the truth of (1) and (2).

These propositions can look plausible and innocuous enough, until one realizes that they must somehow be reconciled with the no-self (*anātman*) doctrine. According to the Buddhists, what we call a self is just a stream of ever-changing *dharmas*. Furthermore, according to the Vijñānavādins, cognitions are intrinsically self-cognizing.[11] It would seem to follow that if an impression or idea (*vijñapti*) is an impression of something defiled, then, since there is no difference between a cognition and one's awareness of it, the *self*-cognition must also be defiled.

In non-Buddhist doctrines, of course, a distinction is drawn between a cognition and one's awareness of that cognition. (This, it would seem, is just another way of stating the distinction between perceptions, on the one hand, and the self that has those perceptions on the other.) In attempting to draw a distinction between the Buddha's cognitions of external objects, on the one hand, and his knowledge that external objects are unreal, on the other, Śāntarakṣita and Kamalaśīla appear to be appealing covertly to the essentially non-Buddhist distinction between cognition and one's awareness of that cognition, i.e. between the self and its perceptions.

It might be possible for a non-Buddhist to hold that a person can remain undefiled despite the fact that he or she has cognitions of defiled things; indeed, it might be possible for a non-Buddhist to hold that a person can remain undefiled despite the fact that he or she has *defiled* cognitions.[12] But this may not be a distinction that the orthodox Buddhist can make. Since the Vijñānavādins denied the subject-object distinction, their doctrines seem to imply that if the Buddha's cognitions are of something defiled, then his cognitions are defiled (i.e. *kliṣṭasya vijñānākāraḥ* = *kliṣṭo vijñānākāraḥ*), and from this it follows (according to the *anātman* doctrine) that if the Buddha's *cognitions* are defiled, then the Buddha himself is defiled.

Note also that Śāntarakṣita and Kamalaśīla consistently refer to the Buddha's mind as one mind among many. This is certainly consistent with the fundamental pluralism and realism of the early Buddhist teachings, but it appears to be quite incompatible with their assertion that the Buddha's knowledge is both omniscient and nondual. Any mind that has a separate identity from other minds and things will have perceptions of minds and objects that are *outside it* (provided that it has awareness of the external world at all). On the other hand, a *nondual* omniscient mind could only be one universal mind. In short, even the doctrine of the *sarvajñatva* of the Buddha as it is found in chapter 26 of the TS(P) appears to lead in the direction of a monistic idealism.

The "Refutation of Other Minds" (Saṃtānāntara-dūṣaṇa) is a work by Ratnakīrti (fl. 1070), a late Vijñānavādin. To judge from the title of the work, one might infer that Ratnakīrti repudiated the proof (*siddhi*) of the existence of other minds which had been developed by his predecessor Dharmakīrti in the Saṃtānāntara-siddhi (SS). There are, however, a number of considerations to complicate the picture.

First of all, there is a passage at the end of the work which states that the view that no other minds exist at all (*para-cittaṃ nāsty-eveti*) is restricted in its application (*avadhāraṇa-kṛta*); here it is said that the view that no other minds exist should not be interpreted in such a way as to undermine the teaching of the Buddha's omniscience. This suggests that the denial of the existence of other minds is to be taken as valid only at the level of absolute truth (*paramārtha-satya*). If this is in fact the case, then Ratnakīrti's refutation (*dūṣaṇa*) of the existence of other minds is not so different from Dharmakīrti's *proof* (*siddhi*) of the existence of other minds in the Saṃtānāntara-siddhi (SS), for in the SS Dharmakīrti also maintained that the belief in the existence of other minds was valid only at the level of relative truth. The SS emphasizes the validity of the inference to other minds at the level of phenomenal truth, whereas the SD emphasizes its invalidity at the level of absolute truth. However, a difference of this sort is presumably a difference of emphasis and not a real difference in doctrine.[1]

It is also unclear in the SD whether the correct view at the level of absolute truth is monism or solipsism. As I shall presently argue, there are a number of reasons for thinking that the *siddhānta* according to the SD is monism, and a number of *other* reasons for thinking that it is solipsism. Although these are two quite different doctrines, it is difficult to say exactly which view the SD endorses.

There are essentially three different sections to this short treatise. In the first part, Ratnakīrti argues against the validity of the opponent's argument for the existence of other minds. In the second part Ratnakīrti offers his own direct disproof (*bādhaka*) of the existence of other minds. In the third part Ratnakīrti tries to persuade us that the view that other minds do not exist is consistent with orthodox Buddhist doctrines (e.g. the omniscience of the Buddha) because the view that other minds are non-existent is "restricted in its application" (*avadhāraṇa-kṛta*). I shall discuss these parts individually, in the order in which they are taken up in the text.

(a) Ratnakīrti begins by asking the question: "Are other minds (*saṃtānāntara*) real or unreal (*sad-asat*)?" The opponent answers that they are real and that their existence is proven through inference (*anumāna*). The inference the opponent describes is essentially the same one that Dharmakīrti defends (in its idealist interpretation) in the Saṃtānāntara-siddhi. First we perceive that our own bodily speech and actions succeed the volitional activity of our own minds, and that such speech and action does not occur when it is not preceded by such volitional activity. It is on this basis that we infer (by analogy) that there are other minds when we observe instances of intelligent speech and action which are not preceded by the volitional activities of our own mind.

The first part of Ratnakīrti's treatise is a critique of this argument. He suggests two alternative ways in which the argument can be interpreted, and concludes that the argument is not valid (at least at the absolute level of truth) because it is invalid according to each of these two interpretations.

The two possibilities that Ratnakīrti considers are these:

(i) The volitional mind (*icchā-citta*) which is involved in this inference is a particular which is perceptible (*dṛśya*).

(ii) The volitional mind which is involved in this inference is volitional mind in general (*icchā-citta-mātra*) which is intrinsically imperceptible.

This way of dividing up the question, however, fails to make at least two very important distinctions:

(1) Ratnakīrti's schema fails to consider the possibility that a person's mind is a *particular* which is intrinsically imperceptible to another person, for (ii) above covers only the possibility that another mind is a universal or general concept (*sāmānya*) that is intrinsically imperceptible to another person. This omission is a

particularly serious flaw in the argument, for this is probably the very possibility that is presupposed in the opponent's argument. Furthermore, it may very well be what the ordinary person instinctively supposes about other minds.

(2) Ratnakīrti's schema fails to distinguish sufficiently between the two different minds that are involved in the inference. In the opponent's inference, there is first of all one's own mind (which is the basis of the inference) and then the other person's mind (which is the object that is inferred). As we shall see when we consider in more detail Ratnakīrti's criticism of the opponent's argument under its second formulation, Ratnakīrti fails to draw this distinction and speaks instead as if the mind that is the basis of the inference is the same thing as the mind that is inferred.

Let us first consider the first objection in more detail.

(i) The possibility that another mind is a particular which is (ordinarily) *perceivable* is easily dismissed by Ratnakīrti. He points out that this possibility is contradicted by the very fact that when we infer the existence of another mind the other mind is *not* perceived. (If it were, he points out, there would be no occasion for making the inference at all.) The opponent then objects that there are some inferences in which the object that is inferred (*anumeya*) is not perceived and yet we do not conclude that the *anumeya* is non-existent; an example would be inferring a fire on a distant mountain on the basis of seeing smoke on the mountain. But Ratnakīrti argues persuasively that the inference to other minds is a very different case. The fire is unseen because it is distant in space, but perception does not reveal to us another mind even when we perceive (in our bodily presence) the speech and actions of others.

It is true that the case of other minds is different in this respect from the case of fire being inferred on the basis of smoke, but it is surely illegitimate for Ratnakīrti to simply *assume* that the fire-smoke case is the only kind of valid inference in which the *anumeya* is imperceptible. What the ordinary person supposes in this matter, presumably, is that other minds are imperceptible *just because they are other minds*, and not because they are (like physical objects) entities that can be located at a great distance in space. There may very well be something wrong with this ordinary supposition, but surely the idea cannot simply be dismissed.

A fire is something that is perceptible, and it can be seen if one is in its presence; another mind, on the other hand, may be intrinsically imperceptible, or at least imperceptible to ordinary perception. If it is true — as some Western analytic philosophers have argued — that "only I can have (or experience) my pain," then the most reasonable view of the matter might very well be that my mind is a particular (*svalakṣaṇa*) that (at least ordinarily) cannot be experienced by anyone *but me*. If this is the correct view about *my* mind, then (the opponent would argue) it is presumably the correct view about *other* peoples' minds. Unless this possibility can be ruled out in advance, it would appear to be illegitimate to argue that other minds are non-existent simply because they are never perceived.

(ii) The second alternative that Ratnakīrti considers is that another mind is a universal or general property [*sāmānya, icchā-(citta)-mātra*].

For the reasons given in chapter 6, a universal is not (at least in the ordinary case) the proper object of inference (*anumeya*), nor — as I argued there — is it clear that Diṅnāga and Dharmakīrti thought that it was. Even Ratnakīrti seems to have been aware of some of the difficulties here, for he observes at one point that "it is only a particular fire which is the cause of [a particular occurrence of] smoke." And at another point he acknowledges the close connection that exists (at least in many cases) between inference and perception. "When we conclude that fire is the cause of smoke," he says, "we conclude that if we were present at the place where smoke occurs, we would see fire."

These are very good reasons for thinking that the object of inference (*anumeya*) is a particular or individual rather than a property. Oddly enough, however, Ratnakirti's conclusion from the aforementioned observation is the following: "This is how we establish that fire in general (*vahni-mātra*) is the cause of smoke in general (*dhūma-mātra*)." And later, in speaking of the connection between inference and perception, he says: "The supposition of perceptibility just means this: If a jar were present at this spot and at this moment it *would* be perceived and *would* be an object of my visual consciousness in general (*madīyasya cakṣur-vijñāna-mātra*)." The foregoing statements are unobjectionable in some ways, but the qualification "it would be perceived by my mind in general" seems to be off the mark. Here the phrase "my mind in general" means "my mind as a property or universal." However, there would appear to be even less justification for speaking of my *own* mind as an (unreal) universal than there is for my referring to *someone else's* mind as a property or universal, and that is because I seem to have immediate and direct access to the contents of my own mind.

Furthermore, Ratnakīrti overlooks the distinction between one's own mind and another person's mind when he considers the possibility that the opponent means "mind in general" when he infers the existence of another mind. His main argument against the inference to other minds under its second formulation is that if another mind were imperceptible (*adṛśya*), then the opponent would be precluded from using the *vyatireka* form of inference; i.e., he could not argue that another mind is the cause of another's speech and actions on the grounds that the appearance of speech and actions does *not* take place when a volitional mind in general is *absent*. According to Ratnakīrti, all such forms of inference presuppose that the *anumeya* of the inference can be established independently through perception (as, e.g., in the case of fire, which is perceptible as well as inferable).

Here Ratnakīrti has apparently misunderstood the nature of the inference that is in question. According to the opponent, the inference to other minds simply amounts to this:

> I first observe in my own case that speech and actions occur when I will them and not otherwise. I then observe (representations of) intelligent speech and actions which I have not willed. I then infer (by analogy) that there must be another mind than my own that is the cause of the (representations of) speech and action in the latter case.

That is to say, in my own case I observe that:

(1) In every case, my intelligent speech and behavior is preceded by my own volition.

(2) Whenever there is no volition in my own case, there is no intelligent speech and behavior on my part.

On the basis of (1) and (2), which are established by *observation* (i.e. self-perception), I *infer* that in the case of others:

(1)′ Their intelligent speech and behavior is always preceded by their volition.

(2)′ Whenever there is no volition on their part, there is in their case no intelligent speech and behavior.

Ratnakīrti appears to argue that if another mind is imperceptible, then the opponent cannot use (2)′ as part of an inference. But this appears to be confused, for the argument in question does not use 2′ as part of an inference, any more than it uses (1)′ as part of an inference. Both (1)′ and (2)′ (which are logically equivalent) are *conclusions* of an argument from analogy that is based on (1) and (2), i.e., the reasoning is entirely from one's own case.

The argumentation of the SD is particularly puzzling because the only possibility that the SD considers is that the inference is based on *mind in general* which is common to my mind and other minds. But this is not a possibility that the opponent even considers. The opponent's argument is obviously based on a claim about what we are directly acquainted with in the case of our own minds, and not on the notion of a mind in general which is neither my mind nor the mind of another. Presumably, when a person uses the inference by analogy to infer the existence of other minds, he does so on the basis of what he directly observes about his own case. The only thing that remains imperceptible (both before and after the person has made this inference) is the *other* person's mind.

(b) Ratnakīrti is concerned in the first section of the Saṃtānāntara-dūṣaṇa to show that there is no interpretation of the opponent's inference to the existence of other minds that can be shown to be tenable. In the second part of the treatise, Ratnakīrti presents his own independent (*svātantrika*) argument against the validity of the inference to other minds. This argument goes as follows:

1. When I am aware of my own mind, I am not aware of the minds of others.

2. When I am aware of my own mind, I am not aware of non-existent entities like hares' horns.

3. Therefore other minds *are* non-existent entities like hares' horns.

I do not think that this is a valid argument. In fact, I do not think that it is any more plausible than the following one:

1.′ When Max is looking at the Eiffel Tower, he does not see the Campanile in Venice.

2.′ When Max is looking at the Eiffel Tower, he does not see the Tower of London.

3.′ Therefore, the Campanile in Venice is not different from the Tower of London.

What Ratnakīrti's argument amounts to is simply the assertion that other minds are non-existent because one is never immediately aware of the existence of other minds in the way that one is immediately aware of the existence of one's own mind. But this may not show that other minds do not *exist*; it may only show that they are not *perceived*. According to the opponent, at any rate, other minds can be *inferred*. Ratnakīrti's argument cannot in itself be taken to show that this inference is invalid, unless one *assumes* that perception is the only valid means of cognition.[2]

Ratnakīrti's argument seems to assume that for something to exist, it must be perceptible. However, the average person may not make this assumption; nor has it been made by most idealists. According to the ordinary person and most idealists (e.g. George Berkeley), there are minds *and* "perceptibles," i.e. both minds and things that are perceived by those minds. This means that the ordinary person (and the "ordinary" idealist) appear to be committed to the view that *other* minds exist as unperceived particulars. This view may be untenable, but merely pointing out that other minds are never perceived does not *prove* that it is untenable.

(c) In the third part of the SD, Ratnakīrti takes up the question of the nature of reality from the ultimate point of view, i.e. from the point of view of the Buddha's cognition.

In three places (see footnotes 3, 8 and 9 to Appendix IV) Ratnakīrti states unequivocally that other minds do not exist. This means that Ratnakīrti is committed to some kind of nondualist view, at least at the level of absolute truth. But which nondualist view? Does he commit himself to solipsism (according to which *my* mind is the only thing that exists) or does he commit himself to monism?[3]

There is, of course, the passage at the end of the SD, where Ratnakīrti says that the view that no other minds exist at all (*para-cittaṃ nāsty-eveti*) is restricted in its application (*avadhāraṇa-kṛta*). This distinction between an absolute and a relative truth would seem to imply that Ratnakīrti was a monist, for it is not at all clear what it would mean to say that one is a dualist at the level of relative truth and a *solipsist* at the level of absolute truth. This is particularly true in Ratnakīrti's case because he wants to defend (at some level of truth) the orthodox doctrine of the Buddha's omniscience. This fact more or less excludes solipsism as a possibility, for it would obviously make no sense for a solipsist to maintain that someone *else* is omniscient.

Although this consideration favors interpreting Ratnakīrti as a monist, the line of argumentation in his treatise actually suggests that he was a solipsist. The SD is essentially a defense of the *sahopalambhādi* principle against the view that there is *any* external object outside consciousness itself (i.e. either external material objects *or* external minds). As was pointed out in the previous chapter, the *sahopalambhādi* principle is ambiguous between the following two interpretations: (1) there is no difference between blue and *my* perception of blue and (2) there is no difference between blue and *someone's* perception of blue. The Saṃtānāntara-siddhi and the Viṃśatikā of Vasubandhu are most naturally interpreted according to the second formulation of the *sahopalambhādi* principle, for they are plainly concerned to show that there is a multiplicity of mind streams and that the idealist can explain how the impressions (*vijñapti*) of these mind streams are correlated with each other. However, this issue is never even considered in the SD, and it is hard to see how it could have been, since Ratnakīrti presents a *svātantrika* argument which is designed to show that other minds could not possibly exist. Thus, while Dharmakīrti was concerned to show that the inference to other minds is valid (at least at the phenomenal level), Ratnakīrti presents an argument to show that other minds are simply unreal. If this *svātantrika* argument is valid, then the question of how the experiences of a multiplicity of mind streams are coordinated with each other cannot even arise.

I do not think that the solipsistic implications of Ratnakīrti's *svātantrika* argument against the existence of other minds can be avoided by appealing — as he does — to the distinction between two kinds of truth. According to Ratnakīrti (and the Mahāyānists generally), the difference between appearance and reality is the difference between two different kinds of *truth*. This means, in effect, that it could make sense to say of some entity X that it is both A and not-A, i.e., A from the point of view of relative truth and not-A from the level of absolute truth, or vice versa. However, the assertion that something is both A and not-A (from the point of view of different kinds of truth) appears to be just as contradictory as the assertion that X is both A and not-A simpliciter. The qualification "according to different levels or kinds of truth" does nothing at all to mitigate the contradiction.

Consider the case of a person walking along in the dusk who mistakes a rope lying in the path for a snake. In this case, the snake is unreal as an external object, though it is *not* unreal as a mental appearance in the person's mind. (This would presumably be true regardless of whether one accepted a materialist, dualist or idealist theory of mind.) In this example it would be highly misleading to say that the snake is both real and unreal. It is only slightly less obvious, however, that it would be incorrect to say that the snake is real from one point of view and false from another point of view, for in the example being considered the snake that is said to be *both real and unreal* does not exist at all. That is to say, there is not one thing — a snake that is both real and unreal — but two different things, or rather *three* different things. There is 1) the rope (which is real); 2) the snake which is *thought* to exist as an external object (which is totally unreal); and 3) the snake as a mental appearance in the person's mind (which is real, though of course this mental appearance is not a snake). If one considers this case carefully, in other words, there is nothing in the picture that can be said to be both real and unreal (or neither real or unreal) at all — not even from the point of view of different levels of truth.

Let us consider one more example where the distinction between appearance and reality is involved. In ordinary language we say things like "The sun rises in the East and sets in the West" even after we have learned that it is the earth that revolves around the sun, and not vice versa. Consider now the following assertion: "The statement that the sun rises in the East and sets in the West is true from the point of view of relative truth but false from the point of view of absolute truth." Such an assertion, it seems to me, would be simply false, for there *is* no sense in which it is true that the sun rises in the East and sets in the West. What *is* true is that it *appears* to someone who is standing on the surface of the earth and looking at the horizon etc. as if the sun were rising. Here the statement "It appears *as if* it were the case that P" is a *different* statement from P itself. What we have, then, is not a case of one statement being both true and false (or neither true nor false) — not even from different points of view or levels of truth — but two entirely different statements.

There are other reasons for rejecting the view that truth is an equivocal concept. For example, Dharmakīrti argues in the SS that other minds exist at the level of phenomenal truth but do not exist at the level of absolute truth. This raises the following question: *How* can minds exist at the phenomenal level if they do not exist at the *absolute* level? For example, how can the impressions and experiences of a multiplicity of mind streams be coordinated at the level of phenomenal truth if they do not even exist at the level of absolute truth? If the Vijñānavādin declines to offer an explanation, the bankruptcy of his appeal to the notion of two different kinds of *truth* is virtually admitted by him. If on the other hand he offers an explanation, we are entitled to ask if the explanation makes sense or is valid, and if the explanation is valid without qualification, the distinction between two different kinds of truth will not even arise.

Logically speaking, therefore, there can be only *one* kind of truth (i.e. something is either true or it isn't).[4]

If Ratnakīrti had been pressed home on all these issues, I believe that he would ultimately have had to abandon the view that inference is a valid form of cognition (*pramāṇa*) and to have embraced solipsism. According to the Vijñānavāda analysis, all perception is essentially self-referential, in the sense that it is closed in on itself and does not give us knowledge of anything beyond itself. This principle will infallibly lead to solipsism unless the validity of some form of *inference* beyond our immediate perceptions is allowed. In so far as Ratnakīrti is unwilling to allow this, his position — as Kajiyama (1965) pointed out — is solipsistic.

Ratnakīrti's appeal to the notion of two different kinds of truth merely serves to obscure the doctrinal difficulties he faced. If one analyzes perception in such a way that perception gives us knowledge of something that lies outside perception itself, or if one allows that legitimate inferences can be made from immediate perceptions to entities that exist outside perception, then there would appear to be two possibilities. Either matter is the object/cause of our perceptions, or some mind or multiplicity of minds other than our own is the object/cause of our perceptions.

According to the formulation of the Vijñānavāda in the Viṃśatikā, the Cheng wei shilun, the Saṃtānāntara-siddhi etc., the object/cause of all our perceptions (at least in the normal waking state) is other minds. Since Ratnakīrti was unwilling to abandon the doctrine of the Buddha's omniscience (much less his existence), it is hard to see how he could have repudiated this standard presentation of the Vijñānavāda doctrines, but much of his argumentation appears to have precisely this consequence.

PART IV:

THE DOCTRINE OF COLLECTIVE HALLUCINATION

IX: *Viṃśatikā and Cheng wei shilun*

The idealist philosophy of the Vijñānavādins, like most of the philosophies of India, was closely connected with religious and doctrinal concerns. The Vijñānavādins believed that their views correctly interpreted the doctrines taught in the Mahāyāna scriptures (*sūtras*). According to these scriptures, the world is nothing but the false ideation of the mind, like a dream.[1] The Śūnyavādins could not deny that "mind only" teachings are found in the *sūtras*, but according to them the view that the world is purely mental was a merely provisional teaching. On their view the ultimate meaning of the Buddha's teachings was that everything is totally void or empty (*atyanta-śūnyatā-vāda*). The Vijñānavādins, however, held that the doctrine of the voidness of all *dharmas* could not be taken literally. On their view this doctrine means that the whole world is nothing but mind.

The Vijñānavādins were also concerned to differentiate their views from those of the other religious thinkers in India, all of whom — except for the classical Sāṃkhya-vādins, the Jainas, and the Pūrva Mīmāṃsakas of the Vedic tradition — were theists (*īśvara-vādins*). On this point, they ran into some serious philosophical problems, for the Vijñānavādins, unlike most other idealists, could not say that the world is mind only in the sense that it exists in God's mind, because as Buddhists they did not accept the doctrine of a supreme being (*īśvara*). Consequently, they could not appeal to the notion of an omniscient intelligence (as Berkeley did, for example) to deal with the problem of unperceived objects.

In the Viṃśatikā, Vasubandhu attempts to thread his way between dualism, on the one hand, and theistically-based idealism, on the other, by appealing to the notion of *karma*. According to Vasubandhu, when you and I are looking at the "same" tree, our experiences are the same — or at least very similar — because we both share the same *karma* that has ripened, and because our minds cooperate in some fashion in hallucinating the "same" tree.

When you and I are "looking at a tree," we naturally suppose that there is some objective thing which exists independently of the minds of either of us. According to Vasubandhu, this opinion is an illusion. According to him, there are really two "trees" — the "tree" that I perceive in my mind, and the "tree" that you perceive in your mind — and no objective, external tree which exists independently of its being perceived. In short, there is nothing but a stream of impressions (*vijñāna, vijñapti*) in the mind streams (*saṃtāna*) of a multiplicity of individuals.[2] The "commonality" of our experience arises, according to this theory, because mind streams influence each other reciprocally (*paras-parataḥ*) through the power of telepathy (*adhipatitva*) (cf. Viṃś. and VV 18).

It is essential to this account that the mind streams really be fully independent entities, even though they cooperate in producing the collective hallucination of the world. For example, Vasubandhu and the other Vijñānavādins surely did not think that the apparently separate minds were just different aspects or manifestations of one mind. For one thing, Vasubandhu and the other Vijñānavādins never endorsed this view. Secondly, the view that the individual mind is simply an appearance or manifestation of one, universal mind was a Vedāntic doctrine, and one that was inconsistent with fundamental Buddhist principles. According to the Vijñānavādins, the appearance of a common "world" of perception is not to be explained by the hypothesis that all minds are essentially "one." Nor is the appearance of "common" (*sādhāraṇa*) objects of perception fortuitous. The Vijñānavādins thought that a common "perceptual object" is constructed via a direct process or dialogue that takes place amongst the different mind streams without the intermediation of matter.

The root text for this doctrine is the Viṃśatikā. Let us look at it a little more closely.[3]

Vasubandhu begins the Viṃśatikā with the assertion that mind is real and that the objects we think we see in the external world are unreal:

> Everything is mind or representation only (*vijñapti-mātram-evaitat*), because there is the appearance of non-existent objects, just as a person suffering from an ophthalmological disorder sees things which do not really exist.[4]

In the next verse of the Viṃśatikā and its autocommentary (VV), Vasubandhu mentions three objections to this idealist view:

First objection. If everything is mind only, then the determination (*niyama*) of time and place would not be possible. In other words, if it were true that the ideas of things arise even though there are no real things corresponding to them, then things should arise anywhere and at any time, as in the case of dreams, and this is contrary to our experience.

Vasubandhu's reply to this objection is a simple denial that dreams are indeterminate in this sense (Viṃś. 3a-b). Vasubandhu claims that the determination of space and time in dreams is just what it is in the waking state, for, he says, the things which are seen in dreams are not seen everywhere nor are they seen always. In other words, dreams are as "determinate" (*niyama*) as waking experiences are, and the distinction between them which the critic wants to uphold does not exist.

Vasubandhu's reply to the first objection (whether it is valid or not) does not reach the question whether the world is in "my" mind (the solipsistic view) or whether it exists in a multiplicity of minds. It is clear from Vasubandhu's reply to the second objection, however, that he believed in a multiplicity of minds. Much of his reply to the second objection, for example, is concerned with showing that a "common" universe or world of experience is compatible with the doctrine that the world exists in a multiplicity of minds.

Second objection. If everything were mind only, then the mind streams (*saṃtānas*) of the individuals in one place and time in the waking state would not be indeterminate (*aniyama*), and this contradicts our actual experience. What he appears to mean by this is that those appearances (*ābhāsa*) which really are mind only, like the sky-hairs seen by those who suffer from ophthalmological disorders, are purely private experiences, and are not seen by by others who are established at the same place and time. But if everything were mind only, this "indeterminacy" would be typical.

Vasubandhu's defense of his views against this objection is presented in terms of a disputed question in Buddhist cosmology. There was disagreement over whether the demons or hell guardians (*naraka-pālas*) who torment the denizens of hell were real beings or not. Vasubandhu's position on this disputed point was that the hell guardians do not really exist because their existence would not be fitting (*ayogāt*). What he meant by this was that asserting the real existence of such things would be problematic from the point of view of fundamental Buddhist doctrines. For example, if such beings were real, then they would experience the torments of hell just as their captives do, and this would violate the law of *karma*, according to which pain and suffering are the exact recompense for actions carried out in this or in previous lifetimes.

Although Vasubandhu held that the *naraka-pālas* were not real, he did not reject the Buddhist doctrine that there are beings that suffer from their *karma* in hell. Furthermore, he maintained that there is at least one sense in which the hell guardians are not the purely private or subjective hallucinations of the denizens of hell, for he held that all the ghosts (*pretas*) in hell see the same "objects" because they share the same *karma* (VV 3).[5] The denizens of hell really are tormented by the hell guardians, dogs, crows, walls of iron which hem the ghosts in and crush them etc., even though all these objects are non-existent (*asat*), for everything happens there according to the governance (*adhipatva*) of the matured or ripened *karma* of those beings. Here Vasubandhu is clearly asserting the commonality of the experience of a multiplicity of mind streams (*saṃtānas*). He argues, however, that *karma* alone ensures this commonality of experience, and not a common world of real, external objects.

Vasubandhu even suggests that the doctrine of *karma* logically *implies* the doctrine of idealism. According to a view which had been held by some Buddhists, the hell guardians are neither mental appearances nor real, sentient beings which actually suffer along with the beings they torment. They are instead special elements (*bhūta-viśeṣas*) which are born due to the *karma* of the inhabitants of hell. These special elements are conceived by the beings of the hell realm as infernal guards etc. (*naraka-pālādi-saṃjñām*), but what the inhabitants are actually seeing are these *bhūta-viśeṣas*, which transform themselves (*pariṇamanti*) so as to frighten the sinners with hand gestures, the clashing of mountains, etc.

It is interesting that Vasubandhu, in replying to this alternative view, concedes that the hell beings exist in some sense (*na te na sambhavanty-eva*). Nevertheless, he thinks that the objects which the sinners experience in hell are nothing but the mental transformations or modifications of those who suffer there. If the birth of beings is from *karma*, he says, then we should simply say that all things are merely transformations of consciousness.[6] Why should special elements or beings (*bhūtas*) be assumed rather than transformations of the various conciousnesses? Moreover, he argues, the doctrine of mere consciousness is preferable to the doctrine that there are real, external objects, because the idealist view holds that the cause of the experience (the latent impression or *vāsanā* of the previous *karma*) is in the same place (the mind stream of the individual) as the "object" which is experienced (the result of the *karma*). This is as it should be, he says, for the impression of the deed is nowhere but in the stream of consciousness of the individual, and consequently the hell guardian who torments the individual as a result of his *karma* should also be there.

Having committed himself to the view that there is nothing in the word but a sequence of representations in a multiplicity of mind streams, Vasubandhu has to show how his formulation of the *karma* doctrine can explain the "commonality" or "universality" of our experiences in the waking state. His view is that the representations (*vijñapti*) of the various mind streams mutually influence each other.[7] Thus, he says, the characteristics or differentiations (*viśeṣa*) of one mind stream arise because of the *viśeṣas* of the representation of another mind stream (*saṃtānāntara*), and not because of the characteristics of an external object.

Third objection. Finally, Vasubandhu considers the objection that his idealist views cannot account for the fact that the good and bad actions which are done in the waking state have consequences, whereas the good and bad actions of the dreamer do not. Vasubandhu says that this difference can be accounted for by the fact that in the dream state the mind is overcome by "dullness." This reply, of course, implies that there is no real, qualitative difference between waking and dreaming.

Although Vasubandhu held that the world is mind only, he apparently did not hold that the world existed completely in the *conscious* minds of sentient beings. It is likely, in fact, that the Vijñānavādins thought that the world exists mostly in the *unconscious* minds of sentient beings.

There seems, for example, to be an explicit appeal to the notion of unconsciously perceived objects in the Triṃśikā. In Triṃś. 3 Vasubandhu says that the store consciousness (*ālaya-vijñāna*) is the "perception, abiding in, and grasping of what is unperceived or inadequately perceived (*asaṃviditaka*)."[8] Unfortunately, there is no auto-commentary by Vasusbandhu on the Triṃśikā, but the detailed commentary by Xuan Zang on the Triṃśikā shows very clearly that he, at any rate, interpreted this verse to refer to unconsciously perceived objects (CWSL 2-4).[9, 10]

Xuan Zang's commentary on the Triṃśikā is of particular interest because it introduces, in the context of a discussion on the nature of the perceived object (*ālambana*), the important notion of potencies or dispositions (*bījas*) which are common to a multiplicity of minds (*sādhāraṇa-bījas*). According to Xuan Zang, the *ālaya-vijñāna* evolves (*pariṇamanti*) into the appearance (*ābhāsa*) of what is called a "receptacle world" (*bhājana-loka*) by the force of the "maturation" (*paripāka*) of these common or universal *bījas*.[11] Furthermore, he says that the mind (*vijñāna*) of each being evolves in this way on its own account, but that the result of this development is "common," so that the "receptacle world" is not "differentiated." In a similar way, he argues, the lights of many lamps which are placed together in the same room are individually distinct, even though the light of the collection of lamps is *as if* it were only one lamp.

Xuan Zang qualifies this doctrine of "common" or "universal" *bījas* in several ways:

(1) A seed (*bīja*) is common to some beings but not to all of them. According to Xuan Zang, the view that the *bījas* are held in common by *all* of the beings in all of the realms of Buddhist cosmology leads to a number of unacceptable consequences. First, the minds of the Buddhas and Bodhisattvas would actually evolve (*pariṇamanti*) into this defiled world of ours. Second, the minds of

unenlightened beings like ourselves would evolve into the "pure lands" of this and other realms. Third, the beings of the so-called "formless realms" (*ārūpya-dhātus*) would continue even from those realms to have their minds evolve in the inferior realms. Xuan Zang found these consequences unacceptable, and therefore maintained that the store consciousness of a being develops only into the "receptacle world" which belongs to the body in which it is born.

(2) A closely related qualification is connected with the distinction which Xuan Zang draws between the force of acts and the force of meditation (*samādhi*), religious vows (*praṇidhi*) etc. In the case of meditation, religious vows etc., he says, there is no fixed rule as to the "receptacle worlds," bodies, realms (*dhātus*) etc. As Poussin observes, this probably refers to the fact that, according to Buddhist doctrine, the mind of a *yogin* or ascetic who possesses the power (*siddhi*) of the divine eye (*divya-cakṣu*) develops into objects which are visible to his sight, even though they belong to a realm which is higher than the one where the *yogin* is born. Such objects would not normally be seen by those individuals in the *yogin's* world who are less yogically developed.

(3) According to Xuan Zang, it is not true that all beings in *one* realm see exactly the same thing. There are, he says, "special objects of experience" for the various classes of beings like ghosts, human beings, gods, animals etc. Even when these different categories of beings are viewing the "same" object in the same world, their experiences are so different that they cannot really be said to see the "same" thing.

(4) Another important qualification is that the minds of various beings manifest *only* as the material objects and physical bodies of oneself and others of a particular world, and not as the *experiences* of other beings. Thus, Xuan Zang says, one can see the ("physical") ear of another person, but one cannot say that one actually hears what another person hears, or — as he puts it — one cannot say that one person's store consciousness develops into the actual sensory consciousness of others.

In CWSL 2-4, Xuan Zang also attempts to deal with another important objection to the mind only doctrine. According to Buddhist doctrine, when a "receptacle world" is going to perish, no beings inhabit it, nor will there be any being which will be reborn there. How, then, can such a world be said to be mind only?[12]

Xuan Zang's answer to this objection is that even if there are no actual beings in a world (*bhājana-loka*) at a particular time, its existence is maintained by the store consciousnesses of the beings who have departed from it or who will be reborn in it. In short, the solution of the problem, according to Xuan Zang, is that a world may exist entirely in the minds of certain beings even if those beings are not actually in the world at that time. A corollary of this view — although it is only implicit in Xuan Zang's text — is that a world can exist entirely in the minds of such beings even though they are not even *conscious* of the existence of that world.[13]

X: *A Critique of the Doctrine of Collective Hallucination*

As was noted in the previous chapter, the Viṃśatikā begins with the statement: "Everything is mind only, because there is the appearance of non-existent objects, just as a person suffering from an ophthalmological disorder sees things which do not really exist." To judge from the rest of the Viṃśatikā, this statement means exactly what it says. It means, for example, that the book you are reading now does not exist: it is a figment of the mind. It means that all the other objects in the room about you, all the articles of furniture, the room itself, the building it is in, even the city and town, the planet and the universe you inhabit, are as unreal as a psychotic's hallucination or the dream you had last night.

There are some fairly obvious and fairly standard objections to this kind of assertion. Vasubandhu mentions some of them in the Viṃśatikā. One natural objection, for example, is that our normal waking perceptions are not like dreams or hallucinations because there is an orderliness and "determinateness" about the world we perceive in our normal waking state which is lacking in dreams and hallucinations. Furthermore, the world which we perceive in our waking state is *commonly* perceived (or so we think) — i.e., it is a public world, rather than a private one, and in this respect is unlike the "world" of dreams and hallucinations. Only *you* can "see" a book that you are hallucinating or dreaming, but anyone with normally functioning senses and mind would perceive the book that you are holding in your hand if he or she were looking at it.

Vasubandhu believed that his formulation of idealism could meet these objections. His formulation of idealism in the Viṃśatikā may be summarized under the following five points:

(1) Everything is mind only (*vijñaptimātram evaitat*) — i.e., matter is totally unreal (*parikalpita*).

(2) There are (at least at the level of relative truth) many minds, all finite and all essentially independent of each other. There is no single, supreme, absolute mind .

(3) Everything is illusory (*asad-arthāvabhāsanāt / yathā taimirikasyāsat-keśa-candrādi-darśanam*).

(4) The world as it appears to each sentient being is determinate (*niyama*). That is to say, it is stable and collectively perceived (or, more exactly, collectively *hallucinated*) by the multiplicity of finite sentient beings.

(5) The fact that the experiences of the multitude of sentient beings are correlated with each other (i.e. that their perceptions are "determinate") is not simply coincidental or fortuitous. It is accounted for by the hypothesis that sentient beings (with some important qualifications) are always in immediate mind-to-mind contact with each other.

It will be convenient in the discussion that follows to have labels for these five propositions. Proposition 1 I shall call the Mind Only Principle; Proposition 2 I shall call the Many Finite Minds Principle; Proposition 3 I shall call the Unreality Principle (and its denial I shall call the *Reality* Principle); Proposition 4 I shall call the Determinateness Principle; and Proposition 5 I shall call the Telepathic Principle. Propositions 1 through 5 may be summarized by saying simply that the Vijñānavādins held that the world was *collectively hallucinated* by the totality of sentient beings. This doctrine I shall call the doctrine of Collective Hallucination.

The Mind Only Principle (MOP) is the criterion we use for classifying a philosophy as idealist; all idealist philosophies have adhered to it, so it is not unique to the Vijñānavāda. The Many Finite Minds Principle (MFMP) *was* unique to the Vijñānavāda, for while many (perhaps most) idealists have accepted the existence of many finite minds, the Vijñānavādins, so far as I know, were the only philosophers in the history of the world (other than solipsists) to accept the Mind Only Principle *and* to deny the existence of a supreme or absolute mind (i.e. to reject both theism and monism). The Unreality Principle is another fairly atypical idealist doctrine. It is not, however, quite unique to the Vijñānavāda, for other philosophical systems (e.g. the Advaita Vedānta of the Śaṃkara school) have also held it. The Determinateness Principle, in itself, is neither idealist nor non-idealist; it simply states what it is that any philosophy (except possibly solipsism) has to explain. The principle that makes the Vijñānavāda the most unique is perhaps the Telepathic Principle (TP). Note that the TP is closely connected with — indeed, is virtually entailed by — the conjunction of the Determinateness Principle, the Mind Only Principle, and that part of the Many Finite Minds Principle that denies the existence of a single, supreme or absolute mind.

Many of the religious (and even non-religious) thinkers in India accepted the existence of telepathy. It was even widely regarded in India as one of the common powers (*siddhis*) which could be developed through the discipline of *yoga* and other meditative and/or spiritual practices.[1] The Vijñānavādins, however, pushed the belief in telepathy further than any other philosopher or school in either the East or the West, at least so far as I know. Although many philosophers have believed in the existence of such a principle — or at least have been willing to entertain it as a theoretical possibility — it was only the Vijñānavādins who put telepathy at the very *center* of their epistemology. Note that in the Vijñānavāda telepathy is not used simply to explain certain odd experimental or spontaneous cases which suggest that information may possibly be transferred from mind to mind without the mediation of the physical senses. In the Vijñānavāda, it is used to explain even *normal* perception.

In the rest of this chapter I shall argue that the concept of telepathy cannot be used to explain normal perception in the way that the Vijñānavādins intended. Specifically, I shall argue that there is a conflict between the Many Finite Minds Principle, on the one hand, and the the Determinateness Principle on the other which the Telepathic Principle does not bridge. The argument is, basically, that the Vijñānavādin has to invoke so *much* telepathy in order to explain the features of normal perception that he ends up, in effect, with a doctrine that is indistinguishable from monistic idealism.

The argument is presented in two stages. In the first part I consider six specific cases of collective hallucination which have been reported in the literature of psychical research.[2] In this first part of the argument I contend that the Telepathic Principle is probably incapable of explaining even supposed cases of collective hallucination. I then extend the argument to the case of normal perception, which is (by definition) more "determinate" than any reported case of collective hallucination.[3]

Let us begin, then, by looking at six of the rather large number of cases of "collective hallucination" that have been reported and discussed in the parapsychological literature:[4]

> *Case 1*: You and your wife are paid a visit by your wife's cousin and her husband. The four of you are eating in the dining room, when the four of you suddenly notice, standing by the dining table, an apparition of your wife. The likeness is exact in every way, except that the double is wearing a dress which is unlike any dress your wife owns. You say quietly "It is Sarah" (your wife's name) in a tone of recognition, whereupon it immediately disappears.
>
> Your wife reports that the apparition seemed to her to be entirely apart from herself or her feelings, like a picture or a statue. Neither you nor the house visitors have ever seen a visual hallucination before, though your wife has had other hallucinations, all of which were connected with ill-health or nervous shock.
>
> *Case 2*: You, Mrs. B, and your daughter, Miss. B, are sleeping together in the same room. In the middle of the night, both of you awaken suddenly, "without assignable cause," and see a female figure in a white garment with dark curly hair hanging down the back. The figure is standing in front of the fireplace, over which there is a mirror. As the two of you are in different beds, you see the figure from different angles, but your perceptions of the figure are exactly what they would be if a real person had been occupying the position where the figure stands. For example, your daughter sees the back of the figure, but not the face, though the face is clearly visible to her in the mirror. You yourself see the figure's face in quarter profile. You and your daughter are alarmed, and exclaim to each other about the presence of the figure. The two of you jump out of bed and make for the door, which had been locked, and which is then found to still *be* locked. When the two of you turn around again, the figure has disappeared.

Case 3: You are having lunch with your mother at home in the middle of the day. In the course of the dinner table conversation, your mother suddenly looks down at something beneath the table. You inquire whether she has dropped something. She says: "No, but I wonder how that cat could have gotten into the room?" Looking underneath the table, you are surprised to see a large white Angora cat beside your mother's chair. You both get up from the table and open the door to let the cat out. The cat walks around the table, goes noiselessly out the door, proceeds half way down the hall, and then turns around and faces the two of you. The cat stares at you for a short time, and then dissolves away, "like a mist," before your very eyes. Neither you nor your mother has a cat, and neither of you can remember having seen such a cat around the place.

The incident makes a rather "unpleasant impression" on you. This feeling is greatly enhanced when, a year later, you and your mother are at your sister's house in another city. You and your mother enter the house in the afternoon after a walk, when, on opening the main door, the two of you are greeted by what appears to be the same white cat. It proceeds down the passage, staring at the two of you with the same "melancholy gaze." When it gets to a closed and locked door in the hallway it again dissolves "into nothing."

Case 4: You are a household servant employed by the L's. One afternoon you and another servant are sitting in the kitchen, when the two of you see the door handle turn, the door open, and Miss L., the daughter of the family, enter the kitchen, walk up to the fire-place and warm her hands before the fire. Both of you notice that she is wearing a pair of green kid gloves. She suddenly disappears before your eyes. The two of you run upstairs to tell Mrs. L, the mother, what you have just seen. The mother herself fears that something may be wrong, but she attempts to quiet the two of you by reminding you that Miss L. always wears black and never green gloves, and that therefore the "ghost" could not have been that of her daughter.

About a half-hour later, the "real" Miss L. enters the house, goes into the kitchen, and warms herself by the fire. She has on a pair of green kid gloves which she had purchased on the way home, having been unable to find a suitable black pair.

Case 5: You are a clergyman, and make an afternoon call at the family home of some members of your church. You are offered an arm-chair, but choose instead to sit on the sofa, which gives you a nice view of the garden. There are two others in the room (including the lady of the house), who sit facing you, and who have their backs to the window. While you are conversing with them on the subject of your visit, you see an old man with a white beard, dark blue overcoat and flat-topped felt hat pass by the window. Immediately afterwards the front door bell rings. The lady of the house is expecting a visit from a friend of hers (a woman), and remarks, "This must be —." You say, "No, it's an old man with a white beard." At this, both of the women express surprise, and begin wondering who it could be. Just then the door of the living room opens, and in walks a physician who is well known to all three of you. As soon as he has shaken hands with everyone, the lady of the house says, "But where is the old man with the white beard?" To which the physician replies, "Yes, where is he?"

It turns out that as the physician had come up the walk towards the front door and had passed the living room window, he had looked into the living room where the three of you had been sitting, and had seen, seated in the arm-chair which you had declined, a person answering exactly to the description of the old man you had seen passing the window, except that the old man with the white beard *he* had seen had not had a hat on. The physician was surprised not to find the old gentleman in the room; hence his reply to the your parishioner's question.

The physician is wearing a brown overcoat, a hat, and no beard, so you could not have mistaken *him* for the old man.

Case 6: You go to work as usual one Thursday morning at around 10:45, and on entering the office find your secretary in conversation with the building manager. Another co-worker, a Mr. H., is standing behind your secretary. You are a bit surprised to see Mr. H. at the office so early, as he does not usually get to the office until around mid-day. You are just about to ask him what brought him in so early, when your secretary begins questioning you about a telegram which you have received. During this time, a Mr. R, from an office upstairs, enters the room and listens to this conversation. There are now (or so it appears to you) five people in the room: yourself, your secretary, the building manager, Mr. H. and Mr. R.

At this point, Mr. R. and the building manager leave the room. There are now (or so it seems to you) three people in the room: you, your secretary, and Mr. H. You are shown the telegram by your secretary, and read it. Then you turn to Mr. H and describe its contents to him. You notice a melancholy look on his face, and observe that he is without a necktie, which is unusual for him. You say to him: "Well, what's the matter with you? You look so sour." He makes no answer, but continues looking at you. You pick up a letter from a table standing between the two of you and read it, and continue to see Mr. H. standing opposite to you. Your secretary says: "Here is a letter from Mr. H" and hands it to you. You are dumbfounded as Mr. H. vanishes on the spot.

Your behavior has astounded your secretary, who (it turns out) had not seen Mr. H. at all. Furthermore, the message from Mr. H. which he hands you — and which was the occasion for the disappearance of Mr. H. from your field of vision — had been written on the previous day (Wednesday), and states that, since he was not feeling well, he would not be coming into the office the next day (Thursday). When Mr. H. does come to the office the next day (Friday), you ask him what he was doing about 10:45 in the morning on the previous day. He replies that he had been having breakfast with his wife about 14 miles away, and that he had never left his house during the day.

You are a bit hesitant to mention your hallucination to Mr. R., the man who works upstairs, but the following Monday you bring yourself around to asking him what he remembered of the office conversation on the preceding Thursday. R. replies that the conversation was about the telegram, and remembers that five people were present: you, the secretary, the building manager, *Mr. H* and himself. Upon further questioning, he tells you that he remembers that H. was standing at the corner of the table, opposite to you. He also tells you it had seemed to him that H.

> had looked quite melancholy, but that he had attributed this to H's annoyance about the conversation that was being held. R. tells you that H. was still standing in the same position when he left the room with the building manager.
>
> Upon informing R. that Mr. *H.* himself says that he was at home all day and never came to the office on Thursday, he becomes positively indignant and insists on questioning the building manager, who had left the room with him. When the manager is asked to reconstruct the events, he reports that he had not seen H. either.

Case reports like these are very puzzling from a philosophical point of view, for (assuming that they have been accurately reported) they tend to strongly subvert the distinction between what is private (mental) and what is public (material). We ordinarily suppose that what one thinks or feels (or hallucinates) is purely private to oneself, and that one's internal mental states (hallucinatory or otherwise) remain private unless they are manifested to others in one's statements, gestures, facial expressions and other outward behavior. The reports of collective hallucination, however, suggest that internal, mental states might not necessarily be private in this sense. Assuming that these cases (and others very much like them) have been accurately reported, we would have to assume that at least on some occasions a direct, telepathic connection operates between individuals. The question here is whether this could be the *whole* explanation of the matter.

Within the field of psychical research, the view that it *can* be the whole explanation of the matter is associated particularly with the name of Edmund Gurney, a classics scholar at Trinity College, Cambridge in the late 19th century. Certain features of these puzzling cases strongly support Gurney's purely telepathic hypothesis. This is especially the case with Cases 5 and 6. In Case 6, for example, Mr. H. appears to only two of the possible percipients, so he only partially satisfies the Determinateness Principle. Similarly, the apparitional old man with the blue coat and white beard of Case 5 fails to satisfy the Determinateness Principle in two different ways, for, besides vanishing suddenly, he appears to one of his percipients as being in one place and to another as being in another place.

Insofar as all six of these cases fail to fully satisfy the Determinateness Principle, we are inclined to regard them as purely hallucinatory. The only peculiar feature about them which seems *non*-hallucinatory is that all six of them are (to varying extents) *collectively* perceived. Gurney's theory attempts to account for this special feature of the "collective" cases by the telepathic hypothesis. According to this theory, collective hallucinations are just as hallucinatory and "non-objective" as single-percipient hallucinations are. The only salient difference between the two cases (i.e. the fact that the former are collectively perceived) is explained by the hypothesis that the (unconscious) minds of the percipients in these cases somehow cooperate in constructing an hallucinatory story, which is then projected by their subconscious minds as an external object.

Gurney's purely telepathic theory is an appealing one as an explanation of at least some aspects of these cases. It is, however, less attractive for other aspects of the cases, especially those which do *not* represent a violation of the Determinateness Principle.

In the first four cases, for example, the objects were reported to behave very much like normal objects during the time that they were collectively perceived. In Case 1 four people were reported to have seen the apparition, and, to judge from the narrative account, the apparition appeared and disappeared to all four percipients at the same time. In Case 2, the apparition's mimicry of a normal object was even greater, for the apparent object behaved optically the way a normal perceptual object would be expected to behave. (Both percipients, for example, reported seeing the apparent perceptual object in the profile that fitted each percipient's respective angle of vision, and one of the percipients reported seeing the face of the figure reflected in a mirror.) In Case 3 the percipients reported seeing a cat which apparently behaved in every respect like a perfectly ordinary cat. Even more puzzling is the fact that the same two percipients reported having had virtually identical experiences on two different occasions, separated spatially by hundreds of miles and by a time interval of more than one year. This raises the question whether we would have to say that the two apparitional cats were in fact *identical*.

These features of the first four cases (and others like them which have been reported in the literature) tend to undermine, at least to some extent, the purely telepathic explanation. The reason, it seems to me, is the more or less *criterial* connection that exists between the Determinateness Principle and the Reality Principle. In other words, the more an apparent perceptual object satisfies the Determinateness Principle (i.e. is collectively perceived and behaves as a normal object, at least during the time that it is collectively perceived), the more we are inclined to regard it as having been, during the time that it was collectively perceived, a real object by *definition*. Another psychical researcher, G. N. M. Tyrrell (1953), critized Gurney's telepathic hypothesis on just these grounds:

> The real crux of the difficulty is not merely that each of the percipients sees at the same time an apparition *more or less* similar to that which the others see; it is that all the percipients see the *same* thing, each from his own point of view in space, just as though it were a material figure. Gurney, apparently, half doubted whether this were so; but I do not think that the evidence, carefully looked into, leaves any reasonable doubt that it is ... It seems therefore that there is scarcely room for doubt that the sensory image of one percipient is correlated with the sensory image of another just as it would be if the two percipients were seeing the same material figure in normal perception...
>
> If it be granted, as I think it reasonably must be, that perception of apparitions is full-blown perception, identical in its features with normal perception, and that in collective cases the various percipients see the *same* figure, each appropriately according to his position and distance from the figure; and that, as the figure moves, the sensory images of all the percipients change exactly as they would if the figure were a material one, then Gurney's theory of collective perception breaks down. For it might be conceived that one percipient should telepathically affect another so as to cause him to see a figure more or less like the one he was seeing himself, but it is inconceivable that the figures should be exactly correlated to one another as in normal perception. Indeed, experimental telepathy suggests the figures seen by the different

percipients would be likely to differ a good deal from one another. [Tyrrell (1953: 70-73).]

Tyrrell thought that such apparitions would have to be explained in terms of "idea patterns" or "thought forms." According to this hypothesis, idea patterns are generated in some fashion or other by a telepathic process of communication on the part of the subconscious minds of the percipients; nevertheless, once generated they have some kind of existence independent of the minds that generate them. Other theorists, like Hornell Hart (1956), have gone even further than Tyrrell and argued that such apparitions require the hypothesis of some kind of ghostly or "astral" *matter* which behaves in strikingly "non-material" ways and which is even more independent of the minds of the percipients involved than Tyrrell's "idea forms." On Hart's hypothesis, for example, the fact that two out of the four percipients in Case 6 saw Mr. H. and others did not is explained, not on the hypothesis that only two of the percipients telepathically cooperated in generating the apparition, but by the hypothesis that Mr. H. had a wandering "astral" or "subtle" body, which for some reason was perceptible to only two out of the four possible percipients.

I believe that this controversy over reported cases of collective hallucination within the field of psychical research is relevant to the philosophical analysis of the Vijñānavāda, for the Vijñānavādins were committed, in effect, to Edmund Gurney's purely *telepathic* explanation of collective hallucinations. According to the Vijñānavādins, the only thing that exists is a succession of mental impressions (*vijñapti*) in the mind streams of a multiplicity of individuals. This view precludes the hypothesis of Tyrrell's "idea forms" just as much as it does Hart's hypothesis of a "subtle" or "astral" matter.

Take the bizarre cat (or cats) of Case 3 as an example. According to the Vijñānavāda, there is no "astral cat" (as Hart and others have suggested); nor is the cat an "idea form" or "thought form" which has some kind of separate or independent existence from the minds of the percipients, as Tyrrell suggested. According to the Vijñānavāda, there in fact is no cat, either as a physical object, an "astral" object, or an "idea form." Any belief to the effect that there is an objective cat of any sort is an error, for there is in fact only the impression (*vijñapti*) of a cat in A's mind and an impression of a cat in B's mind. On this view, there is a cat that A "sees" (i.e. A's cat-percept) and a cat that B "sees" (i.e. B's cat percept), but no cat per se. The fact that both A and B have exactly identical impressions of a cat is explained by the hypothesis that the two minds are in direct, telepathic contact.

The Vijñānavādins' view is therefore identical with Edmund Gurney's purely telepathic theory of the reported cases of collective hallucination. As such, it is subject to the same kinds of objections that Tyrrell, Hart and others have levelled against Gurney's theory. However, the Vijñānavādins wished to extend the telepathic hypothesis to cover the case of *ordinary* perception as well. This, so far as I know, extends the telepathic hypothesis much further than any of its adherents even in the field of psychical research have desired to push it.

The discussion of Cases 1 through 6 has shown, I believe, that even in these cases (which fail to fully satisfy the Determinateness Principle) the purely telepathic theory is to some degree problematic. If this is so, then a fortiori the Vijñānavādins' extension of the telepathic theory to cover *ordinary* perception (i.e. to cover cases which ex hypothesi do fully satisfy the Determinateness Principle) could be expected to be even more problematic. The reasons are purely philosophical, and have nothing to do with the empirical question of whether such "super-ESP" exists.

Let us consider once again Vasubandhu's formulation of the idealism of the Vijñānavāda in the Viṃśatikā. According to Vasubandhu, the experiences of the denizens of hell are purely mental phenomena, like dreams. However, he says, the experiences of the multitude of beings in the hell realms are not purely private. They *are* private in the sense that the experiences are not experiences of anything outside the mind streams of the individuals that experience them, but they are public, too, in the sense that the experiences of the beings who "dream" their torments are *correlated* with each other. The things that the hell beings experience are determined in some fashion by their *karma* and their acquired dispositions (*vāsanās*). According to Vasubandhu, the same thing applies to *our* world. On his view, even *our* world is a Collective Hallucination.

As we have seen, there are problems involved in applying the Vijñānavāda view (i.e. the purely telepathic hypothesis) to the cases of "ordinary" collective hallucination. However, the problems are of a far more serious kind when the purely telepathic theory of perception is applied to all of our ordinary, waking perceptions. The reason is, simply, that ordinary, waking perceptions are in certain essential respects even less like single-percipient hallucinations than the reported cases of collective hallucinations are.

One of the main difficulties confronting the Vijñānavāda doctrine of Collective Hallucination is the fact that an ordinary perceptual object continues to exist indefinitely, and does *not* suddenly vanish without apparent cause on the spot. The purely telepathic hypothesis has some plausibility in the case of "ordinary" collective hallucinations like Cases 1 through 6 above because, given the way the apparitions suddenly arise and vanish, there is no compelling reason to suppose that the apparent perceptual objects continue to exist when the percipients involved cease to perceive them. This is, perhaps, the main reason why we feel some inclination to say that a collective hallucination is simply two identical hallucinations that occur simultaneously to two different people. On the other hand, we are *not* inclined to say, when three people A, B and C are looking at a tree, that there are really three "trees," all of which are purely mental — i.e., the tree-percept in A's mind, the tree-percept in B's mind and the tree-percept in C's mind. One of the reasons, of course, is that ordinary objects (by definition) *fully* satisfy the Determinateness Principle.

In Case 3 there is presumably no question of how the apparitional cat is related to my cat or your cat, or to any other embodied creature or physical object in the world. However, if A, B and C are looking at a real cat, it makes no sense to say that the cat is constructed by the (subconcious) minds of A, B and C *even if* we could attribute to their minds super-ESP, for ordinary cats are not idiosyncratic, sui generis objects. If A, B and C are looking at a real cat, they are not looking at something which simply *looks* (for the moment) *like* a cat. They are looking at a cat whose specific characteristics are to be explained by its birth from other cats, its genetic structure etc. Unlike hallucinated cats, ordinary, real cats belong to a species, genus, family etc. of biological organisms, and it is these generic features, which connect ordinary cats with other cats and other living creatures, which explain the perceptual characteristics which they do have.

This consideration raises problems for any purely phenomenalistic view which would identify perceptual objects with their mental or sensory appearances in the way that Vasubandhu suggests. If we were to take such a phenomenalism seriously, we would have to suppose that the joint percipients of an ordinary cat are free to hallucinate any cat their subconscious minds can agree on hallucinating. But on the assumption that the cat is an ordinary cat — i.e. the kind of object that we have discovered cats to be — this supposition is untenable, for if the cat is a real cat, there is a cellular, genetic and even atomic structure to the cat, which *explains* its phenomenal or perceptual characteristics.

Any phenomenalist who wanted to accommodate this essential feature of ordinary cats within his world view would presumably have to say that A, B and C, if they proceeded to examine an ordinary cat more carefully, would simply make up the microstructure of the cat as they go along. But such a suggestion could not be made to work. The philosophical problem is not just that this hypothesis would require us to invoke an enormous amount of ESP on the part of the percipients. The more fundamental problem is that what A "discovers" about the microstructure of the cat must corroborate not only what B and C "discover" about the micro-structure of the cat; it must also "corroborate" what all other investigators past, present and future "discover" about the microstructure of cats. Furthermore, even if this could be made plausible according to the super-ESP hypothesis, the problem would remain that on this phenomenalistic view it would be A, B and C's previous impression (i.e. hallucination) of the cat which would constrain their later "discoveries" of the microstructure of the cat. However, the view that the phenomenal characteristics of things are epistemologically prior to the structure of things which we discover through scientific methods surely has the matter the wrong way around. Given our present knowledge of the way the world actually works, this hypothesis would violate the fundamental principle that the complex should be explained by the simple, and not the other way around.

Another serious objection to such phenomenalism is that it cannot accommodate the notion that a perceptual object which is seen at at a certain time by a particular percipient or percipients continues to exist at a later time when those percipients are no longer seeing it. As Bishop Berkeley pointed out, this is a fundamental problem with which any idealist philosophy must come to terms. Berkeley's solution of the problem was that "unperceived" objects always exist in God's infinite mind. This solution to the problem, of course, was not available to the Vijñānavādins.

The evidence from Vasubandhu's Triṃśikā 3 and Xuan Zang's commentary on it (CWSL 2-4) suggests that the Vijñānavādins attempted to meet this difficulty — without, of course, abandoning the Many Finite Minds Principle — by extending the notion of perception and knowledge to include the notion of unconsciously (*asaṃvidita*) perceived objects. On this view, all objects which are not *consciously* perceived by some finite mind or other are *unconsciously* perceived. Thus, on the conscious level, pure phenomenalism is preserved, and objects (and/or qualities of those objects) arise and vanish depending on whether or not some sentient being or other actually perceives them. Conscious perception, however, is only one small part of the matter, for beyond the range of ordinary introspection there is a much vaster realm of perception which is unconscious. According to this modified version of the Mind Only and Many Finite Minds Principles, perceptual objects alternate between being perceived consciously (by the "physical" senses) and being perceived unconsciously (perhaps by means of "non-physical" senses). It is this unconscious knowledge, according to CWSL 2-4, that accounts for the impression that we have of a common or universal world of experience which is external to our individual minds.

As was pointed out in the last chapter, Xuan Zang compares the world to the lights of many individual lamps which are placed in a room and which appear *as if* there were only one lamp. This analogy appears to be misleading, however, for it fails to accommodate the crucial fact that it is the coordination or correlation of a virtually uncountable number of *perceptions* that has to be explained. A better analogy would be that of billions of movie projectors (the finite minds of sentient beings) in a very large room (the universe), each projecting its own movie (perceptions). To make this analogy correspond to the Determinateness Principle, we would also have to suppose that all the projectors were, as Vasubandhu puts it, in "mutual correspondence" (*paras-paratah̤*) with each other, so as to give the impression of a common, external world.

By far the most natural way of accounting for correspondences of this extent and detail, of course, would be to suppose that all of the movies were of the same thing, but shot from different points of view. This appears to be the instinctive assumption that is made by common sense. However, this explanation was not available to the Vijñānavādins because the Vijñānavādins held that there is nothing but streams of percepts in the minds of a collection of individuals. This is perhaps the central epistemological problem confronting the Vijñānavāda, and it is pretty clear that Xuan Zang's analogy of the lamps does nothing to resolve or even mitigate it. Even if the hypothesis of super-telepathy could be used to explain the correspondences amongst all these various projectors (i.e. finite minds), the Vijñānavādin apparently has no way of accommodating the common sense notion that there are objects which are not perceived by any finite mind at any given time but which *would* be perceived if there were a finite sentient being in the vicinity looking in its direction with normally functioning senses etc.

It is hard to see how the Vijñānavāda could accommodate this common sense notion without radically reinterpreting the doctrine that objects represent merely a stream of percepts in a multiplicity of finite minds. In order to deal adequately with the problem without abandoning the Mind Only and Many Finite Minds Principles, one would have to suppose that the apparently finite minds of sentient beings are, at the unconscious level, virtually omniscient. Many things even on our planet are not perceived by the senses of any sentient being at any given time; and there is a much larger number of things which go unperceived in this way on other worlds and planets (cf. the "vast chiliocosms" of Buddhist cosmology). To accommodate this "common sense" fact *without* supposing that sentient beings at the unconscious levels of their minds are in fact infinite, the Vijñānavādin would have to show that every object in the universe exists in the mind of some finite mind or other, but not in all minds. It is not clear how this could be done. For example, would "unperceived" objects exist in the unconscious mind of the being that was nearest to it in "space" at any given time? Obviously, a principle of this kind would be arbitrary, and would also be subject to the objection that the locus of an "unperceived" object would always be moving from one unconscious mind to another as sentient beings moved about in "space."

The result of the preceding discussion seems to me to be this. Provided that one is not a solipsist, and that one is prepared to acknowledge the validity and necessity of inferences beyond what is immediately given from moment to moment in the stream of one's own impressions, one has a choice between the following alternatives:

(1) One can adopt the materialist position, and argue that mind is nothing but matter.[5]

(2) One can adopt the dualist position, and argue that a world of matter is the object/cause of our mental impressions.

(3) One can adopt the Kantian position, and argue that there is an external object, but that this object is a mere *Ding an sich* which is essentially unknowable.

(4) One can adopt the idealist position, and argue that everything is nothing but mind. *However*, this position, in order to make any sense, presupposes the existence of an infinite mind.

Although I shall not argue the point here, it seems to me that the second of these alternatives comes closest to the pre-critical view of common sense. It may even be the *correct* metaphysical view. However, it does seem to me that (2) represents a very unstable position between the other alternatives, for it does not take much pushing to making (2) collapse in the direction of either (1), (3) or (4).

To see why, consider the difficulties in the dualist view which were raised by Bishop Berkeley in his refutation of the existence of matter. Berkeley argued that since "direct" perception is essentially just a matter of having certain experiences, matter (as something external to mind or experiences) must be unreal. His reasoning was as follows. Since matter is not directly perceived (i.e. is never part of the actual content of our minds) it must be inferred. But, Berkeley argued, the view that matter is inferred is untenable, because in the inference to matter existing outside of mind one cannot intelligibly describe the thing whose existence is to be inferred.

Compare the kind of inference that the dualist wants to make with that of inferring fire from smoke. (This is not an example that Berkeley actually uses, but it will serve our present purposes.) Berkeley argues, in effect, that since we can know through perception what fire is, we know what it means to infer the existence of fire on the basis of observing smoke. For Berkeley, however, the fire that we know through perception is essentially *mental*. He also argued that using the data of immediate experience to infer the existence of a matter lying entirely outside experience is an entirely different matter from ordinary inferences, for the former inference, according to Berkeley, involves going from perception (i.e. something which is essentially a matter of direct experience) to something which we have never experienced and never could experience. Hence, according to Berkeley, the view that matter exists must be rejected.[6]

It must be conceded that Berkeley's conclusion is odd. However, I do think that Berkeley succeeded in showing that the dualist view and the materialist view, once they have been subjected to examination, are also much odder than they might appear to be pre-critically.[7] It also seems to me that Berkeley's formulation of idealism — though it certainly departs from common sense — is much closer to common sense than it is sometimes thought to be. Berkeley agreed that an object continues to exist when it is no longer perceived by any finite being. However, he insisted that when the tree is not being perceived it continues to exist as the same *kind* of thing it is perceived to be when we *are* perceiving it. (For example, it continues to have green leaves and make a rustling sound when the wind blows through its leaves etc.) This proposition (call it B for Berkeley) is no doubt what we do think, pre-critically, about unperceived objects. For Berkeley, however, proposition B entails that a perceptual object continues to exist *as an essentially mental object*. Here, surely, his views depart from common sense. However, it is not easy to see how to separate Berkeley's conclusion (which common sense rejects) from proposition B (which it surely accepts). This is one of the things that makes the Berkeleian arguments so interesting philosophically.

The most desperate alternative of all is, of course, solipsism. According to the solipsist, there is only one mind: the solipsist's mind. If this doctrine is true, it means that I, Tom Wood, alone exist. If there is anyone out there reading this book that I have written, the doctrine that I, Tom Wood, alone exist is false. Conversely, if you are convinced that the book that you are reading was written by another sentient being, then *you* must conclude that solipsism is false. Only if you could convince yourself that you alone exist could *you* be a convinced and consistent solipsist.[8]

As was pointed out in chapters 6-8, there seem to be some solipsistic tendencies in the later (*nyāyānusārin*) Vijñānavāda. (For example, it is fairly natural to read the *sahopalambhādi* principle in a solipsistic way.) Note, however, that a formulation of idealism like Berkeley's is not solipsistic. Berkeley would have agreed with the *sahopalambhādi* principle in so far as it denies the existence of something existing outside of any mind whatever, but would have rejected the suggestion that the world exists in one's own mind. Berkeley recognized the validity of making inferences beyond one's *own* immediate stream of experience, but he insisted that inference could only take one from something mental to something else that is also mental (i.e. either a mind or something perceived by a mind). We can make such inferences, according to Berkeley, because we are directly acquainted with mind through our own experience. For Berkeley the inference to other minds and to things perceived by other minds is therefore quite natural, for it simply involves inferring from one's own experience to someone *else's* experience. Berkeley argued, however, that the inference from one's own experience to something which is supposed to exist outside one's own and *anyone else's* experience is quite unnatural and in fact unintelligible.

Note also that most formulations of idealism, like Berkeley's, do not involve the assertion that the world is unreal. It is true that many idealist philosophers use phenomena like dreams and illusions to point to the reality of mind and consciousness, and to show that "direct" or "immediate" perception is basically just a matter of having certain experiences of sight, smell, touch, sound etc. However, idealism would involve the view that the world is unreal only if one were to make the further assumption that a perceptual object ceases to exist — as a dream or an hallucination does — when the person or persons who perceive it cease to perceive it. Berkeley rejected this kind of illusionism, but he clearly recognized that an idealist can reject it only by holding that the world exists in an infinite mind. This is the move that the Vijñānavādin, as a Buddhist, did not and could not make.

If the arguments I have presented are sound, the denial of the existence of matter must imply that the world exists, not in my mind or in the mind of a collectivity of independent finite minds, but in an infinite mind. It might be possible to conceive of such a mind either dualistically or monistically, but in any case it seems highly unlikely that one could ever make any sense of the idea that the world is "mind only" without positing an infinite and omniscient mind of one sort or another.

Conclusion

It has been my intention in the preceding chapters to throw some light on the following question: To what extent did the Vijñānavādins believe in some kind of Absolute?

A number of scholars [e.g. A. K. Chatterjee (1975: 133-134) and C. L. Tripathi (1972: 303-304, 334)] have interpreted the Vijñānavāda as an absolute idealism of a fairly typical kind. According to this fairly widespread interpretation, the Vijñānavādins believed in an absolute mind, and were therefore doctrinally quite close to the views of the Advaita Vedānta.[1]

From a purely philosophical point of view, such interpretations are quite natural. Since the Vijñānavādins (for doctrinal reasons) could not have been solipsists, and since it is hard to see how a determinate and non-solipsistic world can be accounted for on idealist lines without invoking an absolute mind of some kind or other, it is not too surprising that many scholars have been tempted to read Vedāntist or quasi-Vedāntist views into the Vijñānavāda. Nevertheless, interpretations of this kind are quite inferential, in the sense that they seem to be based largely on the assumption that the Vijñānavādins must have held such views because that is the only way idealist doctrines can be made plausible or tenable philosophically.

I would agree that many of the Vijñānavādins' doctrines imply — on purely philosophical grounds — the existence of an Absolute of the kind that scholars like Tripathi and Chatterjee have attributed to them. But what this actually means, I think, is that there are compelling philosophical reasons for thinking that the Vijñānavādins *should* have been absolute idealists, even though the texts show rather clearly that they weren't. This way of describing the matter seems preferable because there are many *textual* reasons for thinking that the Vijñānavādins remained faithful to fundamental Buddhist doctrines, all of which are quite incompatible with a metaphysics of absolute idealism. For this reason, one should resist the temptation to interpret the Vijñānavādins as simply crypto-

Vedāntists. The actual situation is a good deal more complex than this.

It is very important, in interpreting the Vijñānavāda, to avoid the assumption that philosophical commitments and doctrinal commitments always lead in the same direction. This may very well be true of a large number of philosophical traditions, but it is particularly worth stressing in the case of the Vijñānavādins, who (like the great majority of the philosophers in India) were concerned to uphold a body of received doctrine. In this respect, the classical Indian philosophers are rather like the medieval scholastic philosophers of the West. Indeed, the charge has been levelled against both classical Indian philosophy and medieval Western philosophy that the philosophers in both traditions were merely religious philosophers and that their work is therefore irrelevant to philosophy as it is now understood in the modern world. Both of these evaluations are unwarranted, of course, but it is true that the philosophers of India usually did philosophize within a dogmatic and religious context and with a dogmatic and religious purpose, and this fact sometimes created certain tensions for them, as indeed it frequently did for the scholastics of the Western medieval tradition as well.

In the case of the Vijñānavāda, caution in this matter must extend even to the interpretation of the assertion that everything is mind only (*citta-mātra*, *vijñāna-mātra*). The passages in the Mahāyāna *sūtras* and the Vijñānavāda *śāstras* that assert that everything is mind only have quite naturally been taken by Western philosophers — and by Indian philosophers influenced by idealist systems like the Advaita Vedānta — as implying a straightforward absolutist doctrine. I believe that this interpetation — at least from a doctrinal point of view — is quite mistaken. It is true that there are some statements in the literature of the Vijñānavāda that can be construed as implying some kind of Absolute, but this Absolute is definitely not (as is generally supposed) an absolute *mind*. The texts are quite explicit on this point, for they consistently describe suchness, the perfected nature etc. as non-mind (*acitta*).

It is surprising to find such an assertion in an idealist philosophy that claims that everything is mind only. However, as was pointed out in chapters 1-3, the doctrinal basis for this assertion can be traced to the oldest Buddhist teachings. These teachings, for the most part, take a wholly negative view of mind. According to the great majority of these texts, mind is only one of the five *skandhas* and, as such, consists of stream of impermanent *dharmas* which are destined to be extinguished in the final *nirvāṇa*.[2]

For an idealist doctrine like the Vijñānavāda, this raises the following problem. If there is an Absolute which is not mind (*acitta*), how can it be said that everything is mind only? Note that if an Absolute is anything at all, then of course it exists, even if it consists merely of intangible, absolute mind. This could hardly be denied without playing fast and loose with terms like "existence" and "non-existence," or meddling with fundamental logical laws like the law of the excluded middle and the law of non-contradiction.

Must we say, therefore, that the state which is said to be *acitta* is simply a state of nothingness or non-being? From a purely logical point of view it would appear that it must be so, since the early Buddhist texts teach that everything is impermanent, and that cessation from *saṃsāra* (i.e. *nirvāṇa*) is to be attained by the cessation of everything that is impermanent. This, in fact, is exactly how the Sautrāntikas, who claimed to base their views exclusively on the canonical *sūtra* teachings, interpreted *nirvāṇa*. According to this school, *nirvāṇa* is not a real or positive *ens* (*bhāva*), but instead is simply the extinction of all the factors or elements (*dharmas*) of existence. The Sautrāntika view appears to be amply supported by the early Buddhist texts. For example, it is supported by 1) the way the doctrine of the four-fold noble truths is formulated, 2) by the straightforward meaning of the terms "*śūnya*" and "*śūnyatā*," and 3) by the fact that the early teachings consistently use a purely negative terminology to describe the summum bonum ("*nirvāṇa*," "*nirodha*," etc.).

This purely negative interpretation of *nirvāṇa* was so orthodox and so well-established that the Vijñānavādins could not have negated it completely, even if they had wanted to. The evidence, in fact, is that they did not even feel the need to so, for the Vijñānavādins, like the Mādhyamikas, held that their views were quite orthodox, and in fact even more Buddhist than the Buddhism of the other schools. Nevertheless, signs of tension between the later and the the earlier teachings are not hard to find.[3]

(1) In Triṃś. 21, Vasubandhu asserts that it is of the very essence of mind that it arises and perishes depending on causes and conditions. In Triṃś. 25, however, Vasubandhu identifies *vijñapti-mātratā* with the immutable suchness (*tathatā*), which in the Mahāyāna is the same thing as emptiness (*śūnyatā*). Triṃś. 21 is quite orthodox (indeed, what it asserts can be found in all the Buddhist texts), but Triṃś. 25 is not, for it identifies the essence of mind (one of the five impermanent *skandhas* of the human personality) with the immutable suchness. Triṃś. 25, therefore, raises questions like the following: If the essence of mind is just emptiness, suchness etc., why do the early texts say that mind or consciousness becomes extinct in *nirvāṇa*? Furthermore, Triṃś. 21 and 25, taken together, lead to a contradiction, for together they imply that mind itself (*vijñaptimātratā*) is not the same thing as the essence or self nature of mind (*vijñāna-svabhāva*). As was argued in chapter 3, this makes no logical sense, nor can it be supported by either Western or Indian grammatical and linguistic analysis.

(2) Since mind is impermanent and dependent on causes and conditions it is *saṃsāric*. Therefore mind, at least within the context of Buddhist doctrine, cannot be regarded as an Absolute. According to Xuan Zang and Sthiramati, therefore, what is immutable is *citta-tā* or *citta-dharmatā*.

On closer analysis, it turns out that this *citta-tā* or *citta-dharmatā* is just emptiness (*śūnyatā*). It is therefore not mind, but non-mind (*acitta*). A rather large number of passages in the Vijñānavāda writings also show that the Vijñānavādins regarded this *citta-dharmatā* or *śūnyatā* as a kind of Absolute (e.g. Triṃś. 29-30, TSN 37-38, MV 1.13-22). Nevertheless, the plain meaning of "*śūnyatā*" in the Buddhist writings and in Sanskrit generally is just "voidness" or "emptiness." Hence questions of the following sort arise: How can the Absolute be identified with *śūnyatā*? And how could *śūnyatā* or *tathatā* be the basis (*āśraya*) for the phenomenal properties of Buddhahood (as Xuan Zang suggests it is in the Cheng wei shilun)?

In order to understand why these contradictions and difficulties arose, it is essential to remember that the Mahāyāna teachings evolved from earlier Buddhist teachings. The earliest Buddhist teachings (i.e. the common body of teachings which are found in the *sūtras* of the Pāli canon and the partial canons that have been preserved in the Chinese and Tibetan Āgamas) do not teach that the aim of the Buddhist life is to be free from both *saṃsāra* and *nirvāṇa* or from both existence and non-existence. According to the earliest Buddhist texts, *nirvāṇa* is simply the release from *saṃsāra* (i.e. existence), all of which is said to be impermanent and necessarily implicated in suffering.

The Mahāyānists modified these early teachings in at least two ways. First of all, they developed the doctine of the *apratiṣṭhita-nirvāṇa*, i.e. the idea of an active, post-Kuśinagarī Buddha who remained active after his physical death for the salvation of all sentient beings. Secondly, they advanced the view that all *dharmas* are in essence already void and in some sense therefore essentially non-existent. In the hands of the Mahāyānists these notions seem, at least at first glance, to involve commitment to some kind of an Absolute.

Nevertheless, the Mahāyānists remained Buddhists doctrinally. As such, they both needed and wanted to fit their own views into the large body of doctrines and texts that were regarded as canonical and authoritative by all the other Buddhist schools, or at least to demonstrate the continuity of their own doctrines with those earlier teachings. Were it not for this fact, the idealist doctrines of the Vijñānavāda might very well have been a good deal more straightforward than they actually are. Much of the difficulty of understanding the Vijñānavāda texts, and many of the intricacies and complexities of these texts, seem to be due to the fact that the Vijñānavādins wanted to reconcile their own doctrines with these earlier, canonical teachings. Given the nature of these earlier teachings, it could have been predicted that the Vijñānavāda doctrines would be confusing and convoluted (and even inconsistent), for the earlier doctrines seem to have been formulated with great care to preclude just the kind of absolutist interpretation that the Vijñānavādins wanted to give them.

APPENDIXES

APPENDIX I

Authors and Texts

This Appendix gives a brief account of some of the important authors and texts referred to in this work: the Abhidharma-kośa-(bhāṣya) [AK(B)] and Abhidharma-kośa-sphuṭārthā-vyākhyā [AKSV], the Madhyānta-vibhāga [MV], Viṃśatikā [Viṃś.], Triṃśikā [Triṃś.], Tri-svabhāva-nirdeśa [TSN], Saṃtānāntara-siddhi [SS], Cheng wei shilun [CWSL], Tattva-saṃgraha-pañjikā [TS(P)], and Saṃtānāntara-dūṣaṇa [SD].

Abhidharma-kośa-(bhāṣya). The Abhidharma-kośa (AK) is work in verse which belongs primarily to the Sarvāstivāda school of the Hīnayāna. The Abhidharma-kośa-bhāṣya (AKB) is a prose commentary on the AK which mainly follows the views of the Sautrāntika school of the Hīnayāna. The AKSV is another commentary by Yaśomitra.

The authorship of the AKB is ascribed to a certain Vasubandhu (fl. 360 C.E.). The prevailing scholarly view seems to be that this same Vasubandhu also wrote the AK, the differences between the two texts being explained on the hypothesis that Vasubandhu changed his views between the time he wrote the AK and the time he wrote the AKB. According to a tradition recorded by Paramārtha (fl. 450 C.E.), which appears to be regarded as reliable by most modern scholars, Vasubandhu continued to change his views even after his composition of the AKB, for according to Paramārtha Vasubandhu was converted to the Mahāyāna by his half-brother Asaṅga after he had written the AKB. According to Paramārtha, the Viṃśatikā and the Triṃśikā were written by the same Vasubandhu who wrote the AKB. This identification of the Vasubandhu who wrote the AKB with Vasubandhu the Vijñānavādin was challenged in 1951 by E. Frauwallner. He received heavy criticism for postulating two different Vasubandhus from P. S. Jaini (1958) and others. Frauwallner (1956: 351; 1961: 131, n. 10) later modified his theory of the two Vasubandhus. According to the modified theory, there were two different Vasubandhus, *both* of whom were converted to the Mahāyāna.

My citations from the Abhidharma literature in the present work are confined to the AK(B) and the AKSV. Confining attention to this work and its related commentaries can be justified on a number of grounds.

First, the AK(B) became at a very early date the most important of the Abhidharma texts. So great was its prestige, in fact, that it was used as an introductory Abhidharma text by many of the other schools of Buddhism. (It was also the only Abhidharma text to be translated in its entirety into the Tibetan canon.) Secondly, even if one were to reject the identity of the two Vasubandhus, the relation between the AK(B) and the Vijñānavāda is obviously very close, as is evidenced by the frequency of the citations of the AK(B) by Vijñānavādin writers like Xuan Zang.

I have also focussed attention on the AK(B) because (as I argue in chapter 1) the Sautrāntika view that the *asaṃskṛta dharmas* are unreal (*adravya, prajñaptisat*) appears to be justified by the earliest Buddhist *sūtras*. I am aware that this claim is controversial, but focussing attention on the AK(B) could easily be justified in the present context even if one were to reject this claim, for the Sautrāntika view that the uncompounded *dharmas* are mere designation (*prajñaptisat*) rather than real entities (*dravya, vastu*) obviously has close affinities with the *Mahāyāna* view that all *dharmas* are void (*sarva-dharma-śūnyatā*). Hence the Sautrāntika Abhidharma has a special importance for the Vijñānavāda even apart from the question of the interpretation of the early Buddhist texts on the subject of the *asaṃskṛtas, nirvāṇa* etc.

For the AK(B) I have used the edition by Dvārikādāsa Śāstrī (DŚ). (References to DŚ are to *kośa-sthāna* and page number.) There is also an earlier edition of the same text by P. Pradhan (1967). Both of these editions are based primarily on the Sanskrit MS. of the AK(B) (dating from the 12th or 13th century) which was discovered by Rāhula Sāṅkṛtyāyana in Tibet at the monastery of Ngor in 1935. A Nepalese Sanskrit MS. of the Sphuṭārthā (Vyākhyā) of Yaśomitra (AKSV) had been discovered somewhat earlier.

Another important source of information on the AK(B) is Xuan Zang's Chinese translation of the text. For the Xuan Zang text I have used the 1971 reprint of the translation into French by de La Vallée Poussin (1923-31). There are significant divergences between the text of the AK(B) as preserved in Poussin's translation and the text of the AK(B) as it is found in the Sanskrit editions of the text by Pradhan and Dvārikādāsa Śāstrī. Dr. Subhadra Jha (1983: ix-x), for example, has compared the Poussin and Pradhan editions of the AK(B) as follows:

> Both the treatises go back to the same source no doubt, but they are not identical in respect of the contents. The work represented in Vallée Poussin's book is more elaborate than that presented in Pradhan's edition, almost at every point, so much so that they form two differing redactions: one smaller version (hence plausibly likely to be considered nearer to the original) and the second a bigger version; the latter may be considered to be based upon an enlarged version of the first work.

Madhyānta-vibhāga (The Discrimination between the Middle and the Extremes). The Madhyānta-vibhāga is undoubtedly a very old Vijñānavāda text. Its authorship is traditionally ascribed to either Maitreyanātha or Ārya Asaṅga (fl. 350 C.E.). There is also a commentary (*bhāṣya*) on the text (MVB) which is ascribed to Vasubandhu, and another commentary (*ṭīkā*) on Vasubandhu's commentary by Sthiramati (MVBṬ). If the *bhāṣya* is authentic, the Madhyānta-vibhāga is indoubtedly an older text than either the Viṃśatikā or the Triṃśikā, which were written by Vasubandhu.

The opening verse of the MVB refers to the author (or promulgator) of the text and to the "speaker" of the text. Sthiramati, in the introduction to the MVBṬ, specifies Maitreyanātha as the "promulgator" (*pranetṛ*), Ārya Asaṅga as the "speaker" (*vaktṛ*), and Vasubandhu as the commentator of the Madhyānta-vibhāga.

There has been much scholarly controversy over the identity of Maitreyanātha. There are references in the Buddhist texts to a Maitreya who is said to be the "future Buddha," i.e., the next individual who is destined to become a full Buddha and revitalize the religion (*dharma*) taught by Gautama Buddha after it has declined and degenerated through the passage of time. Some scholars, like E. Obermiller (1931) have contended that the

Maitreyanātha referred to in the MVBṬ was this future Buddha. According to this view, there was no historical figure by the name of Maitreya who had anything to do with the authorship or promulgation of the MV, and by the term "promulgator" (*pranetṛ*) Sthiramati simply means that the future Buddha, Maitreya, inspired Asaṅga with the teachings from the Tuṣita heaven. Other scholars, notably Hakuju Ui (1929) and G. Tucci (1930), have claimed that Asaṅga did have a human teacher named Maitreya, from whom he received the MV. [However, Tucci (1956: 14, n. 1) seems to have changed his opinion later in the light of Demiéville's (1954) remarks on the subject.] On the view that Maitreya was an historical personage, the real author of the MV was not Asaṅga, but Maitreyanātha.

I have used the edition of the MV by Tatia and Thakur (1967), which appeared as Vol. X of the Tibetan Sanskrit Works Series published by the K. P. Jayaswal Research Institute in Patna.

This edition is based on Rāhula Sāṅkṛtyāyana's photocopies of a Sanskrit MS., found in the monastery of Ngor in Tibet, which are presently in the possession of the Jayaswal Research Institute. The MS. was written in a proto-Maithili-cum-Bengali script which was prevalent in the 11th and 12th centuries in North Eastern India. The orthography of this MS. does not conform to pure classical Sanskrit. (Some consonants, for example, are reduplicated.) Tatia and Thakur removed these orthographic peculiarities in order to make the text conform to classical Sanskrit.

The original Sanskrit text of the *ṭīkā* by Sthiramati was discovered in Nepal by Prof. Sylvain Lévi. This text has been edited by Susumu Yamaguchi (1934). Another text of Sthiramati's *ṭīkā* was also discovered about the same time by G. Tucci.

The text and my own translation of the first chapter of the Madhyānta-vibhāga are given in chapter 1.

Viṃśatikā (The Twenty Verses) and *Triṃśikā* (Thirty Verses). These works were written by Vasubandhu (fl. 360 C.E.), the disciple (and perhaps the half-brother) of Ārya Asaṅga. Vasubandhu is the most important single writer of the Vijñānavāda, and is in a sense the real founder of this school.

Sanskrit MSS. of the Viṃśatikā and Triṃśikā were discovered in Nepal in the 1920s by Prof. Sylvain Lévi and Hemrāj Śarman, Rājguru and chief librarian of the government of Nepal. One MS. contained the Triṃśikā and the commentary on it by Sthiramati; the other contained the Viṃśatikā and Vasubandhu's autocommentary on it (VV). The MS. of the Viṃś. lacked the first page (which included the first two *kārikās* and the commentary on them); Lévi "retranslated" this on the basis of the extant Tibetan and Chinese translations.

My translation of the Triṃśikā appears in chapter 3. My translation of the Viṃśatikā appears in chapter 5.

Cheng wei shilun (Treatise on Mind Only). This is a commentary on the Triṃśikā by Xuan Zang (596-664 C.E.), one of the most important writers of the Vijñānavāda. Xuan Zang's translation of the Triṃśikā and his commentary on the text is written in Chinese; its Sanskrit title was probably Vijñapti-mātratā-siddhi-śāstra. Xuan Zang's Cheng wei shilun is the "root text" or foundational text of the *wei shi* (Consciousness Only) school of Chinese Buddhism.

Xuan Zang's Cheng wei shilun was translated into French by L. de La Vallée Poussin (1928-48) as *La Siddhi de Hiuan-Tsang*. All of my citations from Xuan Zang's work are taken from Poussin's translation. I am also greatly indebted to Poussin's voluminous notes on this text.

The Cheng wei shilun has been translated into English by Wei Tat (1973). His translation usually follows Poussin's French translation of the text rather closely, but lacks Poussin's notes.

Dr. Henry Rosemont, Jr., the editor of the present monograph series, has kindly provided me with the Pin-yin romanizations of the Chinese names and terms used in the text.

Tri-svabhāva-nirdeśa (The Analysis of the Three Natures). The authorship of this work is uncertain.

There are four MSS. of the Tri-svabhāva-nirdeśa. Two of them are in Sanskrit, and two are in Tibetan [Tola and Dragonetti (1983)]. One of the Tibetan translations attributes the text to Vasubandhu; the other attributes it to Nāgārjuna.

The work is definitely not by Nāgārjuna, but the attribution to Nāgārjuna by one of the Tibetan translations does throw some doubt on Vasubandhu's authorship of the text. Furthermore, many of Vasubandhu's authentic works have commentaries on them. The

Tri-svabhāva-nirdeśa does not, and this is a further reason (though certainly not a decisive one) for doubting Vasubandhu's authorship of the work.

One of the two Tibetan translations is found in Vol. 58 of the Bstan-'gyur. This volume of the Bstan-'gyur contains the "five original treatises" of Vasubandhu, i.e. the Triṃśikā, Viṃśatikā, Pañca-skandhaka, Vyākhyā-yukti and the Karma-siddhi. The Tibetan translation of the Tri-svabhāva-nirdeśa which is attributed to Vasubandhu is placed between the Viṃśatikā and the Pañca-skandhaka. This treatise is in 38 verses (*kārikās*), and is entitled "The Exposition of the Three Natures" (Tri-svabhāva-nirdeśa).

The other Tibetan translation is contained in Vol. 17 of the Bstan-'gyur, which contains works ascribed to Nāgārjuna and other Mādhyamikas. This volume of the Bstan-'gyur contains a Tibetan translation of basically the same text as the one found in Vol. 58, except that this translation contains 40 verses, and is attributed to Nāgārjuna. The title of this translation of the text is "On Entering into the Three Natures" (Svabhāva-traya-praveśa-siddhi).

There are four editions of the two Sanskrit MSS.: one by S. Yamaguchi (1931); one by L. de La Vallée Poussin (1932-33); one by S. Mukhopadhyaya (1939); and one by Tola and Dragonetti (1983). I have used the edition by Poussin. Incidentally, the Sanskrit MSS. are apparently not totally reliable, for both Poussin and Yamaguchi corrected their MSS. in the light of the Tibetan translations.

Saṃtānāntara-siddhi (The Proof of the Existence of Other Minds). This work is attributed to Dharmakīrti (fl. 640 C.E.), one of the most important writers of the school of Vijñānavāda logicians. The SS appears to have been inspired largely by Vasubandhu's Viṃśatikā.

Dharmakīrti's text is no longer extant in the Sanskrit, but it has been preserved in Tibetan in the Bstan-'gyur, along with commentaries (also in Tibetan) by the Indian commentator Vinītadeva and the Mongolian monk Ṅag-dbaṅ bstan-dar.

A free rendering of this text is given in Appendix II. The presentation of the text there is based entirely on a comparison of the translation into English by Hidenori Kitagawa (1955) and the translation by H.C. Gupta into English (1969) from Stcherbatsky's earlier translation into the Russian (1922).

Tattva-saṃgraha (A Compendium of True Principles). This is a work by Śāntarakṣita (fl. 750 C.E.). There is an elaborate commentary on it by his disciple Kamalaśīla (fl. 770 C.E.) called the Tattva-saṃgraha-pañjikā (TSP). The only extant Sanskrit text of the TS was discovered by G. Bühler in the Jaina temple of Pārśvanātha at Jaisalmer in 1873; the Pañjikā of Kamalaśīla was found there some years later by C. D. Dalal. These MSS. have been edited by Embar Krishnamacharya (1926) and by Dvārikādāsa Śāstrī (1968). I have followed the Krishnamacharya edition. The text has also been translated into English by Ganganatha Jha (1937).

The relationship of Śāntarakṣita and Kamalaśīla to the Vijñānavāda is a matter of dispute. The prevailing tendency in the Tibetan tradition is to classify them as Yogācāra-Svātantrika-Mādhyamikas, i.e. as Mādhyamikas who have been influenced by Yogācāra ideas. Others classify them as Svātantrika-Mādhyamika-Yogācāras, i.e. as Vijñānavādins who have been influenced by Madhyamaka ideas.

My discussion of these two writers is confined to the TS and the TSP. It seems to me that these are purely Vijñānavādin works. I give my reasons for classifying them as such in Appendix III.

Saṃtānāntara-dūṣaṇa (Refutation of the Existence of Other Minds). This work was written by Ratnakīrti (fl. 1070 C.E.). Just as Dharmakīrti's Saṃtānāntara-siddhi was inspired by Vasubandhu's Viṃśatikā, Ratnakīrti's Saṃtānāntara-dūṣaṇa appears to have been inspired — despite what its title would indicate — by the Saṃtānāntara-siddhi of Dharmakīrti.

Ratnakīrti represents the Vijñānavāda at a very late stage in history, shortly before it and all the other Buddhist schools were destroyed by the invading Muslims. Ratnakīrti's school of the Vijñānavāda was called the "*citrādvaitavāda*" (the doctrine of the nonduality of the variegated appearances of things) and the "*vijñānādvaitavāda*" (the doctrine of the nondual mind). Jñānaśrīmitra (fl. 1025), the teacher (*guru*) of Ratnakīrti, gives the lineage of this school as follows: Maitreyanātha, Ārya Asaṅga,

Vasubandhu, Diṅnāga, Dharmakīrti, and finally Jñānaśrīmitra's own *guru*, Prajñākaragupta.

The only extant Sanskrit MS. of the Saṃtānāntara-dūṣaṇa was discovered by Rāhula Sāṅkṛtyāyana in the monastery of Ngor in Tibet. It is written in proto-Maithili-Bengali script of approximately the 13th century C.E. The MS. is now in the possession of the Bihar Research Society, Patna, and has been edited by Anantalal Thakur (1975), along with other works by Ratnakīrti, in the volume Ratnakīrti-nibandhāvaliḥ.

The text has previously been translated and annotated by Yuichi Kajiyama (1965). My free rendering of the text from the Ratnakīrti-nibandhāvaliḥ is given in Appendix IV.

APPENDIX II

The Saṃtānāntara-siddhi

[Introductory Verse:]

If someone objects that other intellects are inferred after one has observed that one's own action is preceded by one's own intellect, then it is just the same in the case of mind only.

1. Realist: We infer the existence of other minds by first noting in ourselves that our bodily actions and speech are preceded by a movement in our own minds, and then by inferring the existence of other minds by observing the bodily and actions of speech of another person. Hence if mind only *(cittamātra)* were true, bodily actions or speech would not exist, and we would have no basis for inferring the existence of other minds.

Dharmakīrti: The idealist can also infer the existence of other minds, for the idealist also holds that those cognitions (*jñāna*) which appear as the representations (*vijñapti*) consisting of the body and speech of another person cannot occur in the absence of another mind.

2. The realist objects: You may say that you can infer the existence of other minds just as well as *we* can on the grounds that a person's impressions can be caused *directly* by the minds of others, but the inference to other minds is still not reasonable in your case because we do not directly perceive the activity of the mind stream of another person.

Dharmakīrti: You are confused, for the situation is exactly the same in your case as it is in ours. *You* have to admit that we do not perceive the mind activity of another person, which you suppose to be the causal antecedent of the bodily and action of speech of others. Hence your position is no different from ours in this respect.

3. Realist: No, we can know the existence of another mind because one's own mind cannot be the efficient cause of the bodily actions and speech of another person. Therefore our inference to other minds is a good one. The reasoning is simply this: we see the

bodily actions and speech of another, which, on analogy from our own case, we infer to have been preceded by the mind activity of some mind or other. But we can exclude our own case, since one mind does not *directly* cause the impressions of another mind. Hence we validly infer the existence of *another* mind.

Dharmakīrti: Why do you say that one mind cannot be the efficient cause of another mind?

Realist: Because we never feel the mind cause of another mind in our own mind. Second, those actions which are caused by our own mind are always found in us, and not in others. Therefore, if the actions and speech of another were also caused by our own mind, then they should be perceived in the same way as our own actions are, i.e. as occurring in us. But this is not the case. Therefore, we have to admit that the actions of another have their own efficient cause in the mind activity of some *other* mind.

Dharmakīrti: We agree with you that one does not feel the mind cause of another in one's own mind. But that fact does not show what you think it does. What is to be concluded from this fact is that those *representations* of bodily speech and action which appear as external things must have been caused directly by another mind (operating as an efficient cause).

4. Realist: Couldn't it be that those representations (*jñāna*) which appear as external things do not have any efficient cause (*nimitta*) at all?

> [The realist does not really have this doubt, of course. He believes that the immediate, direct cause of our perception of external things is the external things themselves. But he wants to know how the idealist can draw a distinction between things like dreams and the impressions which we have through the senses in the normal waking state.]

Dharmakīrti: If you say that A's impression of B does not have B's mind as its immediate and efficient cause (*nimitta*), then we may be led to admit that nothing has an efficient cause. In that case, for example, even our bodily actions and speech might not have *our* minds as their efficient cause. There certainly is a distinction between those representations which appear as things separated from us and those which are not separated from us. But no distinction between them is possible on the grounds of their having, or not having, an efficient cause. Therefore we cannot admit that only those representations which appear as things connected to us have mind activity as their efficient cause.

Realist: Why not?

Dharmakīrti: Why don't you tell us what the difference is? There is no difference between the case in which the activity of my mind is the cause of my speech and actions, and the case in which some other mind is the cause of other speech and actions. For example, I may shoot an arrow into the air, and the movement of the arrow is not my own movement; nevertheless it has my mind (ultimately) as its cause. Similarly, if someone rocks me or picks me up and whirls me around, I have the sensation of movement even though the (ultimate) cause of the movement and the sensations is a volition and activity of someone else's mind. These examples show that my actions and speech are on the same footing as the actions and speech of others.[1]

You Realists say that we cognize the existence of the mind activity of another person because we do not experience any movement of mind in ourselves when we perceive the actions belonging to others, and so do we. We both believe that speech and bodily actions in every case have a movement of mind as their efficient cause, and hence will not occur when there is no movement of mind. There is therefore no difference between us, except that you make two inferences in each case where we make only one. You first infer from your sensory impressions the external bodily actions and speech of another person, and then on that basis infer the existence of another mind. We however directly infer the existence of another mind on the basis of the representations themselves (*vijñapti-mātra*).

5. [Now the opponent tries an entirely different line of attack.] Realist: If all representations (*vijñapti*) of bodily action and speech are efficiently caused by the movement of mind, why don't you claim that the things we see in dreams also have the movement of other minds as their efficient cause?

Dharmakīrti: This is what we do say! What is wrong with saying that the bodily speech and actions of another person which we see in our dreams have the mind activity of that other person as their cause?[2]

Realist: This is wrong, because the things we see in dreams do not exist.

Dharmakīrti: Why don't the things we see in dreams exist? We perceive *them* just as we do the things we see when we are awake.

Realist: When a person is overcome with sleep and dreams, the consciousness (*vijñāna*) is empty of reality. Dreams are therefore essentially different from the waking state of consciousness, and the things we dream about are essentially different from the things we see in the waking state.

Dharmakīrti: We also allow that this can happen. Sometimes our own mind activity plays a role in our perceptions, as in dreams. However, even in these cases the mind activity of others plays a role, although the effect may be delayed. So it does not follow that *nothing* we see in our dreams has the mind stream of another person as its efficient cause.

> [According to the two commentators of the text, Vinītadeva and Ṅag-dbaṅ bstan-dar, the Realist heretofore in the discussion has been a Sautrāntika, according to whom external objects and other minds have to be inferred on the basis of sensory perception. According to these commentators, the next objection is made by a Vaibhāṣika — a Buddhist realist who is said to hold the view that other minds and bodies are *directly* perceived.]

6. Realist [Vaibhāṣika]: In so far as you have admitted that even in dreams the impressions (*vijñapti*) need not be empty of reality, why not say that *all* the persons we perceive in dreams are other *saṃtānas* (mind streams), and therefore real?[3]

Dharmakīrti: By no means are we to be persuaded that *all* bodily actions and speech which occur in dreams must be caused by another person's mental activity. We do claim that *in one way or another* all representations of bodily actions and speech of *another* person are caused by the *saṃtāna* of another person. But the difference between the state of waking and the state of dreaming is that in the waking state we get most of those representations from a cause operating in the present moment, whereas in the latter case they arise mostly from memories. Though this is the usual case, it is not the *only* case. Sometimes, for example, our dream impressions are caused directly by the activity of another mind stream, as in the case of dreams given by the gods, telepathic dreams etc.

[According to the two traditional commentators, the rest of the text returns to the dispute between the Vijñānavādin and the Sautrāntika. At this point the Vijñānavādin takes the offensive.]

7. Dharmakīrti: Even if bodily actions and speech *were* real entities apart from mental representations (*vijñapti*), how would that help you to cognize the existence of another mind?

Realist [Sautrāntika]: Because the real bodily actions and speech of another person are the effects of the movement of the other person's mind.

Dharmakīrti: How is your case different from ours? For we believe that the *representations* (*vijñapti*) of another person's body and speech are the effects of another person's mind. It is just that we do not believe that there are "real" bodily actions and speech, or external objects, which exist apart from the representations of them. [*Esse est percipi.*] So why not take the simpler course, as we do, and simply say that other minds are inferred directly on the basis of our own immediate impressions of the actions and speech of others?

Realist: No. Signs (*liṅgas*) must be represented in our minds in order to infer the existence of someone else's mind.

Dharmakīrti: If you admit that the possibility of knowing other minds depends on the existence of the representations (*jñāna*) of bodily actions and speech and not upon the existence of bodily actions and speech as real entities apart from our perceptions of them, it is unnecessary to insist on the very complicated process of cognition that you propose. You contend that our representations of another person's bodily actions and speech depend on those real, external actions, and that it is then through the *representations* of these actions that we cognize the existence of another person's mind. But if representations are *necessary* for cognizing another person's mind, why not say, as we do, that they are also sufficient?

On our view, we cognize the existence of other minds by means of the representations themselves, which are caused directly (*nimitta*) by those other minds.

Those impressions (*vijñapti*) which are caused by a movement of one's own mind are experienced as our own, while the impressions caused by other persons are experienced as external things. But this distinction only holds for the majority of cases. Even in the state of sleep the causal relation between the movement of another mind and the representations of the bodily actions and speech resulting therefrom is the same as in the state of waking. However, in the state of illusion (e.g. dreaming) the representations of another person's bodily actions and speech are under the control of a certain additional condition (i.e. coma or unconsciousness), just as the representations of one's own body and speech are. Therefore, it is possible in the illusory state of mind that the subconscious impulses (*vāsanās*) deposited in our consciousness (*vijñāna*) — the efficient cause (*nimitta*) of which is the mind activity of another person — will sometimes start to work only after a certain lapse of time when the other person's mind activity took place. But it will never start to work in the complete absence of the movement of another mind.

Realists: We do not say that perceptions cannot occur unless there are real bodily actions. Illusions and dreams, empty of reality, do occur. But according to our theory, one cognizes the movement of another mind not by means of the representations of those bodily actions, but only by means of the bodily actions themselves. In the state of illusion, such as dreams, there are no real bodily actions; hence what occurs there are only representations or ideas empty of reality, and from these we cannot infer the movement of another mind. In these cases, one can infer only that one's *own* mind is in motion. Therefore your objection is quite beside the point.

Dharmakīrti: What is your basis for drawing a distinction between the state of dreams which comprise mere representations empty of reality and the state of waking in which real entities are involved?

Realists: The state of illusion (e.g. dreaming) is entirely different from the state of waking. Coma, unconsciousness etc. is involved in the former case, but not the latter.

Dharmakīrti: If you say this, then you are admitting that the mind can appear as something external through the force of ignorance (*avidyā*). This is exactly what we say. If you take this line, you will have to say that *all* our perceptions, whether in the waking state or the dreaming state, are nothing but mind. You have therefore contradicted your own position. What a muddle you are in!

8. Realist: Of course, after all the previous observations, we can at least agree on this: that one may reasonably infer the existence of one's own mind cause through the representations (*vijñapti*) of one's own bodily actions and speech. But one cannot say that those representations which belong to one mind stream can *directly* signify the existence of another mind stream. For there is no relationship of material causation (*upādāna-kāraṇa*) between two different mind streams.

Dharmakīrti: Of course, there is a distinction to be made between impressions (*vijñapti*) which are caused by one's own mind-cause and impressions which are caused by another mind-cause. In the former case, the mind-cause is the material cause (*upādāna-kāraṇa*) of the impressions, and in the latter case it is not. However, even in the latter case the impressions of one person's mind stream are causally related to the mind-cause of another person's mind stream. Nevertheless, it is a different kind of causal relation, called "superordinate causation" (*adhipati-pratyaya*).[4]

As a matter of convenience (*upacārāt*), we are prepared to follow ordinary linguistic usage and call all those representations which are caused by some cause or other (i.e. either one's own mind cause or another person's mind-cause) a representation (*vijñapti*), although some of these representations are caused by the mind-cause of another mind stream. There is no harm in doing this as long as we remain clear about what is actually going on.

What *actually* happens is that everyone directly experiences only his or her own representations. However, through the force of subconscious impulses (*vāsanās*), people tend to misinterpret the situation and to think that they are seeing the *same* thing, i.e. something which is in fact external to their own minds. It is similar to two persons with an eye disease who agree that there are two moons in the sky. Here the fact that they suffer from the same eye disease corresponds to the subconcious residue (*vāsanā*) which operates constantly in "normal" perception.

B's impression of his own bodily actions and speech is related through "material" causation with his own mind-cause, whereas A's impression of B's bodily action and speech, though directly caused by B's mind, is only related to B's mind through "superordinate" causation (*adhipati-pratyaya*). It is only for the sake of convenience (*upacārāt*) that we go along with ordinary ways of speaking and call both A's impression of B's bodily action and speech and B's impression of his own bodily action and speech an "impression" (*vijñapti*) of B's bodily action and speech.

> [The discussion now turns to the nature of the inference (*anumāna*) to other minds. At this point in the discussion, according to Kitagawa, the term used for "representation" by both parties is "*liṅga*" (Tib. *rtags*). The term "*liṅga*" was used in Indian logic to denote the "mark" or "sign" which is used in the inference. Suppose, for example, that one infers that there is fire on a mountain on the basis of the fact that there is smoke on the mountain. In this example, the fire is the *sādhya*. The smoke, which provides the grounds for the inference, is called the cause (*hetu*) or mark (*liṅga*) of the inference.]

9. Realists: You say that you can know another mind by means of such marks (*liṅga*) as the consciousness of bodily actions and speech, which are the effect. But for you there is the following problem. Does your knowledge of another mind refer to the other mind itself as an object (*artha*) or not? If it does, then you are implicitly assuming the existence of an external object (*bāhyārtha*), i.e. the other person's mind. If you say that your knowledge does *not* refer to another mind as an external object, how can another mind be known? For you cannot prove the existence of another mind unless you know the independent nature (*svabhāva*) of that other mind.

Dharmakīrti: Your system is subject to the same fault. You say that a person cognizes another person's mind through perceiving the real (i.e. physical) bodily actions and speech of that person. But this does not help. For in your inference and in ours, the possession of real knowledge of another person's mind would entail that one knows the specific forms of the other person's mind just as he knows the specific forms of his own mind. But this inference cannot give us. And without the cognition of these specific forms, how can one claim that he grasps the independent nature (*svabhāva*) of another mind?

Realists: Of course one cannot cognize the specific forms of another mind through its marks (*liṅga*). The knowledge of another person's mind which is given through inference is the knowledge of a general concept.[5]

Dharmakīrti: What do you mean by "general concept"? Is it another mind itself, or is it not? Or is it something which is inexpressible? If the general concept you reach by inference is not another mind itself, or is just something inexpressible, how can you say that one can cognize another mind itself through inference (*anumāna*)?

In fact it is impossible for a general concept reached through inference to be another mind itself. For if this were possible, one would be able to know the specific forms of another mind, and this is something inference does not allow us to do. Inference cannot grasp the independent nature of things (*svabhāva*).

Even though inference does not grasp the independent nature of things, it is still valid in so far as it does not betray us for the practical purposes of our lives, and provided we understand that its validity is limited to that domain (*vyavahāra-satya*). In this respect, the inference to other people's minds is no different from any other kind of inference. Even in the case of inferring fire on the basis of the smoke, the inference does not give one the self nature (*svabhāva*) of fire. If it did, the absurdity would arise that there would be no distinction between the object of perception and that of inference. If this were the case, one would have to say that whatever could be cognized by inference (*anumāna*) could be cognized by perception (*pratyakṣa*), and whatever could *not* be cognized by perception could not be cognized by inference either.

This would lead to absurd results. It would mean, for example, that we could not cognize either past or future occurrences through inference because we cannot do so through perception. It would also mean that when we infer the existence of fire (e.g. on the basis of smoke) we should feel the sensory qualities of fire just as we do when we directly perceive fire. But this too is absurd.

Even though inference (*anumāna*) is different from perception (*pratyakṣa*), inference is valid in the sense that it will not betray us in the predictions that we make for the ordinary purposes of life. Inference enables me to predict fire on the mountain on the basis of the fact that there is smoke on the mountain: since such predictions are always verified, the inference is valid. Similarly, inference enables me to predict another person's behavior as a sentient being on the basis of what I perceive of his past action and behavior. But inference does not give us fire itself or the self nature (*svabhāva*) of fire, nor does it give us mind itself or the self nature (*svabhāva*) of mind.

Realist: Your account of the validity of cognition in general will not do. You say that knowledge is valid simply because it enables one to pursue his daily life (*vyavahāra*) successfully. But this is not an adequate account of the validity of knowledge. For we can infer dream-fire on the basis of dream-smoke, and such inferences will not betray us for all the purposes of our dream-life. But in the case of a dream all of our knowledge is illusory.

Dharmakīrti: This is not quite true. We maintain that since impressions of bodily action and speech never occur without an antecedent mind activity, one may infer the existence of other minds even on the basis of cognition in a dream. We have already explained [see ¶7 above] that in dreams we are subjected to the power of illusion, and sometimes the representations of another person's bodily actions and speech occur only after a considerable lapse of time from the moment when the other person's mind activity occurred. Therefore it is necessary to draw a distinction between the state of waking, which involves the influence of another mind stream operating at the *same* time, and the state of dreaming, which frequently involves the activation of memories. Even in the state of dreaming our inference to the existence of another mind is valid in the context of the dream itself. Consequently, it cannot be said that cognition in the dreaming state is not valid, whereas cognition in the waking state is.

[Dharmakīrti has argued in the immediately preceding discussion that inference does not give us knowledge of the self nature (*svabhāva*) of other minds or mind itself, but only truths about a general concept. But what about perception (*pratyakṣa*)? Since the Buddhist *sūtras* themselves refer to the power of the Buddhas and *yogins* to directly know other minds (*yogi-pratyakṣa*), one might expect Dharmakīrti to allow that one can know the self nature of other minds through *yogic perception*. The opponent now raises this as an objection.]

10. Realist: All right, we will yield to you on the point that inference cannot grasp the independent nature of another mind, and that inference to other minds is only valid in the sense that it does not betray us for the ordinary purposes of life. Still, how do you explain the fact that *yogins* are able to know another person's mind by direct perception? If the *yogin* can know the independent nature of another mind by perception (*pratyakṣa*), what he grasps should be something external to him, but this you cannot accept, for your position is that there is nothing external to perception. On the other hand, if you maintain that *yogins* cannot know the independent, self nature of other minds, how can you call *yogi-pratyakṣa* knowledge? You cannot say that *yogi-pratyakṣa* does not grasp the independent nature (*svabhāva*) of things; if you did, such perception would be invalid, for even according to your definitions, perception which fails to grasp the independent self nature of things is a contradiction in terms.

Dharmakīrti: Even if another mind is known in some sense by the *yogins* who have not completely abandoned the erroneous distinction of subject and object, the validity of their knowledge is limited to the fact that it does not betray them in daily life. As long as the *yogins* have not abandoned the subject-object distinction, they have not attained the full stature of the Buddha.

By the power of meditation the *yogin* can have such clear representations that they appear to him almost like the specific forms of the mind of another person, just as deities will bestow grace on a person by appearing in their dreams etc. So even the *yogin* does not directly grasp another person's mind through his representations. He can be said to know another person's mind only in the sense that the representations which appear in his own mind have the same form (*ākāra*) as those in another person's mind. Therefore *yogi-pratyakṣa* is called perception only for the sake of convenience. As long as the essential distinctions are made, we go along with this way of speaking, for the representations which appear to the *yogin* are so clear that they look almost like the specific forms of another mind.

[The ultimate question for the Buddhist, of course, is the Buddha's cognition, for the Buddha's cognition is by definition the cognition of things as they really are (*yathā-bhūtam*). One might well ask at this point: How about the Buddha? Can he know another mind or not?

Although the text does not represent the opponent as making this objection, one can imagine him arguing against Dharmakīrti as follows. By definition the Buddha is free from the tendency of making the distinction between subject and object. Now if you believe that the Buddha can know another mind itself, then you have to admit the existence of something which is external to cognition. But if you say he cannot, then even the knowledge of the Buddha does not represent a thing as it really is. The result is that either answer you make will be inadmissible.

Dharmakīrti does not raise this question or directly answer it. He simply concludes his treatise with the following statement.

Dharmakīrti: The Buddha cognizes everything, but his cognition cannot be grasped by analytical thinking.

APPENDIX III

A Note on the Tattva-saṃgraha-(pañjikā) as a Vijñānavāda Text

In the present work I cite the views of Śāntarakṣita and Kamalaśīla in the Tattva-saṃgraha-(pañjikā) as Vijñānavādin views. In the Tibetan tradition, however, Śāntarakṣita and Kamalaśīla are regarded as belonging to the Svātantrika-Madhyamaka school, i.e. as Mādhyamikas who were merely influenced by Yogācāra ideas. If this Tibetan tradition were entirely correct, it would be inadmissible to include the TS(P) in a discussion of the Vijñānavāda. I shall, therefore, give my reasons for thinking that these are purely Vijñānavādin works.

(1) Throughout these two works, the Vijñānavāda is presented as the correct view (*siddhānta*), and it is nowhere suggested that it is merely a provisional view. Some of these passages have already been cited in the text (e.g. TSP 3317-3318, cited above, pp. 145-46), but there are several others which have not been cited. One of the more interesting of these is TSP 3645, at the end of the work, where Kamalaśīla speaks of his own views as based on the Vijñānavāda (*yeyam-asmābhir-vijñānavāda-sthitair-nirākāra-cintā* ...).

(2) In the TS and the TSP, Śāntarakṣita and Kamalaśīla cite Diṅnāga and Dharmakīrti as authorities, but never cite a Mādhyamika writer as an authority.

(3) Śāntarakṣita occasionally mentions views that may very well have been Mādhyamika views, but there are no occasions in either work where specifically Mādhyamika views are *endorsed*. An interesting example is TS 1916, where Śāntarakṣita refers to those wise persons (*su-dhiyaḥ)* who believe in a "non-fixed" *(apratiṣṭhita) nirvāṇa*. Kamalaśīla's commentary on the verse specifies that these "wise persons" were the Mādhyamikas. Significantly, the view is not endorsed by either writer as the *siddhānta*. Śāntarakṣita cites this view, not to endorse it, but simply to point out that the opponent has presented an argument which does not apply to all of the Buddhist schools.

(4) Perhaps the weightiest consideration in this matter, however, is that the authors endorse views which could *not* have

been endorsed by the Mādhyamikas. A number of instances could be cited, but I shall confine myself to a particularly interesting one.

According to the Madhyamaka, no *dharmas* are born and none ever perish. The Mādhyamikas meant such statements quite literally, i.e. according to the Mādhyamikas, it cannot be said that anything comes to exist in the causal process, nor can it be said that anything, having once existed, ceases to be. Things do not arise and perish, on this view, since they are always non-existent and void (*śūnya/m*).

The analysis of causality in the first chapter of the Tattva-saṃgraha-(pañjikā) is inconsistent with this view, however, for the authors clearly assert that in the causal process the effect is non-existent at one moment, *existent* in the middle moment, and non-existent in a later moment.

The clearest statement of this can be found in TS(P) 31-33. There an opponent (a Sāṃkhyavādin) asserts that according to the Buddhists a non-existent entity is produced by the causal process. The opponent alleges that this view makes no sense. Kamalaśīla's reply to this objection is as follows (TSP 31):

> We do not say that a non-existent entity is produced (*na hy-asmābhiḥ 'abhāvaḥ kriyate'*)...Our view is that a real thing itself is produced (*'vastv-eva kriyate'*) which previously did not exist (*pūrvaṃ pratipāditam*), which is reasonable because before its production the entity cannot be seen, and because it is unreasonable to say that an effect which already exists (*niṣpanna*) is produced. The effect is said to be produced by that cause (*kāraṇa*) whose mere proximity originates it (*yasya ca kāraṇasya sannidhānamātreṇa tat-tathā-bhūtam-udeti, tena tat-kriyate iti vyapadiśyate*)...

To this the opponent objects:

> If you say that it is the non-existent that is produced (*yady 'asad-evotpadyate'*), then what is the meaning of the Buddhist *sūtras* which say that neither the existent nor the non-existent is produced (*'anutpannā mahāmate sarva-dharmāḥ, sad-asator-anutpannatvāt'*)?

Śāntarakṣita replies (TS 32):

> The origination of a thing is merely its becoming (*bhāva*), and this cannot be related (*sambadhyate*) either with something that exists or with something that does not exist. It is related merely to a conception which is non-existent.
>
> *utpādo vastu-bhāvas-tu so 'satā na satā tathā /*
> *sambadhyate kalpikayā kevalaṃ tv-asatā dhiyā //33//*

What this means, as the following verse (33) and Kamalaśīla's commentary makes clear, is simply this. At one moment, we observe an entity; at another moment we observe another entity; and in the third moment we observe yet another entity. There is no identity between the entities that arise in the causal sequence; hence it makes no sense to say, as the Sāṃkhyavādin does, that the effect exists in the cause. The real or correct meaning of the assertion that what is non-existent is produced, therefore, is that a given entity is preceded in a causal sequence of events by some entity which is different from it, and which is its immediate cause. The apparent reference in ordinary speech to a non-existent entity which is "produced" in the causal process is therefore purely conceptual (*vikalpa*), i.e. a mere *façon de parler* (*prajñapti*).

The realist analysis of causation found in TS 31-33 is stated unequivocally elsewhere as well, e.g. in TSP 1851 and in the TSP's commentary on the introductory verses of the TS.

Since this kind of realist analysis of the causal process is quite antithetical to the Mādhyamikas' own views, the TS(P), at any rate, appears to be a purely Vijñānavādin work.

APPENDIX IV

Saṃtānāntara-dūṣaṇa

Ratnakīrti: We have shown [in previous works] that the whole aggregate of insentient things (*jaḍa-padārtha-rāśa*) is a nondual appearance (*advaya-rūpa*) in our own minds (*sva-citta-pratibhāsātmani*) like a dream or magical illusion (*svapna-māyā*), because no distinction can be drawn between things and our perception of them (*sahopalambhādi*). We now address the following question: are other minds (*saṃtānāntara*) real or unreal (*sad-asat*)?

(a) [The opponent]: They are real (*asti*), and their existence is proved through inference (*anumāna*). The inference is as follows. First we perceive that our own actions and speech (*vyāhāra-vyavahāra*) are preceded by the activity of our own wishful mind (*icchā-citta*). Whenever there is such an activity of our wishful minds, bodily action and speech follow, and whenever such activity is absent, they do not follow [*anvaya-vyatireka* proof], and this establishes that our wishful minds are the cause of our speech and actions. It is on this basis that we infer another mind to be the cause of other speech and actions, even though we do not directly perceive that other mind. Thus the existence of another mind stream (*saṃtānāntara*) is proved.

Ratnakīrti: Can this wishful mind (*icchā-citta*), which is to be established as the cause (*kāraṇa*) of speech and actions, be seen by the person who infers, or is it only a generality or universal (*icchā-mātra*) which has no relation to the distinction of "seen" and "unseen" *(dṛśyādṛśya-viśeṣaṇānapekṣam-icchāmātram*)?[1]

(1) Let us consider the first alternative, according to which the wishful mind is held to be a particular, rather than a universal or generality. If you favor the first alternative, and say that it is a particular that is by nature perceivable (*dṛśya*), your view is untenable because when we make the inference the wishful mind of the other person is not perceived. There is no perceived entity of this sort when inference takes place, and the non-existence (*abhāva*) of your supposed perceivable entity (*dṛśya*) is shown by this very fact. It would be absurd to say that the wishful mind of the

other person is perceived at the time the inference is made, for in that case what would be the use of the inference? If we actually perceived fire on a mountain, we would not need to infer its existence on the basis of perceiving smoke. If fire is negated by non-perception, we may be able to infer its existence through smoke, but if fire itself is seen, inference is of no use.

In the case of the smoke-fire inference the fire is distant in space (*deśa-viprakarṣa*), and the fire is not seen because it is remote in space. Consequently, it is true in this particular case that we cannot infer from the fact that fire is not seen that it does not exist. But the non-perception of other minds is entirely different. What we want to know is whether we can infer that there is another mind *here* when we perceive (in our presence) bodily actions and speech which do not belong to us. To say that the other mind is remote in space would contradict common sense (*alaukika*).

(2) Suppose you choose the second alternative, and say that the cause of the appearance (*ābhāsa*) of bodily actions and speech that are not one's own is a wishful mind in general (*icchā-citta-mātra*) which is common to one's own and another's personality (*sva-para-saṃtāna-sādhāraṇa*) and which is not related to the distinction of "seen" and "unseen." What proof (*pramāṇa*) could you use to establish this?

In this case another mind would be imperceptible (*adṛśya*). In this case you are precluded from using the *vyatireka* form of inference, i.e. arguing that another mind is the cause of another's bodily speech and actions on the grounds that the appearance of bodily speech and actions does not take place when a wishful mind in general is *absent*. For this could be done only if one could first establish the non-existence (*abhāva*) of a wishful mind in general (*icchā-citta-mātra*), which is common to oneself and another person, by means of self-consciousness (*sva-saṃvedana*) or any other proof.

It is entirely different in the case of legitimate inferences, as for example inferring fire on the basis of smoke. In this case we can establish through perception that fire is absent before smoke is produced. When we conclude that fire is the cause of smoke, we conclude that if we *were* present at the place where smoke occurs, we would see the fire. This is how we establish that fire in general (*vahni-mātra*) is the cause of smoke in general (*dhūma-mātra*), even though in the case of a specific inference the fire is remote in space and time. However, fire in general (*vahni-mātra*) is inaccessible and imperceptible in essence (*svabhāva-viprakṛṣṭa*), and so we cannot say that fire in general is the cause of a particular occurrence of smoke. It is only a particular fire which is the cause of a particular occurrence of smoke. Similarly, we cannot say that a wishful mind in general, common to oneself and another person, is the cause of another person's speech and actions on the grounds that whenever a wishful mind in general is *not* present another person's actions and speech do not occur (*vyatireka*), for a wishful mind in general is *essentially* non-perceptible and inaccessible (*viprakṛṣṭa*).

Nor can you argue that mind in general is *not* inaccessible in essence (*svabhāva-viprakṛṣṭa*) when it is taken in relation to self-consciousness in general (*sva-saṃvedana-mātrāpekṣā*). You might say, for example, that the fire which we saw yesterday by one sense perception (*indriya-vijñāna*) is not cognized by the same sense-perception today, but that this does not preclude us from saying that fire in general (*agni-mātra*) is perceptible (*dṛśya*) with reference to visual perception in general (*cakṣu-vijñāna-mātrāpekṣā*). Similarly, you might argue that one can say that a wishful mind in general, though common to one's own and another's personality, is perceptible (*dṛśya*) in relation to self-consciousness in general (*sva-saṃvedana-mātrāpekṣā*).

If you were to argue in this way, we would reply that you are misusing the term "in general" (*mātra-śabda*). According to the way you are using the term "in general," it includes *any* person's sense-perception (*indriya-vijñāna*); as such it refers to a sense-perception which is neither connected nor unconnected with the inferrer (*anumātṛ-puruṣa-saṃbandha-asaṃbandhābhyām-aviśeṣitam*). If one were to use the term in this way, nothing would be inaccessible in essence (*svabhāva-viprakṛṣṭa*): you would have to say, for example, that demons (*piśācas*) are perceptible (*dṛśya*) just because some *yogins* have developed the power to see them. Therefore, the words "in general" should be applied only when we disregard the specific characteristics (*svalakṣaṇa*) of things but do not disregard their connection with the person who infers. It was to avoid just such a misunderstanding that Dharmottara said: "The definition of perception (*pratyakṣa-lakṣaṇa*) must be made from the standpoint of a single observer."[2]

Therefore the supposition of perceptibility (*dṛśyatā-saṃbhāvanā*) just means this: If a jar were present at this spot and at this moment it *would* be perceived and *would* be an object of *my* visual consciousness in general (*madīyasya cakṣur-vijñāna-mātra*). But we cannot say that another person's mind (*para-citta*) is perceptible in this sense. For we cannot argue that if another person's mind were present, that it would be an object of my self-consciousness in general (*madīyasya sva-saṃvedana-mātra*).

> [The preceding arguments have been directed solely against the validity of the opponent's arguments for the existence of other minds, i.e. they have been what the Indian logicians called *prāsaṅgika* arguments. Now Ratnakīrti argues directly against the thesis that the foregoing arguments were intended to support, i.e. he now presents *svātantrika* arguments against the thesis that other minds really exist.]

(b) Some people say that there is neither a proof (*sādhaka*) nor a disproof (*bādhaka*) of other minds, and hence that the whole matter is just doubtful or indeterminate (*saṃdeha*). But this is not so. Here is the disproof (*bādhaka*):

> If the mind of another person were possible, then it would be different (*bheda*) from our own mind (*sva-saṃtāna*); otherwise it would not be different from our own mind which *is* manifested (*prakāśamāna*). But there is no such difference between them. Therefore another mind is neither identical (*abheda*) nor different (*bheda*) from our mind and is non-existent (*abhāva*) like a universal (*sāmānya*) or the "horn of a hare" (*śaśa-viṣāṇa*).[3]

How then can you say that the matter is doubtful or indeterminate? On your view, our mind would necessarily (*avaśya*) be different from another mind. Such difference would be the self nature (*svabhāva*) of our mind, and would necessarily be perceived when our own mind (*sva-saṃtāna*) was being perceived.

A different mind, however, is never seen, for if it were seen it would manifest as the limit or boundary of our own mind. As Jñānaśrīmitra says:

> If one's own mind were different (*bhinna*) from another, its limit should be manifest; if it is not manifest, it is not so cognized.

and

> Not even a shade of difference is seen between one's mind and another's mind; how then can the two be different?[4]

When one's own mind alone (*sva-saṃtāna-mātra*) manifests, no difference manifests itself between our own mind and any non-existent entity like a hare's horn. Since no difference can be observed in our own minds between another mind and a hare's horn, neither the difference nor the non-difference of another mind ever manifests in our own minds. Therefore another mind is not different from a non-existent entity like a hare's horn. Since the difference between one's own mind and another's mind is never perceived, one cannot say that there is such a difference. If you maintain that there is a difference, you are merely clinging to an artificial mode of speech (*vacana-racana*).

If you say that distinctness between one's own mind and another exists even though the boundary (*avadhi*) between them is never seen, on the grounds that we innately feel compassion for other sentient beings, the answer is that doubt is possible with respect to other minds.[5]

Furthermore, how can you distinguish between other minds (which you hold to be real) and external objects (which you hold to be unreal)? Let us agree, as Vijñānavādins, that external objects (*bāhyārtha*) do not manifest to anyone at any time. How can you infer from this that external objects do not exist if you allow that external minds do not manifest to anyone at any time and yet *they* exist? Since there is no difference in this respect between other minds and external objects, how can you be Vijñānavādins and belong to the same school of thought that we do?

There is the same objection if you try to maintain that the boundary (*avadhi*) between a previous cognition (*saṃvitti*) and a later cognition is cognized even though such a boundary is not seen. This is analogous to the case of other minds. According to you, the difference (*paratva*) between an earlier cognition and a later cognition — i.e. the relation between cause and effect — is manifested (*avabhāsamāna*) just like variegated appearances like blue etc. (*nīlādi-citrākāravat*), but this contradicts the teaching of the revered Dharmakīrti:

> Causality pertains only to the relative truth (*saṃvṛtti*).[6]
>
> [I.e. you want to maintain that the difference between one mind and another mind, and the difference between one moment of cognition and a later moment, and the relation between cause and effect, are matters of perception. But in that case all such distinctions and notions would be absolutely, rather than relatively true, which is not the correct view.]

Indeed, your view is contradicted by all of the considerations which go to establish our own view. How can you fail to doubt the existence of another mind, when we have shown in other works with respect to the entire realm of apparently diversified entities (*citrākāra-cakra*) that the mere fact that something is visible (*prakāśamānatva*) shows that everything is nondual (*advaita*) and devoid of perceived differences (*bheda*).[7]

[The opponent objects]: But what is your proof (*pramāṇa*) for establishing the non-existence (*abhāva*) of another person's mind? You cannot do it through perception, for perception has as its object only a reality to be affirmed (*vidhi-viṣaya*), and is therefore incapable of proving a negative judgement. (I.e. one can prove that *x* exists if *x* is perceived, but you cannot prove that *x* is non-existent on the grounds that it is *not* perceived.) Nor can you establish the non-existence of another person's mind through inference, for inference can only prove the non-existence of a perceptible object (*dṛśya*) and is not capable of proving the non-existence of another person's mind, which is by nature imperceptible (*adṛśya*).

[Ratnakīrti]: This is not correct. If another mind could exist, then it should be a determinate entity (*niyata-bhāva*), and therefore different from one's own mind. If an entity *x*, being perceived, does not appear in the form (*rūpa*) of *y*, then it is not possible to say that *x* exists in the form of *y*, just as blue does not exist in the form of yellow. Now when one's own mind is perceived it is not seen in a form which is different from another mind. Therefore, according to the form of argument called "non-perception of the nature of the denied object" (*svabhāvānupalabdhi*), we have to deny the identity of one's own mind and this other mind which is said to be different from it.

Nor is our inference illegitimate (*asiddha*). For if a distinct thing (*bheda*) is manifested clearly, then the limit (*avadhi*) of that thing is also manifested; conversely, if no limit is manifested, then there is no manifestation of a distinct thing, just as a hare's horn never appears as a thing distinct from our own mind. Since we thereby disprove that one's own mind and another's mind are different, and since it is inadmissible that one's own mind and another mind are the same (*abheda*), the fact that another mind is neither the same nor different from one's own mind is clearly established. Since other minds are thereby shown to be devoid of reality (*vastutā-apahati*), like a universal (*sāmānya*),[8] how can you say that the question of other minds is merely doubtful or indeterminate on the grounds that there is no disproof?

(c) Moreover, your doubt about the existence of other minds belongs to the realm of unenlightened people only. What did Bhagavān Buddha say about this? If even his words leave a doubt on this matter, how could he be omniscient (*sarvajñatā*)? We say: "The Buddha never asserted the existence of another mind in any fashion, and this shows that he was omniscient." How is this? We have already considered your inference which takes as its object another mind stream (*saṃtānāntara-viṣaya*). This inference, even if it were valid, could not establish the Buddha's omniscience because omniscience must be direct, not indirect. If you say that another mind is known by the mind of the Buddha through perception (*pratyakṣa*), this too would be wrong, for in that case there would remain the distinction between the Buddha's mind and another person's mind (*grāhya-grāhaka-bhāva*). This would involve admitting the reality of external objects (*bāhyārtha*) in a roundabout way, and how could this be right?

The view we attribute to the Buddha is: "No other minds exist at all" (*para-cittaṃ nāsty-eveti*).[9] This assertion is restricted in its application (*avadhāraṇa-kṛta*) and does not have the fault of destroying the Buddha's omniscience. As long as there is the obscuration (*saṃvṛti*) in the form of erroneous conceptions involving the grasping of differences, there will be doubts about the existence of other minds. Our statement is made only in this context — i.e. in order to enlighten others — and therefore is not guilty of the fault of self-contradiction (*svacana-virodha*). Indeed, we do not even say that in our own case (*abhimatam-asmākam*) there is no doubt whatsoever about whether other minds are objects of perception (*saṃtānāntara-viṣaya*). Our proof that other minds do not exist is similar to our proof that things are nondual (*advaya*); consequently the allegation of self-contradiction (*svacana-virodha*) etc. and its refutation do not apply to the same level (*naika-niyataḥ*).

With respect to the mere existence of the variegated appearances of things (*citrākāra-saṃbhāva-mātrena*), Prajñākaragupta dispelled the darkness of the Vedānta:

> "Perception grasps itself, and nothing else" etc.[10]

If someone objects that this is just the *ātmavāda* [i.e. the Vedānta], the answer is No, because self-consciousness manifests in various appearances or forms (*citrākāra-saṃvedanāt*).[11]

NOTES

NOTES

Notes to Introduction

1. Thus Vasubandhu begins his Viṃśatikā-vṛtti with the following statement:

> In the Mahāyāna it is clearly established that all the three worlds are mind only (*vijñaptimātra*). ... Here "*citta*," "*manas*," "*vijñāna*" and "*vijñapti*" are synonyms (*paryāyāḥ*). "Mind" includes all the mental associates as well.

Then, as if to make his commitment to idealism perfectly unequivocal, he adds:

> The suffix "-only" (*-mātra*) is used to deny the existence of external objects (*mātram-ity-artha-pratiṣedhārtham*).

2. The number of constituent elements (*dharmas*) assigned to each of these five groups varied from school to school.

3. The Vijñanavādins gave an idealist orientation to the traditional teaching of the five groups (*pañca-skandhas*). For example, the Abhidharma-samuccaya (an Abhidharma work of the Vijñanavāda school) begins by enumerating the standard five groups and then asks: "Why are there only five of these groups?" The answer is that there are only five because the self (*ātman*) *appears* (*pratibhāsate*) as form, feeling, impulses, cognition and consciousness.

4. The Mahāyānists used the term "Mahāyāna" (Great Vehicle) to refer to their own views, and the term "Hīnayāna" (Inferior Vehicle) to refer to those Buddhists who did not accept some of the Mahāyānists' central doctrines.

5. The Vijñanavādins called this special causal efficiency "*adhipati-pratyaya*." This was a traditional Abhidharma term that the Vijñanavādins appear to have taken over and adapted to their own purposes.

Notes to Chapter 1: Madhyānta-vibhāga (lakṣaṇa-pariccheda)

1. Cf. AKB ii.55 [DŚ ii. 326-327]. In this passage the Sarvāstivādin contends that the scriptural passages which speak of *nirvāṇa* as the destruction (*nirodha*) and absolute non-appearance (*aprādur-bhāva*) of suffering mean that in *nirvāṇa* suffering does not manifest (*nāsmin prādur-bhāva iti*). The Sautrāntika, on the other hand, contends that such passages simply mean that *nirvāṇa* involves the deliverance of the mind-stuff, like the extinction of a flame (*pradyotasyeva nirvāṇam vimokṣas-tasya cetasaḥ*); consequently, *nirvāṇa* is simply non-existence, and it is thus that the deliverance of the mind-stuff of the Buddha is accomplished (*yathā pradyotasya nirvāṇam-abhāvaḥ; evaṃ bhagavato 'pi cetaso vimokṣa iti*). Yaśomitra's gloss (AKSV) specifies that in this passage "*nāsmin prādur-bhāva iti*" means that *nirvāṇa* is what accomplishes the non-manifestation of suffering (*adhikaraṇa-sādhanam-iti*) and that for the Sautrāntika "*aprādur-bhāva*" is a matter of sheer non-existence (*aprādur-bhāva = aprādhur-bhūti*), i.e., that for the Sautrāntika the non-appearance of pain is not a matter of what *nirvāṇa* effects, but of what it is.

Candrakīrti (MMKV 25.4-9) gives exactly the same analysis of the dispute between the Sarvāstivādin and the Sautrāntika. He characterizes the Sarvāstivādins (MMKV 25.4) as holding that *nirvāṇa* is a real thing (*bhāva, nirodhātmakaḥ padārthaḥ*). The Sarvāstivādin replies to the Sautrāntika, who holds that *nirvāṇa* is just simple extinction (like the going out of a light) by arguing that this simile must be understood to mean that *nirvāṇa* is the real element of existence (*dharma*) *in which* the release from suffering occurs (*asminn-iti nirvāṇākhye dharme sati bhavati ... tatrāpi yasmin sati cetaso vimokṣu bhavatīti veditavyam-iti*). On the other hand, Candrakīrti (MMKV 25.9) represents the Sautrāntika as holding that *nirvāṇa* is mere nothingness (*abhāva*).

The Sarvāstivādins also regarded space (*ākāśa*) as a real, uncompounded (*asaṃskṛta*) entity (*dharma, dravya*), like *nirvāṇa*. The Sautrāntikas, however, argued that space is not an independent reality like matter, sensation etc.; it is just that when we fail to encounter resistance we say that there is space (*ākāśa*). Hence, according to the Sarvāstivādins, both *nirvāṇa* and space are real entities (*dravya*), whereas for the Sautrāntikas both are simply unreal (*adravya*).

2. Here I take it as a given of modern scholarly research that the earliest identifiable Buddhist teachings are contained in the extant *sūtras* which are the common property of the Pāli canon and the very incomplete canons which exist in Sanskrit, Tibetan and Chinese. (The extant Sanskrit fragments appear to belong to the Sarvāstivāda; the Chinese Āgamas appear to belong to a number of the other Hīnayāna schools as well.) For an introduction to this topic, see Warder (1980: 3-16) and Minh Chau (1964).

3. Cf. AKB i.7 (DŚ i.27): "The going out (*niḥsaraṇam* = *niḥsāraḥ*) is the extinction (*nirvāṇa*) of all the conditioned *dharmas*." (Yaśomitra specifies that this is the *nirupadhi-śeṣa-nirvāṇa*.) Note that this appears to be meant as a *definition* of *nirvāṇa*, as it is in many other similar passages.

4. Aggi-vacchagotta-sutta, Majjhima-nikāya, sutta 72. [I have used the Horner translation in Conze et. al. (1954: ¶107, p. 106).]

5. Ud. VIII says that there is (*atthi*) a condition which, among other things, is not "nothingness" (*ākiñcañña*). However, this cannot be read as a *denial* that the "end of ill" is mere nothingness, for "*ākiñcañña*" in the old texts is a technical term which refers to a state of unconsciousness rather than a state of nothingness pure and simple. This is clear even in this passage from the Udāna, for this "nothingness" is mentioned between the sphere of infinite consciousness and the condition of neither-consciousness-nor-unconsciousness. Since "*ākiñcañña*" in this passage must refer to unconsciousness or the consciousness of nothingness rather than nothingness per se, the passage cannot be construed as denying that *nirvāṇa* is simply a state of extinction or nothingness. (For more on "*ākiñcañña*," see H. G. A. Van Zeyst, "*ākiñcaññāyatana*," EB.)

6. In the following I have used the PTS translation.

7. Since the analogy of the forest plays an important role in the Cūḷa-suññata-sutta, it is of interest to note that Viṃśatikā 20 also uses the term "*śūnyatva*" (absence, devoidness, desolation) in speaking of a Purāṇic legend about the forest-dwelling sages; i.e.

"How else, indeed, did the wrath of the sage (*ṛṣi*) bring about the desolation (*śūnyatva*) of the Daṇḍaka forest?"

8. For example, Saṃyutta-nikāya IV, 54 says that the world is said to be empty because it is empty of self or what belongs to the self, and then it specifies that the eye, one's physical body, visual consciousness, and impressions of the eye are empty of self and of what belongs to the self. So, too, its says, are the ear, nose, tongue, body and mind (and their respective sense-data, consciousnesses and impressions) empty of self and of what belongs to the self. Likewise for all feelings which arise, conditioned by the impression on the eye, ear, nose, tongue, body and mind, whether it be pleasant or painful or neither pleasant nor painful etc.

9. In Buddhism the term "*vijñāna*" is used to refer to both mind (*citta, manas*) and consciousness (*cetanā, cit*). In this work I shall of course be following the Buddhist usage, and will therefore not distinguish between "*vijñāna*" as "*cit*" (i.e. consciousness itself) and "*vijñāna*" as "*citta*" (i.e. as mind), although this distinction is made in some other Indian schools (e.g. the Advaita Vedānta).

10. See Conze (1975: 177, 190, 209, 226, 249, and 278); Aṣṭa-sāhasrikā-prajñā-pāramitā-sūtra, ed. Rajendralal Mitra (1888: 273, 298, 341, 379-380, 424, 482).

11. According to the Yogācārins, the Mādhyamikas denied the existence of mind as well as the external world. The following passage from Xuan Zang's Cheng wei shilun is typical of such criticisms of the Mādhyamikas. Here Xuan Zang argues that the Mādhyamikas have misunderstood the Mahāyānist doctrine that all *dharmas* are void or without a self nature (*sarve dharmā niḥsvabhāvāḥ*):

> Kārikās 23-25 [of the Triṃśikā] show that the dictum of the *sūtras* that all *dharmas* are devoid of self nature must not be taken literally. Intelligent people will guard against the mistake of interpreting this to mean that, in a sweeping manner, the *dharmas* are entirely unreal. [Poussin (1928-48): 561.]

Xuan Zang does not explicitly mention the Śūnyavādins or Mādhyamikas in this passage, but there can be no doubt that they were the object of his criticism in this and similar passages, for Kui

Ji, his immediate disciple and commentator, names them as such. [See Poussin (1928-48: 188, n. 1), where Bhāvaviveka is specified by Kui Ji as a nihilist who "denies the existence of mind (*vijñāna*) and all the *dharmas*."]

Harsh Narain (1963), in an important paper which does not seem to me to have received the attention that it deserves, has shown that this charge of nihilism was levelled against the Mādhyamikas by the Vijñanavādins and by all the other Buddhist and non-Buddhist schools in India as well. On this issue, see also de La Vallée Poussin (1917, 1932-33).

12. E.g. "All the three worlds are nothing but mind" (*citta-mātram idaṃ yad idaṃ traidhātukam*), Daśabhūmika-sūtra (Rahder, p. 49). This is cited almost verbatim by Vasubandhu at the outset of his autocommentary on the Viṃśatikā [S. Lévi (1925: 3)].

13. See, for example, Lindtner (1986: 240, 243, 245-48, 254), who discusses passages from some of the writings of Bhāvaviveka (and the Ratna-pradīpa, whose authorship is disputed) where it is maintained that the *cittamātra* doctrine is at best a provisional truth (*saṃvṛti-prajñā*).

14. In this connection it is important to note that the question whether the mind is empty or void is not the same thing as the question whether the mind is a material thing or object (*vastu, artha, viṣaya*).

Neither the Vijñanavādins nor any other Buddhist school held that mind is a *thing* like a physical object. Even according to the traditional Buddhist Abhidharma, for example, what we call "things" consist of constituent *dharmas* belonging to the *rūpa-skandha*. All the *dharmas* comprising the groups of feeling, perception, impulses and mind were thought to be different from these *rūpa-dharmas*. [Cf. AKB 44a-b (DŚ i.123): "Mind is formless and immaterial" (*manas-tv-amūrttivad*), and AKB 43 (DŚ i.118-119), which argues that there is no contradiction in vision being single even though one sees with two physical eyes because mind is not material and is not fixed in one place (*na cāśraya-vicchedād viccheda-prasaṅgaḥ; vijñānasya deśāpratiṣṭhitatvād rūpavad-iti*).]

Most Indian philosophers were in agreement that mind is by its very nature (*svabhāva*) intangible, ungraspable, etc. Consequently, the mere fact that the Vijñanavādins, like most of the other Indian schools, held that mind is intangible etc. does not mean that they, or the other Indian schools generally, held that the mind is non-existent. Of all the various schools of philosophy in India, it was only the Mādhyamikas and perhaps some of the materialists (Lokāyatas) who — for very different reasons — maintained that the mind is actually unreal and non-existent (*śūnya, abhāva*).

15. Thus Udāna VIII. ix describes *nibbāna* as follows:

> The body is broken, perceiving is dissolved, all feelings are quiescent, impulses have ceased, and consciousness (*viññāṇa*) has reached its end.

This fundamental doctrine of the early *sūtras* and collected sayings is carried forward in the Abhidharma literature. Cf. AK ii.41b-c (DŚ ii. 233): "the trance state of unconsciousness is the cessation of the mind stuff and the associated mental factors (*āsaṃjñikam-asaṃjñiṣu nirodhaś-citta-caittānām*); AKB ii.43 (DŚ ii.237): the ordinary people cannot attain the state of cessation of consciousness (*nirodha-samāpatti*) because they fear annihilation; it is attained only by the force of the Buddhist path; it is the state of deliverance of the Ārya who has attained the *dharma* of *nirvāṇa* (*na hi pṛthag-janā nirodha-samāpattim-utpādayituṃ śaknuvanti; uccheda-bhīrutvād, ārya-mārga-balena cotpādanād, dṛṣṭa-dharma-nirvāṇasya tad-adhimuktiḥ*).

The Sarvāstivādins held that these *samāpattis* were real entities or *dharmas* (*dravyasat*), whereas the Sautrāntikas maintained that the cessation of consciousness was not a real entity, but only a verbal designation (*prajñaptisat*) (cf. AKB ii.44). Since the Sautrāntikas refused to regard negative concepts like the cessation of consciousness as denoting real entities, they held (unlike the Sarvāstivādins) that a subtle consciousness continued to exist in the trance states; hence they believed that in these states consciousness was attenuated rather than actually destroyed. [The Vijñānavādins were in agreement with the Sautrāntikas on this point, and identified the subtle consciousness that remained in the *samāpattis* with the store consciousness (*ālaya-vijñāna*).] However, even the

Sautrāntikas agreed that this subtle consciousness is extinguished in the final *nirvāṇa* of total extinction (*nirupadhi-śeṣa-nirvāṇa*).

The cessation of *vijñāna* in *nirvāṇa* is a fundamental Buddhist tenet, and many other passages like the one from the Udāna could be cited. It was so orthodox a teaching, in fact, that even the Mādhyamikas could not deny it. For example, in MMKV 25.3 Candrakīrti says that in the pure state of *nirvāṇa* without any basis (*nivṛtau nirupadhi-śeṣe nirvāṇa-dhātau*) none of the three factors of existence like actions and defilements exist, and that this is the unanimous verdict of all the Buddhist schools (*evaṃ ca sarvavādinām-abhimatam*). However, as a Mādhyamika Candrakīrti also believed that *dharmas* are literally void and non-existent; hence in the passage that follows this statement he says that *dharmas* are never real, just as the snake in the standard rope-snake illusion is never real. In other words, what the early Buddhist texts present as a state to be *attained* is taken by Candrakīrti to characterize the ultimate nature of things (*paramārtha*) even *now*. This radical view made the Mādhyamikas unique, since all the other schools maintained that *saṃsāra* is real and that it is extinguished in *nirvāṇa*, however much they might have disagreed about the nature of *saṃsāra* and *nirvāṇa* in other respects.

16. In ordinary Sanskrit and in the traditional Buddhist teachings, "*śūnya*" is associated with non-existence and devoidness. While the possibility cannot be dismissed on a priori grounds that the Mahāyānists used the terms "*śūnya*," "*śūnyatā*" etc. in a non-standard sense, there are some telling considerations against this hypothesis. First of all, no ancient or medieval Buddhist writer, to my knowledge, ever stated that he, or Buddhist philosophers generally, used these terms in a sense which they did not have in ordinary language, nor to my knowledge did any of their opponents take the Buddhists to be using these terms in a special sense which they did not have in ordinary language. [In fact, the most common charge levelled against the Buddhists by the other schools was that they were nihilists (*vaināśikas, śūnyavādins*).] Secondly, I think that it can be shown that the Buddhist texts themselves — beginning with texts like the Cūḷa-suññata-sutta and continuing through to the

demise of Buddhism during the Muslim invasions — use these terms in their ordinary sense.

At first sight MV 1.13 might suggest that the Vijñānavādins used these terms in a non-standard way. This passage says (in effect) that emptiness is not existence (because it is the non-existence of duality), and that it is not non-existence (because it is the existence of the non-existence of that duality). However, it will be shown shortly that these latter kinds of assertions (e.g. that *śūnyatā* is existence because it is the existence of the nonexistence of duality) are actually the exceptions that prove the rule, for the existence of the non-existence of duality is surely *non-existence*, not existence.

17. Those who are unfamiliar with Buddhist doctrine might find it odd that the self (*ātman*) is described in the text as an external object, since in most philosophies the self is taken to be internal and private, and is contrasted with other minds and physical objects, which are taken to be external. However, it must not be forgotten that in Buddhist philosophy the self is held to be unreal. In holding that the self is an unreal appearance the Vijñanavādins were not departing from any of the other Buddhist schools (except possibly the non-orthodox Pudgalavādins). The Vijñanavādins' departure from the traditional Buddhist teachings lies instead in the assertion that external objects are *also* unreal appearances.

18. Actually, on Russell's view neither the expression "*x* is bald" in (2) nor "*x* exists" in (1) is treated as a predicate in a subject-predicate sentence. However, as I shall point out shortly, "*x* is bald" and "*x* exists" are treated very differently in Russell's analysis.

19. According to Buddhist philosophy, something that is strictly pure (*anāsrava*) and uncompounded (*asaṃskṛta*) cannot be the cause or effect of anything.

20. Xuan Zang's Cheng wei shilun (Vijñapti-mātratā-siddhi), a commentary on Vasubandhu's Triṃśikā, was written in Chinese. For all my citations from this important work I am wholly indebted to Poussin's translation (1928-48) from the Chinese into the French.

21. How, then is the principle of the mind (*di*) and the nature of the mind (*citta-dharmatā*) related to mind? This puzzle will engage

our attention once again in chapter 3, where it will be discussed in some detail.

22. Furthermore, to equate the essence of mind with the non-existence of mind would involve committing the fallacy of "hypostasizing the negative." Vide supra, p. 4.

23. It should be noted, however, that the doctrine of the innately pure mind is a very old teaching which can be traced back as far as the Aṅguttara-nikāya of the Pāli canon. For example, AN 1.6.1 says: "This mind is pure; it is soiled by impurities which are adventitious to it" (P. *pabhassaram idaṃ bhikkhave cittaṃ tañ ca kho āgantukehi upakkilesehi upakkiliṭṭhaṃ*). Later Buddhist schools, like the proto-Mahāyānist school of the Mahāsaṃghika-Ekavyāvahārika-Lokottaravādins, made much of this doctrine. The doctrine of the innately pure mind also appears in the Vimalakīrti-nirdeśa-sūtra, the Laṅkāvatāra-sūtra and the Śrīmālādevī-sūtra. It also came to play an important role in Ch'an and Vajrayāna Buddhism.

24. Note that the "*asat*" of MV 1.3 must mean that the mind is deceptive or false, and not that it is non-existent. MV 1.7 is another verse that makes no sense unless it is interpreted according to the doctrine of *other* emptiness. MV 1.7 says that perception has the same nature as non-perception. This looks like a contradiction (and perhaps even like a nihilistic assertion), but the *kārikā* is only asserting that perception is in fact *deceptive*. In the waking state we think that there is something outside us when we "perceive" things. According to the Vijñanavādins, however, the objects which we "perceive" in the waking state are no more outside us than the things we see in dreams and hallucinations. In this sense, so-called perceptions are in fact objectless; hence they are really no different from "non-perceptions" like dreams and hallucinations.

25. This *sutta* is found in the Saṃyutta-nikāya of the Pāli canon (SN XI, 2, ¶20, PTS). (I have used the PTS English translation.) Interestingly, this *sutta* is the only one to be cited by name by Nāgārjuna in his Mūla-madhyamaka-kārikā (MMK 15.7). In his commentary on this verse Candrakīrti remarks that the *sūtra* is found in the *nikāyas* (*sūtra* collections) of all the Buddhist schools (*idaṃ ca sūtraṃ sarva nikāyeṣu paṭhyate*).

26. Cf. AK 1.8: "The impure *dharmas* comprise the aggregate of grasping; they are full of strife; they are also suffering, origination, the world, the abode of wrong views and *existence*" (*ye sāsravā upādāna-skandhās-te saraṇā api / duḥkhaṃ samudayo loko dṛṣṭi-sthānaṃ* bhavaś-*ca*).

Notes to Chapter 2: Tri-svabhāva-nirdeśa

1. Although the TSN asserts in some places that the three natures are identical (TSN 10c; TSN 18-21), there are other passages which clearly imply that there are three *different* self natures. TSN 17, for example, says that the imagined nature and dependent nature are impure, whereas the perfected nature is pure. Obviously, if *a* has a property P that *b* does not have, then *a* cannot be identical with *b*; hence, because of TSN 17 alone, the perfected nature must be different from the other two natures. Similarly, in the Vijñanavāda the dependent nature is said to exist (cf. MV 1.1), whereas the imagined nature (i.e. the unreal external object) is said to be non-existent. Hence the dependent nature cannot be said to be the same thing as the imagined nature, on pain of contradiction. For such reasons the three natures cannot be identical just as a matter of simple logic.

2. Inconsistencies of a somewhat different kind will be noted in the next chapter, which discusses the Triṃśikā.

3. Note that the perfected nature cannot be identified with either of the other two natures. On the one hand, the perfected nature cannot be identified with the imagined nature, for the imagined nature is just the non-existent external object or duality. On the other hand, the perfected nature cannot be identified with the dependent nature, for the dependent nature is ever-changing, whereas the perfected nature must be unchanging. What, then, *is* the perfected nature?

4. This verse, or at least the part of it that says that the imagined nature (*kalpita-svabhāva*) has the characteristic of existence, contradicts Triṃśikā 20cd, which (for very good reasons) says that that which is purely imaginary has no self nature at all (*parikalpita evāsau svabhāvo na sa vidyate*), and Triṃś. 17, which

says that what is imagined does not exist. Discrepancies like these — there are others — seem to me to cast doubt on Vasubandhu's authorship of the TSN.

5. Obviously, a materialist would give a very different account of perceptual illusions than the one given here. A reductive or eliminative materialist, in fact, would give an analysis of perceptual illusions diametrically opposed to the one given by the Vijñanavāda. [For more on materialism, see the papers by Feyerabend, U. T. Place, Richard Rorty and J. J. C. Smart in Borst (1970).]

According to the Vijñanavāda, all external objects are illusions and are therefore nothing but mind. According to eliminative materialism, however, *mind* is non-existent and all mental processes — including illusions of the kind referred to in the TSN — are nothing but matter (i.e. brain processes).

I shall not enter into this kind of dispute here. My principal concern here is to analyze the doctrines of the Vijñanavāda, and I am therefore taking a non-materialist analysis of perception and perceptual illusions for granted for the purposes of the present discussion.

6. There are three other places where the TSN uses the notion of something's being "deceptive": TSN 20a (*yathākhyānam asadbhāvāt*), TSN 21b (*yathākhyānāsvabhāva*) and TSN 26c (*atathābhāva*). These passages parallel the use of "*asat*" in MV 1.3.

Notes to Chapter 3: Triṃśikā

1. The same principle was also clearly established in the Abhidharma literature, as the following citations will show:

(a) AK i.18cd (DŚ i.54): "A *dharma* is included in one *skandha*, one *āyatana*, one *dhātu* and *its own self nature*, because it is distinct from the nature of any other" (*sarva-saṃgraha ekena skandhenāyatanena ca / dhātunā ca svabhāvena parabhāva-viyogataḥ*). This, at any rate, appears to be Xuan Zang's reading of AK i.18; Poussin reconstructs as follows: *parabhāva-viyuktatvāt sva-bhāvenaiva saṃgrahaḥ*).

(b) AKB ii.46 (DŚ ii.262) (which gives the Sautrāntika view): "The characteristics of things are not different from the things themselves ... the qualities of a great man are not different from the man himself ... the characteristics of cowness are not different from a cow" (*katham idānīṃ sa eva dharmo lakṣyas-tasyaiva ca laksaṇaṃ yokṣyate ... mahā-puruṣa-lakṣaṇāni mahāpuruṣān-nānyāni ... gotva-lakṣaṇāni gor-nānyāni*).

In this connection Xuan Zang also has [AKB ii.46 (Poussin Tome 1, p. 236)]: "color (*rūpa*) and the essence of color (*svabhāva*) are not different things." According to Xuan Zang, apparently, this was one doctrine that even the Sautrāntikas and the Sarvāstivādins held in common.

(c) Cf. also AKB ii.72 (DŚ ii.370): "[There is one] act of mental attention which has as its object the special characteristics of things, as in the statement '*color is what is colorful* (or what makes things colorful)' (*svalakṣaṇa-manaskāraḥ, tad-yathā — "rūpaṇālakṣaṇaṃ rūpam" ity-evam-ādi*).

2. *aparaḥ punar-iti paratantra-svabhāvaḥ / nanv-ayaṃ bhāva etasya māyāvat parapratyayenotpatteḥ / ataś-ca yathā prakhyāti tathāsyotpattir-nāstīti ato 'sya utpatti-niḥsvabhāvatety-ucyate / dharmāṇām paramārthaś-ca sa yatas-tathatāpi sa iti / paramaṃ hi lokottara-jñānaṃ niruttaratvāt-tasyārthaḥ paramārthaḥ / atha vā ākāśavat sarvatraika-rasārthena vaimalyāvikārāthena ca / pariniṣpannaḥ svabhāvaḥ paramārtha ucyate / sa yasmāt pariniṣpannaḥ svabhāvaḥ sarvadharmāṇāṃ paratantrātmakānāṃ paramārthaḥ tad-dharmateti kṛtvā tasmāt pariniṣpanna eva kṛtvā svabhāvaḥ paramārtha-niḥsvabhāvatā pariniṣpannasyābhāva-svabhāvatvāt.*

Notes to Chapter 4: Triṃśikā and Tri-svabhāva-nirdeśa

1. Alex and Hideko Wayman (1974: 100).
2. Chapter 1, fn. 15.
3. AK i.4 (DŚ i.16) says that the impure *dharmas* are all the compounded *dharmas* except those which belong to the Path (*saṃskṛtā mārga-varjitāḥ sāsravāḥ*); an exception to the general rule is made for those *dharmas* which belong to the path because vices do not cling to them (*āsravās-teṣu yasmāt-samanuśerate*). AKB i.4 explains: "It is true that there are desires that are born from taking the truth of the path to extinction (*nirodha-mārga-*

satyālambanā) as an object, but even in this case the vices do not cling to them." In other words, an exception is made for the compounded *dharmas* that belong to the noble eight-fold path because these *dharmas* tend towards extinction, i.e. towards what is by nature uncompounded (*asaṃskṛta*). Of course, even these pure compounded *dharmas* belonging to the path are extinguished in the final *nirvāṇa* without remainder (*nirupadhi-śeṣa-nirvāṇa*).

4. Poussin (1928-48: 681).
5. Ibid: 675.
6. Ibid: 695.
7. Ibid: 695-696.
8. Ibid: 698-699.
9. As was noted in n. 3 above, the Abhidharma-kośa allows that the *dharmas* pertaining to the *ārya-mārga* (noble path) can be considered pure because they tend towards what is uncompounded (*asaṃskṛta*), i.e. the extinction of the *nirupadhi-śeṣa-nirvāṇa*. The problem in this connection is to see how the *skandhas* and *guṇas* of the Buddha in the *apratiṣṭhita-nirvāṇa* could be considered pure even in this attenuated sense, for the early Mahāyāna texts that refer to the *apratiṣṭhita-nirvāṇa* emphasize that the Buddha enters this state by *renouncing* the extinction of the *nirupadhi-śeṣa-nirvāṇa*.
10. Ibid: 676-677.
11. All cited by Poussin, ibid, 703.
12. The *eka-yāna* doctrine is found mostly in the Tathāgata-garbha group of texts. Xuan Zang's rejection of this doctrine is one of a number of indications that the writings of the Vijñanavādins should not be identified with the *sūtras* and *śāstras* of the Tathāgata-garbha school. There are important similarities between the two classes of texts, but there are differences as well.
13. Poussin (1928-48: 704-705).
14. For this reason it seems to me that Triṃś. 15, which asserts that the five sense consciousness arise in the *ālaya-vijñāna* like waves on the surface of water, is somewhat suspect from a doctrinal point of view.

15. This would seem to be a particularly pointed question, since the *svābhāvika-kāya* is said to be all-pervading, nondual and one and the same for all the Buddhas.

16. Poussin (1928-48: 700-701).

17. It is true that the Buddhist texts frequently refer to the all-pervadingness of space (*ākāśa*). However, unlike some of the other Indian philosophical schools which regarded space as some kind of invisible substance (like the ether of some pre-relativistic cosmologies), the early Buddhists described space as a sheer non-entity. When space (*ākāśa*) is understood in this way, saying that space is all-pervading is of course metaphorical.

As noted above in chapter 1, fn. 1, there was a difference of opinion amongst the Ābhidharmikas over the analysis of the *asaṃskṛta-dharmas*, including space. The Sautrāntikas held that space was a mere verbal designation, on the grounds that "space" (*ākāśa*) is simply a term we use to refer to the absence of resistance (*pratighatva*) etc. This appears to have been the prevailing view, as well as the most orthodox one, in the Buddhist schools. [For more on *ākāśa* see Bareau (1955).] This issue had great importance for the Abhidharma, because *nirvāṇa* had been linked with space (*ākāśa*) as an *asaṃskṛta dharma*; consequently, the analysis or interpretation of space had obvious implications for the analysis of *nirvāṇa* as well.

Notes to Chapter 5: Viṃśatikā and Cheng wei shilun

1. The following passages from some of the later (*nyāyānusārin*) Vijñanavādins illustrate this view:

(i) Diṅnāga, Ālambana-parīkṣā 6ab: "That which is an interior form appears as if it were something external" (*yad-antar-jñeya-rūpaṃ tu-bahirvad-abhāsate*).

(ii) Dharmakīrti, Pramāṇa-viniścaya I, 55b: "There is no difference between the color blue and the cognition of blue, because they are always found together (*sahopalambha-niyamād abhedo nīla-tad-dhiyoḥ*).

(iii) Prajñākaragupta, Pramāṇa-vārttika-bhāṣya, III, 327: "Perception is of itself, and of nothing else" (*ātmā sa tasyānubhavaḥ sa ca nānyasya kasyacit*).

2. As I show in Chapter 7, which discusses the Tattva-saṃgraha-(pañjikā) of Śāntarakṣita and Kamalaśīla, this meant that the Buddha knew all things, i.e. was *literally* omniscient. This appears to have been a fundamental Mahāyāna doctrine, and one that was held by many Hīnayāna schools as well. For a breakdown of the views of the Hīnayānists on this question, see Bareau (1955).

3. Xuan Zang, of course, was not the only one to hold this view. For example, essentially the same distinction is mentioned by Vinītadeva in his commentary on Dharmakīrti's Saṃtānāntara-siddhi [Stcherbatksy (1922: 382)].

4. "Viṃśatikā" means "Twenty Verses," but the work that we now have has twenty-two verses. This is puzzling, and it seems to have puzzled some of the old writers as well, for Poussin (1928-48: 425) mentions that Kui Ji discusses why the Twenty Verses has 20, 21, 22 and 23 *kārikās* in different recensions. Unfortunately, Poussin did not translate the passage.

Notes to Chapter 6: Saṃtānāntara-siddhi

1. Grounds for questioning the standard interpretation of Diṅnāga's *apoha* theory of universals can be found in Hattori (1968), Franco (1984) and Herzberger (1986).

Hattori (1968: 83-85, note 1.27) has discussed PS(V) 1.3d and its interpretation by Śāntarakṣita and Kamalaśīla. Śāntarakṣita and Kamalaśīla attempted to find a reading of PS(V) 1.3d which would be consistent with a strict *apoha* theory of universals. Hattori (like Franco) is critical of their interpretation. Their arguments, he says, "even if they are not actually false in their conclusion, seem not to be faithful to the original thought of the ... passage."

Franco (1984) has pointed to textual evidence which indicates that some of the later Buddhist logicians attributed to Diṅnāga the view that universals are real entities. [They did so, apparently, on the basis of PS(V) 1.3d.] Franco himself has offered a new non-realist interpretation of PS(V) 1.3d, but his reading seems less straightforward to me on purely linguistic grounds than the interpretation that commits Diṅnāga to a realist view of universals.

Herzberger (1986) has argued that for Diṅnāga a universal is (or names) a spatio-temporal quality that qualifies spatio-temporal individuals (p. 112). She also argues that for Diṅnāga universals are "abstracted out of sense experience" and, as such, have a "temporary status" (p. 117).

I find these issues intriguing, but will not pursue them here. The author of the SS, in any case, clearly had in mind a purely nominalistic account of universals.

2. By drawing the parallel between Russell, on the one hand, and Diṅnāga and Dharmakīrti on the other, I do not mean to suggest that their epistemological views were identical. To mention only one difference, in his *Problems of Philosophy* Russell was an out-and-out Platonist, whereas Diṅnāga and Dharmakīrti seem to have held that universals are at best mental constructions. Nevertheless, up to a certain point Russell, Diṅnāga and Dharmakīrti appear to draw the distinction between inference and perception in very similar ways.

3. As Hattori himself has noted (1968: 81, note 1.17), "Diṅnāga's theory of a sharp distinction between the objects of *pratyakṣa* and *anumāna* is hardly applicable to the case of recognition."

Although the objections may be intuitively somewhat clearer in cases of recognition etc., the philosophical objections to the "two objects" view are essentially the same in the case of a previously *un*perceived object.

4. It is rather difficult, it seems to me, to reconcile Hattori's translation of *k.* $2b_2$-c_1, which speaks of the object (*prameya*) as possessing two aspects (*lakṣaṇa*), with his statement (1968: 80, n. 1.14) that "...there cannot be anything which possesses both *sva-lakṣaṇa* and *sāmānya-lakṣaṇa* at the same time."

5. There are other passages in the PS(V) which support this reading of Diṅnāga's use of the term "*viṣaya*." For example, PSV ad PV 1.4ab (ibid., p. 26; p. 87, n. 1.33) says that a *viṣaya* is common to many cases, for it is an object of mental cognition as well as the cognition of other mind streams (*viṣayo hi mano-vijñānānya-*

saṃtānika-vijñāna-hetutvāt sādhāraṇam). The most natural way of reading this is to take "*viṣaya*" as referrring to a non-intentional object.

6. Support for the latter analysis of the compounds "*sāmānya-lakṣaṇa-viṣayam,*" "*sva-lakṣaṇa-viṣayam*" and "*sva-sāmānya-lakṣaṇābhyām-anyat-prameyam*" can be found in passages in the Abhidharma literature which speak of the *dharmas* as supporting both the special and the general characteristic, e.g.:

(a) AKB i.2 [DŚ i.12]: "*Dharma*: because it supports its own-characteristics" (*sva-lakṣaṇa-dhāraṇād dharmaḥ*).

(b) AKSV i.4 [DŚ i.16]: "*Dharmas*: because they support self characteristics and general characteristics" (*sva-sāmānya-lakṣaṇa-dhāraṇād dharmāḥ.*"

(c) AKB i.12 [DŚ i.42]: "[The earth, water, fire and wind] are called great elements (*mahābhūtāni*) because they support their own characters (*sva-lakṣaṇa*) and the secondary or derived matters (*upādāya-rūpa*).

(d) AKSV i.12; [DŚ i.42]: "There are eighteen *dhātus* because there are eighteen that support their own characteristics and the general characteristics" (*aṣṭādaśa dhātavas-tu sva-sāmānya-lakṣaṇa-dhāraṇāt*).

7. One objection to Hattori's interpretation of PS(V) 1.2 is the following. According to the "two objects" interpretation, a *sāmānya* is unreal (*asat, prajñaptisat*). This, I think, makes it rather hard to speak of a *viṣaya* which *is* a universal, for the expression "an unreal *viṣaya*," interpreted non-intentionally, is an oxymoron.

This problem does not arise, of course, if the term "*viṣaya*" in PS(V) 1.2 is interpreted intentionally. Nor does it arise if the compounds are analyzed as adjectival *karmadhāraya* compounds. But on these readings the meaning of the passage must be that there is one object of cognition which is known in two different ways.

8. Nyāya-darśana (1967: 320). These fragments have been discussed by (among others) B. K. Matilal (1968) and R. P. Hayes (1988). Hayes' work is particularly helpful in interpreting this passage because it includes translations (from the Tibetan) of Jinendrabuddhi's Ṭīkā on the PS(V), called the Viśālāmalavatī.

9. This distinction is found in Jñānaśrīmitra (JNA 166: 16ff), Ratnakīrti (RNA 102: 13-17; ibid., 136: 2-3) and the Tarka-bhāṣā of Mokṣākaragupta (TB: 22). According to Kajiyama (1966: 59, n. 137), the Buddhists may have borrowed this distinction from the Jaina writer Māṇikyanandin.

10. It goes without saying that as an idealist Dharmakīrti believed that all so-called physical objects are in fact purely intentional objects. The question here is whether he also held that other *minds* are purely intentional objects of *my* mind's inferences.

11. The view that Diṅnāga and Dharmakīrti were idealists has recently been challenged. Warder (1980) and Singh (1984) have recently argued that they were Sautrāntikas. Since theirs remains the minority view, I have not felt it necessary to present any defense of the prevailing scholarly view against their criticisms. However, I should perhaps say something here about their interpretation of the Saṃtānāntara-siddhi.

The following was the only comment that Warder had to make about the SS in his *Indian Buddhism* (1980: 471):

> [The Saṃtānāntara-siddhi] is a monograph on a special philosophical problem: the inference of the existence of other minds than one's own (i.e. against the solipsist position). Observing that our own purposive actions are preceded by intelligence (i.e. mental activity), when we see similar actions on the part of others we may infer that these also are preceded by intelligence, in other words that other minds exist.

A few years later, in his Foreword to Singh's work (1984: ix), Warder went further and stated that the SS "appears to be a Sautrāntika critique of Vaibhāṣika doctrine, not a Vijñānavāda work." However, he did not present there (nor has he presented anywhere else, so far as I know) any evidence or argumentation to support this claim.

Singh has also asserted that the SS is a Sautrāntika work (1984: 51-58). According to Singh, Stcherbatsky and Kitagawa have simply misinterpreted the text through having been misled by Vinītadeva's commentary on it. Surprisingly, Singh even seems to believe that he has actually shown that the SS is a Sautrāntika text in his book, despite the fact that he has not offered an alternative translation of the text nor, for that matter, an alternative, word-by-word translation of a single passage of the text. Given the importance of this text to his whole line of argument, one might have expected Singh to have employed a higher standard of argumentation and evidence on this point than the one he actually employs.

It seems to me that any serious attempt at a refutation of the prevailing scholarly opinion about this text would have to contain a literal, word-by-word translation of it. Such a translation would have to provide an alternative reading of the text that could withstand scrutiny by other scholars who are in a position to evaluate it against the Tibetan text. As it is, we are left more or less with the bare, unsubstantiated assertion that Vinītadeva, Stcherbatsky (1922), Kitagawa (1955) and Poussin (1918) have simply misunderstood the text. This is not impossible, of course, but on purely a priori grounds it is not very likely, and to date neither Warder nor Singh seems to have provided the kind of evidence that would be required to make us think that it is likely.

There is also a discussion of the SS and a translation of some of its verses in Piatigorsky (1983). Although Piatigorsky criticizes Stcherbatsky on certain points, his translations of the selected *kārikās* from the SS appear to me to allow only an idealist interpretation of the work.

N. J. Shah (1967: 300) refers to an unpublished "restoration" of the SS by Muni Jambūvijaya.This is presumably the retranslation to which R. K. Sharma (1985: 68, n. 1) refers, which he says he was unable to obtain. It would be interesting to see whether Muni Jambūvijaya's translation of the SS provides support for or against the prevailing (i.e. Vijñānavādin) interpretation of the text.

12. The only argument for the existence of other minds that Dharmakīrti considers is the argument by analogy. The inference to other minds may actually be much more complicated and subtle than this. Nevertheless, it would seem that *any* argument proposed by a non-solipsistic idealist would have to hold that the object in the inference to other minds is real (*svābhāvika*).

For an introduction to the contemporary Western analysis of the belief in other minds see J. M. Shorter (1967).

13. Cf. Stcherbatsky (1978: 36-41, Introduction, Section X), Chatterjee (1975: 133-34) and Tripathi (1972: 303-04, 334).

14. Gnoli (1960: xxiv-xxv, n. 3) has made this identification on the basis of citations in Kāśmīra Śaivite works which he has been able to trace to the Tibetan canon.

Notes to Chapter 7: Tattva-saṃgraha-(pañjikā)

1. Kamalaśīla was the immediate disciple of Śāntarakṣita. The TSP is a lengthy commentary on his *guru's* work.

It is a matter of dispute whether Śāntarakṣita and Kamalaśīla were affiliated primarily with the Madhyamaka school or with the Yogācāra school. Adherents of the latter view refer to them as Svātantrika-Mādhyamika-Yogācāras; adherents of the former view refer to them as Yogācāra-Svātantrika-Mādhyamikas. It is argued in Appendix III that the TS(P), at any rate, is a *purely* Vijñānavāda text.

2. Citations are to Dvārikādāsa Śāstrī (1968). Krishnamacharya counts 3,646 verses; Dvārikādāsa Śāstrī (1968) counts 3,645. To find the same verse in Śāstrī's edition, one must often subtract one from the number of the corresponding verse in the Krishnamacharya edition.

3. This, however, was not the view of Śāntarakṣita-Kamalaśīla. For example, chapter 18 (*anumāna-parīkṣā*) of the TS(P) defends the validity of inference in general (and Diṅnāga's *trairūpya* theory of inference, in particular) against criticism.

One possibility to consider, of course, is that Śāntarakṣita and Kamalaśīla held that inference is a *pramāṇa*, but only at the level of relative truth. However, as I have argued in the previous chapter, consigning inference to a domain of "relative" truth cannot in fact be distinguished from the view that perception is the *only* means of knowledge.

4. Obviously, a solipsist cannot hold the view that someone *else* is omniscient, for according to the solipsist the only mind that exists is *his* mind.

5. They could not have been absolute idealists, either, for the doctrine of an absolute mind was anathematized very early in the

history of Buddhism. For example, Majjhima-nikāya I.329, No. 49 proscribes the following view:

> There is a consciousness which the eye does not see, which does not have boundaries, and which shines in all places. It cannot be perceived even as the earthiness of the earth cannot be perceived, even as the wateriness of the water.
>
> *viññaṇaṃ anidassanaṃ anantaṃ sabbatopabhaṃ taṃ paṭhaviya paṭhavattena ananubhūtaṃ āpassa āpattena ananubhūtaṃ.*

Similarly, in MN I.326, No. 49 the following opinion of Baka the Brahmā is declared to be "pernicious" (*pāpakam*):

> It is permanent. It is eternal. It is always existent. It is independent existence. It has the *dharma* of non-perishing. Truly it is not born, does not become old, does not die, does not disappear, and is not born again. Further, no liberation superior to it exists elsewhere.
>
> *idaṃ niccaṃ idaṃ dhuvaṃ idaṃ sassataṃ idaṃ kevalaṃ idaṃ acavanadhammaṃ idam hi na jāyati na jīyati na mīyati na cavati na upapjjati, ito ca pan 'aññaṃ uttariṃ nissaraṇaṃ natthīti*

Presumably, in this passage the eternal and unchanging existence that is referred to is an absolute consciousness.

The foregoing passages and their translation are taken from H. Nakamura (1983: 138).

6. At any rate, if inference is involved, it is not an inference by analogy based on the perception of the bodily actions and speech of others.

7. The doctrine of the omniscience of the Buddha was by no means a purely Mahāyānist doctrine. It became, at a comparatively early date, the prevailing view in the Hīnayānist schools as well. For a breakdown of the Hīnayānist schools on this question, see Bareau (1955). See also Jaini's citation (op. cit., pp. 83-86) of a passage from the Paramattha-mañjūsā, a commentary on Buddhaghoṣa's Viśuddhi-magga by Dhammapāla (fl. 5th-6th century C.E.).

8. According to Dr. Jaini (1974: 87, n. 42), Śāntarakṣita rejected the view that the Buddha is literally omniscient, whereas "later" Buddhists like Kamalaśīla accepted it.

I cannot agree with Dr. Jaini that there is a difference in this respect between the views of Śāntarakṣita and Kamalaśīla, for the view that the Buddha is literally omniscient is stated quite unequivocally by Śāntarakṣita himself in the following verses: TS 3267-8, 3308, 3313, 3329, 3333, 3336, 3338, 3339, 3344-6, 3412, 3419, 3595 and 3626.

9. However, TS 2030, cited at the beginning of this chapter (pp. 133-35), indicates that Śāntarakṣita did not always hold this doctrine consistently.

10. Jha's translation links "*bāhyaṃ ca vastu*" with "*nirvikalpaka-jñāna-gocara*" rather than with "*vikalpa-viṣayam-āropitākāra*." Thus his translation reads:

> [The Buddha] recognizes the object of the Conceptual Cognition as only imposed (unreal), while He looks upon the real external object, — which is envisaged by the Non-conceptual Cognition, — as something quite different, and real; how then can He be said to be 'mistaken'?"

This translation must be a mistake, since idealism cannot be true if the object of the *nirvikalpa-jñāna* is a real, external object (*bāhya*, *vastu*). This appears to be one of the relatively few instances where Jha's translation is misleading.

11. Cf. PS(V) 1.12ab, Hattori (1968: 30):

> Some may hold that cognition also, like a thing of color, etc., is cognized by means of a separate cognition. This is not true because
>
> k.12a-b_1. if a cognition were cognized by a separate cognition, there would be an infinite regression.

This view even extended to the denial that in any *literal* sense a cognition grasps itself. Cf. TS 2000:

> There can be no self-cognition of the cognition in the sense of action or the active agent, because one thing that is without parts cannot have three natures.

That is to say, according to TS 2000 cognitions are inherently self-cognizing, and in a thoroughly nondual way. According to this verse, it is not possible to separate a cognition into a grasping aspect and an aspect that is grasped by it. A cognition and the cognition of that cognition are simply one and the same thing.

12. This distinction is the basis of Śaṃkarācārya's critique of the Vijñanavāda in Bṛhad-āraṇyakopaniṣad-bhāṣya (BUB) 2.3.6, BUB 4.3.7, and Brahma-sūtra-bhāṣya 2.2.28-31. I analyze Śaṃkara's critique of the Vijñanavāda in Wood (1990).

Notes to Chapter 8: Saṃtānāntara-dūṣaṇa

1. It is unlikely that Ratnakīrti undertook a categorical and straightforward refutation of the Saṃtānāntara-siddhi, for Ratnakīrti revered Dharmakīrti and called him "Bhagavān" and the "one teacher of the whole world" (*bhuvanaika-guru*).

2. As has been previously noted, the view of the earlier (*āgamānusārī) Vijñānavādins* was that there are two, and only two, valid means of knowledge, i.e. perception and inference. Ratnakīrti's *refutation (bādhaka*) of other minds in the SD is another interesting and illuminating example of the tendency amongst the later *nyāyānusārī* Vijñānavādins to reject this view in favor of the far more radical one that perception is the only (absolutely) valid mode of knowledge. The later Vijñānavādins were probably led to this rejection or devaluation of inference as a *pramāṇa* by their rejection, on idealist grounds, of the Sautrāntika view that the existence of matter can be validly inferred.

3. In the introduction to his translation of the SD, Y. Kajiyama (1965) uses the terms "monist" and "solipsist" interchangeably. However, these are terms which are taken from Western philosophy, and in Western philosophy they have different connotations.

This point has been noted by A. C. S. McDermott (1973: 174, n. 34). It appears, however, that Dr. McDermott wants to avoid, not only solipsism, but also the conclusion that the ultimate level of reality (*paramārtha*) is nondual or monistic, for she says (p. 170):

> That the issue of solipsism seems to arise in conjunction with discussions of Yogācāra philosophy is merely symptomatic of the extent to which *avidyā* is still operative. For the very ability to raise the question of whether there is one or a multiplicity of streams of psychic energy itself presupposes the activation of the *vāsanās* in the *ālayavijñāna*. But ... both *ālayavijñāna* and its *vāsanās* ultimately dissolve under the impact of Mādhyamika dialectic.

Dr. McDermott's view that reality is ultimately neither dual nor nondual is subject to objections. Even if it could be established that *thoughts* of unity and multiplicity disappear from the mind when Buddhahood is attained, it surely does not follow that the state that is attained is neither dual nor nondual. It is not clear to me how one can assert that the state itself is neither dual nor nondual without violating the laws of logic (e.g. the law of the excluded middle).

4. Some philosophers have argued that there are cases where one must invoke a third truth value (neither true nor false), as for example when one utters "The king of France is bald" when there is no king of France. According to these philosophers, one should say that this assertion is neither true nor false when there is no king of France. However, this does not seem to be the same thing as the distinction between an absolute and a relative truth. The former is a question about the number of truth values; the second involves the question whether truth is a univocal concept.

Notes to Chapter 9: Viṃśatikā and Cheng wei shilun

1. For example, Vasubandhu's statement at the outset of his autocommentary on the Viṃśatikā (VV), that all the three realms (*dhātus*) are mind only, can be found almost verbatim in the Daśa-bhūmika-sūtra: *cittamātram idaṃ yad idaṃ traidhātukam* [Rahder (1926: 49)].

2. The Vijñanavādins used the term "mind stream" (*citta-saṃtāna*) because, as Buddhists, they did not believe in the existence of a self (*ātman*) which remains the same through time.

3. A translation and the Sanskrit text of the Viṃśatikā have been given in chapter 5 of Part III.

4. *vijñaptimātram-evaitad-asad-arthāvabhasanāt*
yathā taimirikasyāsat-keśa-candrādi-darśanam

The first *kārikā* and its commentary are missing in the only extant MS. of the Sanskrit text, which was discovered by Hemrāj Śarman and Prof. Sylvain Lévi in Nepal. I have used Lévi's reconstruction into the Sanskrit, which he based on the Chinese and Tibetan translations of the text.

5. Literally, "all the ghosts (*pretas*) and not just one see the river of pus in hell (*pretāḥ sarve 'pi pūya-pūrṇāṃ nadīṃ paśyanti naika eva)* because they are in the same state of *karma* which has ripened *(tulya-karma-vipākāvasthā*). (VV 3)

6. *yadi tat-karmabhis-tatra bhūtānāṃ saṃbhavas-tathā*
iṣyate pariṇāmaś-ca kiṃ vijñānasya neṣyate

7. *sarveṣāṃ hi sattvānām-anyonya-vijñapty-ādhipatyena mithyo vijñapter-niyamo bhavati yathā-yogaṃ / mithya iti paras-parataḥ / uktaḥ saṃtānāntara-vijñapti-viśeṣāt-saṃtānāntare vijñapti-viśeṣa ut-padyate nārtha-viśeṣāt* (VV 18). (Cf. SS *sūtras* ¶62-63; Kitagawa: 98-99, Stcherbatsky: 368-369).

8. "*Ālaya-vijñāna*" means "store consciousness." The Vijñāna-vādins postulated such a consciousness in order to explain how a person could be affected by the *karmic* consequences of actions done by the person in the past. According to the Yogācārins, this is accounted for by the fact that actions establish dispositions or tendencies (*vāsanās*) which persist in the *ālaya-vijñāna* until the individual reaps the fruit of his *karma*.

The *ālaya-vijñāna* was also invoked to explain the apparent continuity of our experiences. According to Buddhist philosophy, what we call a self (*ātman*) is in fact an ever-changing stream of mental phenomena, which arise and perish depending on their causes and conditions. The Buddhist philosophers recognized, however, that there is the impression of a self (*ātma-moha*) and that this impression is connected with memory and a sense of continuity in our experiences. The Vijñanavādins wanted to account for this feeling of personal identity or continuity through the hypothesis of a store consciousness that contains the seeds (*bījas*) or impulses (*vāsanās*) from past experiences which operate in the present to create one's sense of personal identity.

There are some similarities between the doctrine of the *ālaya-vijñāna* and the *ātman* doctrine of the Hindu schools, but the two doctrines are certainly not identical. For example, as Triṃś. 4d says, the *ālaya-vijñāna* is constantly changing, like a torrent of water. This is not true of the *ātman* of the Hindu schools, for though the *ātman* may manifest different properties at different times, it was thought to be unchanging in itself. The *ātman* doctrine presupposes a metaphysical distinction between an entity and its properties and the view that entities themselves persist through time. These views the Mahāyānists did not accept.

9. Poussin (1928-48: 135-142).

10. In the Buddhist texts the term "*asaṃvidita(ka)*" is most commonly used to refer to the object (*ālambana*) and aspect (*ākāra*) of very subtle states of trance consciousness; in this sense its best translation is perhaps "imperceptible" or "subtle" (*anusūkṣma*). [See Tola and Dragonetti (1983: 260-261, n. 24), who cite in this connection Sthiramati's Triṃśikā-bhāṣya, the Karma-siddhi-prakaraṇa, and the CWSL of Xuan Zang.]

What Xuan Zang says in CWSL pp. 135-142 about the *bhājana-loka*, *sādhāraṇa-bījas* etc. is not incompatible with this more common usage of the term "*asaṃvidita*." Thus, I do not think that the more general usage of the term precludes interpreting Xuan Zang's remarks in CWSL 135-142 as an explication of the notion of unconscious perception, which is how I interpret him.

11. Here Xuan Zang appears to be addressing the same problem that Vasubandhu had addressed earlier in the Viṃśatikā. You and I can look at a tree and (so we suppose) see the same thing, or at least have perceptions that are very similar and which are coordinated in a systematic way. The question is: how is this possible if there is nothing in the world but the representations of consciousness of the mind streams of a multiplicity of individuals?

Xuan Zang's suggestion is that our experiences are coordinated because of the existence of these *sādhāraṇa-bījas*.

12. This problem is reminiscent of Berkeley's conundrum about the ontological status of unperceived objects. If an object must be perceived in order to exist (as Berkeley argued), what happens to it when no finite being is around to perceive it? Berkeley's solution to this problem was that things continue to exist because they are always perceived by God. This particular solution, of course, would have been unacceptable to Xuan Zang even if it had occurred to him, for as a Buddhist he rejected the notion of a supreme being.

13. The passages in question occur in the CWSL's commentary on Triṃśikā 2-4. This seems to me to show that Xuan Zang took Vasubandhu's Triṃś. 2-4 to assert the existence of mental objects that are perceived unconsciously (*asaṃvidita*) and that may be said to exist entirely in the unconscious mind.

Notes to Chapter 10: A Critique of the Doctrine of Collective Hallucination

1. Viṃś. 19-20 is an interesting example of the Vijñanavādins' attitude towards these *siddhis*.

Having argued in the preceding verses that waking perceptions are essentially the same as dreams, and that the appearance of a real, external world arises from the fact that perceptions are mutually determined (*paras-parataḥ*), Vasubandhu asserts in Viṃś. 19 that death itself is a transformation which can be brought about by the mental representations (*vijñapti*) of another being. He proceeds to explain this idea (in VV 19) in terms of the powers which demons (*piśācas*), magicians (*ṛddhivan*) and sages (*ṛṣis*) were reputed to have of killing others, causing others to lose their memories, have dreams etc. He also (Viṃś. 20) cites the authority of the Buddha in this connection, who is said to have used a Purāṇic legend about the destruction of the Daṇḍaka forest and its inhabitants by the mental power of the *ṛṣis* to illustrate his teaching that such "mental" crimes are even worse than crimes of body and speech.

2. It goes without saying that there is a great deal of controversy over the evidentiality of reported cases of "collective hallucination." We need not enter into this controversy here, however, for the following case reports are cited simply as thought-experiments to clarify the Vijñanavādins' doctrine of Collective Hallucination. I shall, therefore, usually omit the qualification "assuming that report R is evidential" in what follows, partly because it is too tedious to keep repeating it.

It would, however, be highly inappropriate and misleading to impute any scepticism on such matters to the Vijñanavādins. Anyone who is sceptical about telepathy will undoubtedly find the views of the Vijñanavādins strange, but our understanding of the Vijñanavādins is not going to be advanced by somehow or other pretending that their views were different from what they were. I do not think that it can be emphasized too much that for the Vijñanavādins *all* perception is essentially telepathic.

3. It is important to distinguish between collective hallucinations in the purely parapsychological sense and the doctrines of the Vijñanavādins, who maintained that *everything* is a collective hallucination. I shall occasionally (when necessary or appropriate) distinguish between a collective hallucination (uncapitalized letters) and the doctrine of Collective Hallucination (capitalized letters). The term "collective hallucination" refers to cases like (1)-(5) to be discussed below; "Collective Hallucination" refers to the Vijñanavādin doctrine that the whole world (*idaṃ sarvam*) is nothing but an hallucination.

4. Obviously, whenever one is interested in the evidentiality of such reports, it is crucial to know exactly who reported what and when. These cases, however, are presented here only as thought-experiments, and in order to make the presentation simpler (and in order to make them more vivid) I have put all of them in the second-person. Nevertheless the details of the cases as reported have not been essentially altered. The case reports I cite can be found in the following sources:

Case 1: Gurney and Myers (1886), vol. 2: 217-218.

Case 2: *Journal*, Society for Psychical Research (SPR), vol. VI: 145. Cited in Mrs. Sidgwick (1922): 363-364.

Case 3: Professor Sidgwick's Committee (1894): 305-306.
Case 4: Gurney and Myers, vol. 2: 626.
Case 5: Ibid.: 199-200.
Case 6: Ibid.: 211-212.

5. Materialism now comes in two basic varieties: reductive and non-reductive. According to non-reductive materialism, mind is identical — specifically, *contingently* identical — with a property of matter. One of the problems with this view is that many of the kinds of difficulties involved in explaining the relationship between mind and matter seem to reappear within non-reductive materialism as the problem of explaining how a material substratum can be related to its mental properties. Some have tried to escape this difficulty through reductive or eliminative materialism. According to this view, neither mind nor mental properties exist; both are held to be as unreal as demons or phlogiston.

For more on materialism, see the papers in Borst (1970). For an interesting recent attack on the notion of contingent identity and its application by the materialist to the mind-body problem, see Kripke (1980).

6. Thus, the view that Kant later adopted had, in all its essential points, been anticipated by Berkeley, who argued forcefully against it.

7. That is, although either dualism or materialism might be the correct view, they prove, on examination, to be rather far removed from common sense.

8. For a powerful critique of solipsism see Russell (1948: 175-181). There Russell argues persuasively that the doctrine of solipsism becomes more and more implausible and untenable as it is made more consistent.

Notes to Conclusion

1. This interpretration has not been confined to contemporary scholars. Very similar views were attributed to the Vijñanavādins even by the Mādhyamikas.

For example, Lindtner (1986: 250) cites a passage from a Mādhyamika work, the Ratna-pradīpa (RP), which argues (*reductio ad absurdum*) that if the Vijñanavādins were right in maintaining that everything is mind only (*cittamātra*), then when a person sees a jar he should also perceive the mental contents (*citta-saṃtāna*) of all other living beings; in this way, every living being would have the intuition (*abhijñā*) of the minds of others (*para-citta*). The Mādhyamikas also argued (ibid, p. 252) that the Vijñanavādin doctrine that cognitions are self-cognizing (*svasaṃvedana*) is identical with the *ātman* doctrine of the Vedānta. (In this connection Lindtner cites the RP, the Tarka-jvālā and the Kara-tala-ratna.) According to the author of the RP, the Vijñānavādins believed in an *ātman* which is eternal (*nitya*), one (*eka*), omnipresent (*vyāpin*) and incorporeal (*amūrta*). The author of the RP also says, with considerable indignation: "The Yogācāras do not understand *pudgala-nairātmya* and they do not understand *dharma-nairātmya* either, because of their tremendous clinging to self (*ahaṃkāra*)."

2. As was noted in chapter 1, the anomalous doctrine of the innate purity of the mind in AN 1.6.1 is a notable exception to this general rule.

3. The following two examples were discussed in chapter 3.

Notes to Appendix II

1. In giving the gist of *sūtras* 17-20, I have followed Stcherbatsky's translation a little more closely than Kitagawa's.

2. In the rest of ¶5 I anticipate somewhat a line of argument that appears in full force only later in the text. Dharmakīrti, as an idealist, maintains that all that we ever directly perceive — whether in dreams or the waking state — are our own cognitions or sense data. In this respect, impressions in our minds in the waking state are on the same footing as the impressions we have in our minds in the dreaming state. The only difference that Dharmakīrti allows between the waking state and the dreaming state is that in the former my percepts are caused directly (and at the same time) by the direct, telepathic influence of other minds on my own. In the dreaming state, however, my mind is in a kind of coma and is weak; in this state, therefore, the impressions that occur in sleep arise as memories of previous impressions. Note that in refusing to draw any

qualitative distinction between dreams and the waking state, Dharmakīrti is just following the lead of Vasubandhu (cf. Viṃś. 18).

3. I have omitted *sūtra* 43 in my synopsis of the text. As Harish Gupta notes (1969: 360-361), Stcherbatsky's translation diverges from Kitagawa's in the translation of *sūtra* 43. Both are in agreement in the interpretation of the central point, which is that the idealist argues that the inference to other minds can be made on the basis of impressions (*vijñapti*) alone. However, Kitagawa takes *sūtra* 43 to be an argument of the realist opponent, who is said to argue that representations are not needed to infer the existence of one's own mind. In a footnote he explains his interpretation as follows: "I suppose that the Realists are referring to the fact that we can know the movements of our own hands, feet etc. without perceiving them."

Stcherbatsky, on the other hand, takes *sūtra* 43 to be a continuation of the argument in *sūtra* 42. This seems to me to make more sense logically, though I am in no position to judge which reading is preferable linguistically. This disputed point does not appear to be a crucial one, however, and I have therefore omitted the translation of *sūtra* 43 in my own free rendering of the text.

4. Here is the key to the whole line of argument. For Dharmakīrti, there is a direct, telepathic link between one mind stream and another (*especially* in the waking state). Both Stcherbatsky (p. 341) and Kitagawa (p. 98) give "*adhipati-pratyaya*" as the Sanskrit equivalent of the Tibetan term which is used to name this linking force. This is significant, for this is the term that Vasubandhu uses in Viṃś. 18 (*adhipatitva*) in connection with the assertion that different mind streams are mutually related (*paraspparataḥ*) with each other. This clearly links the Saṃtānāntara-siddhi with the Viṃśatikā.

5. Stcherbatsky translates the relevant term in *sūtra* ¶69 as "general concept"; Kitagawa translates it as "generality." These terms would seem to indicate that the Sanskrit original was "*sāmānya*," which is usually translated as "universal." Similarly, the particular, which is the aspect of the object which is *perceived*, may have been "*svalakṣaṇa*." Cf. Nyāya-bindu 1.12 (*tasya viṣayaḥ*

svalakṣaṇam) and 1.16-17: *anyat sāmānya-lakṣaṇam* /16/; *so 'numānasya viṣayaḥ* //17//.

Notes to Appendix IV

1. In "*vijñapti-mātra*" or "*citta-mātra*," the suffix "*-mātra*" means "only." In the SD, however, the suffix "*-mātra*" usually appears in the compound "*icchā-(citta)-mātra*" where it means "volition in general" etc. In the SD, in other words, the suffix "*-mātra*" is usually used to refer to a corresponding property or universal, or to the entire class or totality of things of a certain kind.

2. NBṬ (BB 23: 7-8), cited by Y. Kajiyama.

3. This last sentence is Ratnakīrti's statement of the correct view (*siddhānta*) about the existence of other minds. The statement that other minds are non-existent like a universal is based on the *apoha* theory of universals.

4. The text refers to the Pravacana-pradīpa-śrī-sākāra-saṃgraha. Kajiyama cites Sākāra-siddhi (JNA: 458) and Sākāra-saṃgraha (ibid, v. 185).

5. The Sanskrit of the text is not very clear at this point. I have followed Kajiyama's translation as being as good a suggestion as any.

6. The text cites the Vārttika-kāra (i.e. Dharmakīrti). Kajiyama identifies this with *pratyakṣa-pariccheda* 4d. PV II.4 [Śāstrī (1968: 101-02)] reads:

> *aśaktaṃ sarvam-iti ced bījāder-aṅkurādiṣu* /
> *dṛṣṭā śaktiḥ; matā sā cet saṃvṛtyā; 'stu yathā tathā* //

7. Ratnakīrti's school of the Vijñānavāda was called the "*vijñānādvaita-vāda*" (the doctrine of the nondual mind) and the "*citrākārādvaita-vāda*" (the doctrine of the nonduality of the variegated appearances of things).

8. This is the second statement of the *siddhānta*.

9. This is Ratnakīrti's third and last statement of the *siddhānta*.

10. Kajiyama cites PVB III.327 (*pratyakṣa-pariccheda*, R. Sāṅkṛtyāyana, 1953 ed.):

> *ātmā sa tasyānubhavaḥ sa ca nānyasya kasya cit /*
> *pratyakṣa-prativedyattvam-api tasya tad-ātmatā //*

11. Rāhula Sāṅkṛtyāyana's photocopy of the Sanskrit MS. becomes largely illegible at this point. I have not attempted a translation of his suggested readings or reconstructions of the last few lines of the text.

BIBLIOGRAPHY

BIBLIOGRAPHY

Abbreviations

AL(B)	*Adyar Library (Bulletin)*
AO	*Acta Orientalia*
AS	*Asiatische Studien*
BB	*Bibliotheca Buddhica*
BBh	*Bauddha Bhāratī*
BEFEO	*Bulletin de l'École française d'Extrême-Orient*
BEHE	*Bibliothèque de l'École des Hautes Études*
BI	*Bibliotheca Indica*
BSO(A)S	*Bulletin of the School of Oriental (and African) Studies*
BST	*Buddhist Sanskrit Texts*
BT	*Bulletin of Tibetology*
EB	*Encyclopedia of Buddhism*
ERE	*Encyclopedia of Religion and Ethics*
EW	*East and West*
GOS	*Gaekwad's Oriental Series*
HOS	*Harvard Oriental Series*
IHQ	*Indian Historical Quarterly*
ISPP	*Indian Studies Past and Present*
JAOS	*Journal of the American Oriental Society*
JBORS	*Journal of the Bihar and Orissa Research Society*
JGIS	*Journal of the Greater India Society*
JGJRI	*Journal of the Ganganatha Jha Research Institute*
JIABS	*Journal of the International Association of Buddhist Studies*
JIBSt	*Journal of Indian and Buddhist Studies*
JIP	*Journal of Indian Philosophy*
JPTS	*Journal of the Pali Text Society*
JRAS	*Journal of the Royal Asiatic Society*
KPJRI	*K. P. Jayaswal Research Institute*
KSS	*Kashi Sanskrit Series*
LM	*Le Muséon*
MCB	*Mélanges chinois et bouddhiques*

ÖAW	*Österreichische Akademie der Wissenschaften*
PEFEO	*Publications de l'École française d'Extrême-Orient*
PEW	*Philosophy East and West*
PSPR	*Proceedings of the Society for Psychical Research*
PTS	*Pali Text Society*
SACPMS	*Society for Asian and Comparative Philosophy Monograph Series*
SOR	*Serie Orientale Roma*
TP	*T'oung Pao*
TSWS	*Tibetan Sanskrit Works Series*
VBS	*Viśva-Bhāratī Studies*
WZKM	*Wiener Zeitschrift für die Kunde des Morgenlandes*
WZKSOA	*Wiener Zeitschrift für die Kunde Süd- und Ostasiens und Archiv für indische Philosophie*

BIBLIOGRAPHY

In the following bibliography (which is not intended to be exhaustive) I have sometimes cited more than one edition of a given text. In certain cases, I have specified the edition that has actually been cited in the text with an asterisk.

Pāli and Sanskrit Texts: Editions and Sanskrit Fragments, Reconstructions and "Retranslations"

Abhidharmadīpa with Vibhāṣāprabhāvṛtti, critically edited with notes and introduction. Jaini, P. S. (1977). Patna: TSWS 4.

Abhidharmakośa

* Dvārikādāsa Śāstrī (1970-73). *Abhidharmakośa with Vasubandhu's Bhāṣya and Yaśomitra's Sphuṭārthaṭīkā.* Kośasthānas 1-8, 4 vol. Vārāṇasī: BBh.

Pradhan, P. (1975). *Abhidharmakośabhāṣya of Vasubandhu.* 2nd rev. ed. Patna: TSWS 8.

Abhidharmasamuccaya

Gokhale, V. V. (1947). "Fragments from the Abhidharma-samuccaya of Asaṅga." JRAS Bombay 23: 13-38.

Pradhan, P. (1950). *Abhidharmasamuccaya of Asaṅga.* Santiniketan: VBS 12.

Abhisamayālaṃkāra

* Stcherbatsky, Th. and E. Obermiller (1929). *Abhisamayālaṃkāra-(prajñāpāramitā-upadeśa-śāstra): The Work of Bodhisattva Maitreya,* edited, explained and translated. Leningrad: BB.

Vaidya, P. L. (1960). *Aṣṭasāhasrikā Prajñāpāramitā with Haribhadra's Abhisamayālaṃkārāloka.* Darbhanga: BST.

Ālambanaparīkṣā

Aiyaswami Shastri, N. (1942). *Ālambanaparīkṣā and Vṛtti of Diṅnāga with the Commentary of Dharmapāla.* Madras: AL.

Tola, Fernando and Carmen Dragonetti (1982). "Dignāga's *Ālambanaparīkṣāvṛtti*." JIP 10: 105-134.

Aṅguttara-Nikāya. Morris, R. (1885-1910). 6 vol. London: PTS.

Aṣṭādhyāyī (Pāṇini's Grammatik). O. Böhtlingk (1887). Leipzig.

Aṣṭasāhasrikāprajñāpāramitāsūtra

Mitra, Rajendralal (1888). *Aṣṭasāhasrikāprajñāpāramitāsūtra*. BI 110.

Vaidya, P. L. (1960). *Aṣṭasāhasrikā Prajñāpāramitā with Haribhadra's Commentary called Āloka*. Darbhanga: BST 4.

Daśabhūmikasūtra et Bodhisattvabhūmi, chapitres Vihāra et Bhūmi, publiés avec une introduction et des notes. Rahder, J. (1926). Paris, Louvain: Société Belge d'Études Orientales.

Dvādaśāraṃ Nayacakram of Ācārya Śrī Mallavādi Kṣamāśramaṇa. Vol II. Jambūvijaya, Muni (1976). Śrī Ātmānand Jain Granthamālā Series. Bhavnagar: No. 94.

Jñānaśrīmitranibandhāvaliḥ (Buddhist Philosophical Works of Jñānaśrīmitra). Thakur, A. (1959). Patna: TSWS 5.

Madhyamakaśāstra of Nāgārjuna with the Commentary Prasannapadā of Candrakīrti. Dvārikādāsa Śāstrī (1983). Vārāṇasī: BBh.

Madhyāntavibhāga

Nagao, G. M. (1964). *Madhyāntavibhāga-bhāṣya*. Tokyo.

* Tatia, N. and Thakur, A. (1967). *Madhyānta-vibhāga-bhāṣya*. Patna: TSWS 10.

Yamaguchi, Susumu (1934). *Madhyāntavibhāgaṭīkā: exposition systématique du Yogācāravijñaptivāda*. Nagoya.

Mahāyāna-sūtrālaṃkāra: exposé de la doctrine du Grand Véhicule. Lévi, Sylvain (1907, 1911). Édité et traduit. 2 vol. Texte: Tome 1. Paris: BEHE.

Majjhima-Nikāya. Vol. 1: Trenckner, V. Vol. 2-3: Chalmers, R. Vol. 4, index: Rhys Davids, C. A. F. (1888-1925). London: PTS.

Nyāyabindu

Gangopadhyaya, M. (1971). *Vinītadeva's Nyāyabindu-ṭīkā.* Sanskrit original reconstructed from the extant Tibetan version with English translation and annotations. Calcutta: ISPP 1971.

* Malvania, D. (1971). *Dharmottarapradīpa of Paṇḍita Durveka Miśra*, being a sub-commentary on Dharmottara's *Nyāya-binduṭīkā*, a commentary on Dharmakīrti's *Nyāyabindu.* Patna:TSWS 2. [First edition, 1955.]

Śrīnivāsa Śāstrī (1975). *Nyāyabindu of Dharmakīrti with Dharmottara's Ṭīkā.* Meerut.

Stcherbatsky, T. (1918). *Nyāyabindu of Dharmakīrti, with Dharmottara's Ṭīkā.* Leningrad: BB 7.

Nyāyadarśana of Gautama, with the *Bhāṣya* of Vātsyāyana, the *Vārttika* of Uddyotakara, the *Tātparyaṭīkā* of Vācaspati & the *Pariśuddhi* of Udayana [Volume 1 Chapter 1]. Thakur, A. (1967). Vaisali, Muzaffarpur.

Pramāṇasamuccaya

Hattori, Masaaki (1968). *Dignāga, On Perception, being the Pratyakṣapariccheda of Dignāga's Pramāṇasamuccaya.* Cambridge, Mass.: HOS 47.

Katsura, Shoryu (1975). "New Sanskrit Fragments of the Pramāṇasamuccaya." JIP 3: 67-78.

Rangaswamy Iyengar, H. R. (1930). *Pramana Samuccaya, edited and restored into Sanskrit with Vṛitti, Tīka and Notes.* Mysore.

Pramāṇavārttika

* Dvārikādāsa Śāstrī (1968). *Pramāṇavārttikam of Ācārya Dharmakīrti, with the Commentary 'Vṛtti' of Ācārya Manorathanandin.* Vārāṇasī: BBh 3.

Gnoli, Raniero (1960). *The Pramāṇavārttikam of Dharmakīrti: the first chapter with the autocommentary.* Roma: SOR 23.

Malvania, D. (1959). *Svārthānumāna chapter of the Pramāṇavārttika of Dharmakīrti with autocommentary*. Vārāṇasī.

Sāṅkṛtyāyana, Rāhula (1938-40). *Pramāṇavārttika of Dharmakīrti with a Commentary by Manorathanandin*. JBORS 24.

Sāṅkṛtyāyana, Rāhula (1953). *Pramāṇavārtikabhāṣyam (Vārtikālaṅkāraḥ) of Prajñākaragupta, being a commentary on Dharmakīrti's Pramāṇavārttikam*. Patna: TSWS 1.

Pramāṇaviniścaya

Steinkellner, Ernst (1973, 79). *Dharmakīrti's Pramāṇaviniścayaḥ: Zweites Kapitel: Svārthānumānam*. Vols. 12, 15. Wien: ÖAW.

Vetter, Tilmann (1966). *Dharmakīrti's Pramāṇaviniścayaḥ. 1. Kapitel: Pratyakṣam*. Wien: ÖAW.

Ratnakīrti-nibandhāvaliḥ (Buddhist Nyāya Works of Ratnakīrti). Thakur, A. (1975). Patna: TSWS 3.

Saddharmalaṅkāvatārasūtram. Vaidya, P. L. (1963). Darbhanga: BTS.

Saddharmapuṇḍarīkasūtra. Vaidya, P. L. (1960). Darbhanga: BTS.

Saṃtānāntaradūṣaṇa. See *Ratnakīrtinibandhāvaliḥ*.

Tarkabhāṣā and Vādasthāna of Mokṣākaragupta and Jitāripāda. Rangaswami Iyengar, H. R. (1952). Mysore.

Saṃyutta-Nikāya. Feer, L. 6 vol. (1884-1904). London: PTS.

Tattvasaṃgraha

* Dvārikādāsa Śāstrī (1968). *Tattvasaṅgraha of Ācārya Śāntarakṣita with the Commentary Pañjikā of Śrī Kamalaśīla*. 2 vol. Vārāṇasī: BBh.

Krishnamacharya, E. (1926). *Tattvasaṃgraha of Śāntarakṣita with the Commentary of Kamalaśīla*. Baroda: GOS 30-31.

Triṃśikā. See *Vijñaptimātratāsiddhi*.

Trisvabhāvanirdeśa

* La Vallée Poussin, L. de (1932-33). "Le petit traité de Vasubandhu-Nāgārjuna sur les trois natures." MCB 2: 146-161. Paris.

Mukhopadhyaya, S. (1939). *The Trisvabhāvanirdeśa of Vasubandhu*. Calcutta: VBS 4.

Tola, Fernando and Carmen Dragonetti (1983). "The *Trisvabhāvakārikā* of Vasubandhu." JIP 11: 225-266.

Yamaguchi, S. (1931). *Trisvabhāvanirdeśa*, edited in Tibetan and Sanskrit and translated into Japanese. Shukyo Kenkyu (Journal of Religious Studies) 8: 121-30; 186-207. Japan.

Udānaṃ. Steinthal, P. (1885). London: PTS.

Vaiśeṣikasūtra of Kaṇāda with the Commentary of Candrānanda. Jambūvijaya, Muni (1961). Baroda: GOS 136. [Appendix 7: 153-219, contains "retranslations" of portions of the Pramāṇa-samuccaya from Tibetan into Sanskrit].

Vijñaptimātratāsiddhi. Deux traités de Vasubandhu: Viṃśatikā et Triṃśikā. Lévi, Sylvain (1925). Paris: BEHE.

Viṃśatikā. See *Vijñaptimātratāsiddhi*.

Vyākaraṇamahābhāṣya (Patañjali). F. Kielhorn, revised third edition by K. V. Abhyankar (1965). Poona: BORI. [First published 1880.]

Other Works

Aiyaswami Shastri, N. (1967), ed./tr (Tibetan). "Bahyartha Siddhi Karika" (of Śubhagupta). Gangtok: BT IV, 2: 1-96.

Anacker, S. (1984). *Seven works of Vasubandhu: the Buddhist psychological doctor*. Delhi.

Bandyopadhyay, N. (1979). "The Buddhist Theory of Relation between *pramā* and *pramāṇa*." JIP 7: 43-78.

Bareau, André (1955). *Les sectes bouddhiques du Petit Véhicule.* PEFEO.

Berkeley, George (1948). *Works*, ed. T. Gessup and A. Luce. London. [Includes *Three Dialogues between Hylas and Philonous* and *A Treatise Concerning the Principles of Human Knowledge.*]

Bhattacharya, Vidhusekhara (1934). "Evolution of the Vijñānavāda." IHQ 10: 1-11.

Borst, C. V. (1970), ed. *The Mind-Brain Identity Theory.* New York.

Broad, C. D.

(1954) "Phantasms of the Living and of the Dead." PSPR 50: 51-66.

(1962) *Lectures on Psychical Research*: Incorporating the Perrot Lectures given in Cambridge University in 1959 and 1960. London.

Chatterjee, A. K. (1975). *The Yogācāra Idealism.* 2nd rev. ed. Vārāṇasī.

Conze, E. et. al. (1954), ed./trs. *Buddhist Texts through the Ages.* New York.

Conze, E.

(1954) *Abhisamayālaṅkāra*. Roma: SOR 6.

(1975) *The Perfection of Wisdom in Eight Thousand Lines and Its Verse Summary.* [English translation.] Bolinas, California.

Cousins, L. et. al. (1974), eds. *Buddhist Studies in Honour of I. B. Horner.* Dordrecht.

Dasgupta, Surendra Nath

(1928) "Philosophy of Vasubandhu in Viṃśatikā and Triṃśikā." IHQ 4: 36-43.

(1962) *Indian Idealism*. Cambridge. [First publication, 1933.]

Demiéville, P. (1954). *La Yogācārabhūmi de Saṅgharakṣa*. BEFEO 44.

Evans, R. D. and B. K. Matilal (1986), eds. *Buddhist Logic and Epistemology*. Dordrecht.

Feyerabend, Paul (1963). "Materialism and the mind-body problem." *Review of Metaphysics* XVII. In Borst (1970).

Franco, Eli (1984). "On the Interpretation of Pramāṇasamuccaya(vṛtti) I, 3d*." JIP 12: 389-400.

Frauwallner, Erich

(1930-36) "Beiträge zur Apohalehre." WZKM 37 (1930): 259-283, 39 (1932): 247-285; 40 (1933): 51-94; 42 (1935): 93-102; 44 (1936): 233-287.

(1951) *On the date of the Buddhist Master of the Law Vasubandhu*. SOR 3.

(1954) "Die Reihenfolge und Entstehung der Werke Dharmakīrti's." *Asiatica, Festschrift Friedrich Weller*. Leipzig: 142-54.

(1956) *Die Philosophie des Buddhismus*. Berlin.

(1959) "Dignāga, sein Werk und seine Entwicklung." WZKSOA 3: 83-164.

(1961) "Landmarks in the History of Indian Logic," WZKOA 5: 125-148.

Green, Celia and Charles McCreery (1977). *Apparitions*. Oxford.

Gurney, Edmund, F. W. H. Myers and F. Podmore (1886). *Phantasms of the Living*. London.

Hamilton, Clarence H.

(1931) "Hsüan Chuang and the Wei Shih Philosophy." JAOS 51: 291-308.

(1933) "K'uei Chi's commentary on *Wei-Shih-Er-Shih-Lun*." JAOS 53: 144-151.

(1938) *Wei Shi Er Shih Lun, or The Treatise in Twenty Stanzas on Representation-Only by Vasubandhu*. New Haven: American Oriental Society.

Hart, Hornell et. al. (1956). "Six Theories about Apparitions." PSPR: 53-239.

Hattori, Masaaki (1980). "*Apoha* and *Pratibhā*." In Nagatomi et al. (1980).

Hayes, Richard P.

(1986) "Review of Amar Singh's *The heart of Buddhist philosophy: Diṅnāga and Dharmakīrti*." JIABS 9(2): 166-172.

(1988) *Dignāga on the Interpretation of Signs*. Boston.

Herzberger, Radhika (1986). *Bhartṛhari and the Buddhists: An Essay in the Development of Fifth and Sixth Century Indian Thought*. Dordrecht.

Horner, I. B. (1957), tr. *The Collection of the Middle Length Sayings (Majjhima-Nikāya)*. Vol. II. London: PTS.

Jaini, P. S.

(1958) "On the theory of the two Vasubandhus." BSOAS 21: 48-53.

(1974) "On the Sarvajñatva (Omniscience) of Mahāvīra and the Buddha." In Cousins (1974): 71-90.

Jayatilleke, K. N. (1963). *Early Buddhist Theory of Knowledge*. London.

Jha, Ganganatha (1937), tr. *The Tattvasaṃgraha of Śāntarakṣita with the Commentary of Kamalaśīla*. Baroda: GOS 80, 83.

Jha, Subhadra (1983). *The Abhidharmakośa of Vasubandhu*: with the commentary, annotated and rendered into French from the Chinese by Louis de la Vallée Poussin and Sanskrit text edited by Prahlad Pradhan; both translated into English by Subhadra Jha. Patna: TSWS 23.

Kajiyama, Yuichi

(1965) "Buddhist Solipsism: A free translation of Ratnakīrti's *Saṃtānāntaradūṣaṇa*." JIBSt 13 (January): 435-420.

(1966) "An Introduction to Buddhist Philosophy: An Annotated Translation of the Tarkabhāṣā of Mokṣākaragupta." Memoirs of the Faculty of Letters. Kyoto University No. 10: 1-173. Kyoto.

(1968-69) "Bhāvaviveka, Sthiramati and Dharmapāla." WZKSOA 12-13: 193-203.

Katsura, Shoryu (1984). "Dharmakīrti's Theory of Truth." JIP 12: 215-235.

Kitagawa, Hidenori (1955). "A Refutation of Solipsism" (annotated translation of *Saṃtānāntarasiddhi*). JGIS 14-15: 55-73, 97-110.

Kochumuttom, Thomas (1982). *A Buddhist doctrine of experience: a new translation and interpretation of the works of Vasubandhu the Yogācārin*. Delhi.

Kripke, Saul (1980). *Naming and Necessity*. Cambridge, Mass.

La Vallée Poussin, L. de

(1912) *Viṃśakakārikāprakaraṇa: Traité des vingt ślokas avec le commentaire de l'auteur.* LM: 13: 53-90.

(1917) "Madhyamaka," "Nihilism (Buddhist)," "Nirvāṇa," "Philosophy (Buddhist)." ERE: New York.

(1918) Review of *Bibliotheca Buddhica, XIX: Tibetan Translation of Dharmakīrti's Saṃtānāntarasiddhi and Vinītadeva's Saṃtānāntarasiddhiṭīkā*, by Th. de Stcherbatskoï, Petrograd, 1916. BSOS, 1918, pp. 130-32.

(1928-48) *Vijñaptimātratāsiddhi: La Siddhi de Hiuan-tsang,* traduite et annotée. 3 vol. Paris.

(1930-37) "Documents d'Abhidharma." I: BEFEO (1930) 1-28, 247-298. II: MCB (1932) 1: 65-125. III: MCB 5 (1936-37) 1-87.

(1932-33) "Refléxions sur le madhyamaka." MCB 2: 1-146.

(1933) "The Mādhyamika and Tathatā." IHQ 9, No. 1: 30-31.

(1971) *L'Abhidharmakośa de Vasubandhu,* traduit et annoté. MCB 16: 1-6. [Revised edition of the 1923-31 translation.]

Lamotte, Étienne

(1935) *Saṃdhinirmocana-sūtra: L'explication des mystères.* Texte tibétain édité et traduit. Louvain, Paris.

(1973) *La Somme du Grand Véhicule d'Asaṅga* (*Mahāyānasaṃgraha*), I-II. Louvain: Institut Orientaliste.

Lindtner, Christian

(1984) "Marginalia to Dharmakīrti's Pramāṇa-viniścaya I-II." WZKSOA 28: 149-75.

(1986) "Bhavya's Critique of Yogācāra in the *Madhyamaka-ratnapradīpa,* Chapter IV." In Evans (1986): 239-263.

Marsh, Robert Charles (1971), ed. *Logic and Knowledge: essays 1901- 1950.* New York.

Matilal, B. K.

(1968) "Diṅnāga's Remark on the Concept of *anumeya.*" JGJRI 24: 151-160.

(1974) "A Critique of Buddhist Idealism." In Cousins (1974): 139-169.

May, Jacques (1971). "La philosophie bouddhique idéaliste." AS 25: 265-323.

McDermott, A. Charlene S. (1973). "Asaṅga's Defense of *Ālayavijñāna*." JIP 2: 167-174.

Minh Chau, Bhikṣu Thich (1964). *The Chinese Madhyama Āgama and the Pāli Majjhima Nikāya (A Comparative Study)*. Saigon.

Mookerjee, Satkari (1935). *The Buddhist Philosophy of Universal Flux: An Exposition of the Philosophy of Critical Realism as Expounded by the School of Dignāga*. Calcutta.

Nagatomi, Masatoshi (1960). "The Framework of the Pramāṇavārttika, Book 1." JAOS 79: 263-266.

Nagatomi, Masatoshi et. al. (1980), eds. *Sanskrit and Indian Studies: Essays in Honour of Daniel H. H. Ingalls*. Dordrecht.

Nakamura, Hajime (1983). *A History of Early Vedānta Philosophy*. Part One. Delhi.

Narain, Harsh (1963). "*Śūnyavāda*: A Reinterpretation." PEW 13: 311-338.

Obermiller, E. (1931). "The sublime science of the great vehicle to salvation," AO 9.

Péri, N. (1911). "À propos de la date de Vasubandhu." BEFEO 11: 339-390.

Piatigorsky, Alexander (1983). "Some Remarks on 'Other Stream.'" In *Buddhist Studies: Ancient and Modern*, ed. P. Denwood and A. Piatigorsky, pp. 124-52. London.

Place, U. T. (1956). "Is consciousness a brain process?" *British Journal of Psychiatry* XLVII (1956). In Borst (1970).

Professor Sidgwick's Committee (1894). "Report on the Census of Hallucinations." PSPR 10: 25-422.

Rahula, Walpola (1971). *Le compendium de la superdoctrine (philosophie) (Abhidharmasamuccaya) d'Asaṅga*. Paris: PEFEO.

Reat, Noble Ross (1985). "A Buddhist Proof for the Existence of God." JIP 13: 265-272.

Rorty, Richard (1965). "Mind-body identity, privacy and categories." *Review of Metaphysics* XIX. In Borst (1970).

Ruegg, David Seyfort (1969). *La Théorie du Tathāgatagarbha et du gotra*. Paris: PEFEO 70.

Russell, Bertrand

(1905) "On Denoting." *Mind* 16: 479-493. In Marsh (1971).

(1948) *Human Knowledge: Its Scope and Limits*. New York.

(1959) *Problems of Philosophy*. New York.

Sakurabe, H. (1952). "On Frauwallner's dating of Vasubandhu." JIBSt 1.1: 202-208.

Schmithausen, L. (1967). "Sautrāntika-Voraussetzungen in Viṃśatikā und Triṃśikā." WZKSOA 11: 109-36.

Shah, Nagin J. (1967). *Akalaṅka's Criticism of Dharmakīrti's Philosophy*. Ahmedabad.

Sharma, Ramesh Kumar (1985). "Dharmakīrti on the Existence of Other Minds." JIP 13: 55-71.

Shorter, J. M. (1967). "Other Minds." In *Encyclopedia of Philosophy*, ed. Paul Edwards. New York.

Sidgwick, Mrs. Henry (1922). "Phantasms of the Living." PSPR 33.

Singh, Amar (1984). *The Heart of Buddhist Philosophy: Diṅnāga and Dharmakīrti*. Delhi.

Smart, J. J. C.

(1959) "Sensations and brain processes." *The Philosophical Review* LXVIII. In Borst (1970).

(1962) "Brain processes and incorrigibility." *Australian Journal of Philosophy* XL. In Borst (1970).

Staal, J. F.

(1967) "Indian Logic." *Encyclopedia of Philosophy*, ed. Paul Edwards. New York.

(1973) "The Concept of *Pakṣa* in Indian Logic." JIP 2: 156-166.

Stcherbatsky, Th.

(1922) "Establishment of the Existence of Other Minds: A free translation of Dharmakīrti's *Saṃtānāntara-siddhi* and Vinītadeva's *Saṃtānāntarasiddhi-ṭīkā*," translated into Russian with Vinītadeva's *ṭīkā*. St. Petersburg. [This in turn has been translated into English by H. C. Gupta in ISPP 10 (1969): 335-383.]

(1962) *Buddhist Logic.* 2 Vols. New York. [Reprint of 1930-32 translation.]

(1978) *The Conception of Buddhist Nirvāṇa*, with comprehensive analysis and introduction by Jaideva Singh. Reprint of the 2nd enlarged and revised edition. Delhi. [First published Leningrad 1927.]

Tachikawa, M. (1970-72). "A Sixth-Century Manual of Indian Logic: A Translation of the *Nyāya-praveśa*." JIP 1: 111-145.

Takukusu, J.

(1904) "Paramārtha's Life of Vasubandhu translated from the Chinese." TP 2.5: 269-296, 461-466, 620.

(1905) "A Study of Paramārtha's life of Vasubandhu and the date of Vasubandhu." JRAS 33-53.

Tripathi, C. L.

(1969) "The Nature of 'Reality' in Yogācāra Buddhism." *East and West* 19: 474-484.

(1972) *The Problem of Knowledge in Yogācāra Buddhism.* Vārāṇasī.

Tucci, G.

(1930) *On Some Aspects of the Doctrines of Maitreya(nātha) and Asaṅga*. Calcutta.

(1956) *Minor Buddhist Texts, Part I.* Roma: SOR 9.

Tyrrell, G. N. M. (1953). *Apparitions*. London.

Ueda, Yoshifumi (1967). "Two Main Streams of Thought in Yogācāra Philosophy." PEW: 155-166.

Ui, H. (1929). "Maitreya as a historical personage." In *Indian Studies in Honor of Charles Rockwell Lanman*. Cambridge, Mass.

Van Zeyst, H. G. A. (1961). "Ākiñcaññāyatana." EB. Colombo.

Vetter, Tilmann (1964). *Erkenntnisprobleme bei Dharmakīrti*. Wien: ÖAW.

Warder, A. K.

(1975) "Objects." JIP 3: 355-361.

(1980) *Indian Buddhism*. 2nd rev. ed. Delhi.

Wayman, Alex (1965). "The Yogācāra Idealism." PEW 15: 65-74.

Wayman, Alex and Hideko (1974), trs. *The Lion's Roar of Queen Srīmālā*. New York.

Wei Tat (1973), tr. *Ch'eng Wei-Shih Lun: The Doctrine of Mere-Consciousness*. Hong Kong.

Wood, Thomas E. (1990). *The Māṇḍūkya Upaniṣad and the Āgama Śāstra: An Investigation into the Meaning of the Vedānta*. Honolulu: SACPMS 8.

Woodward, F. L. (1948). *The Minor Anthologies of the Pali Canon. Part II. Udāna: Verses of Uplift and Itivuttaka: As it was said.* London: PTS.

Woodward, F. L. and E. M. Hare (1932-36). *The Book of the Gradual Sayings*. London: PTS.

INDEX

INDEX

ABOUT THE AUTHOR

Thomas Wood received his B.A. and Ph.D. in philosophy from the University of California at Berkeley. He has taught Eastern and Western philosophy at the California State University at Fresno and the State University of New York at New Paltz.

SOCIETY FOR ASIAN AND COMPARATIVE PHILOSOPHY
MONOGRAPH SERIES
Henry Rosemont, Jr., Editor

No. 1 *The Sage and Society: The Life and Thought of Ho Hsin-Yin,* by Ronald Dimberg, 1974

No. 2 *Studies in Comparative Aesthetics,* by Eliot Deutsch, 1975

No. 3 *Centrality and Commonality: An Essay on* Chung-Yung, by Tu Wei-Ming, 1976 (out of print)

No. 4 *Discourse on the Natural Theology of the Chinese,* by Gottfried W. Leibniz, translated with an introduction, notes, and commentary by Henry Rosemont, Jr., and Daniel J. Cook, 1977 (out of print)

No. 5 *The Logic of Gotama,* by Kisor Kumar Chakrabarti, 1978 (out of print)

No. 6 *Commentary on the* Lao Tzu *by Wang Pi,* translated by Ariane Rump, introduction by Wing-tsit Chan, 1979

No. 7 *Han Fei Tzu's Political Theory,* by Wang Hsiao-po and Leo S. Chang, 1986

No. 8 *The Māṇḍūkya Upaniṣad and the Agama Śāstra: An Investigation into the Meaning of the Vedānta,* by Thomas E. Wood, 1990

No. 9 *Mind Only: A Philosophical and Doctrinal Analysis of the Vijñānavāda,* by Thomas E. Wood, 1991

Title orders should be directed to the University of Hawaii Press, 2849 Kolowalu Street, Honolulu, Hawaii, 96822. Manuscripts should be directed to Professor Henry Rosemont, Jr., Department of Philosophy, St. Mary's College, St. Mary's City, Maryland 20686.